World History
HL

8~
Scan

D0787816

The World Is Our Witness

The Historic Journey of the Nisga'a into Canada

Tom Molloy
with
Donald Ward

FIFTH
HOUSE
PUBLISHERS

For Corinne, Jennifer, Alison, Kathryn, and Hanna

Copyright © 2000 Tom Molloy

All rights reserved. No part of this publication may be reproduced, stored in a retrieval system, or transmitted, in any form or by any means, electronic, mechanical, recording, or otherwise, without the prior written permission of the publisher, except in the case of a reviewer, who may quote brief passages in a review to print in a magazine or newspaper, or broadcast on radio or television. In the case of photocopying or other reprographic copying, users must obtain a licence from the Canadian Copyright Licencing Agency.

Front cover and chapter opening photograph, ceremonial Nisga'a mask, by Gary Fiegehen, ©Nisga'a Nation
Cover and interior design by John Luckhurst / GDL

The publisher gratefully acknowledges the support of The Canada Council for the Arts and the Department of Canadian Heritage.

THE CANADA COUNCIL | LE CONSEIL DES ARTS
FOR THE ARTS | DU CANADA
SINCE 1957 | DEPUIS 1957

We acknowledge the financial support of the Government of Canada through the Book Publishing Industry Development Program for our publishing activities.

Printed in Canada.

00 01 02 03 04 / 5 4 3 2 1

Canadian cataloguing in publication data

Molloy, Tom, 1940–

The world is our witness

Includes bibliographical references and index.
ISBN 1–894004–47–7

1. Nisga'a Indians—British Columbia—Treaties. 2. Nisga'a Indians—Canada—Government relations. 3. Nisga'a Indians—British Columbia—Government relations. 4. Nisga'a Indians—British Columbia—Claims. I. Title.
KE7749.N5M64 2000   346.71104'32'0899741
C00-910353-8   KF8228.N5M64 2000

Published in Canada by
Fifth House Ltd.
A Fitzhenry & Whiteside Company
1511-1800 4 St. SW
Calgary, Alberta, Canada
T2S 2S5

Published in the U.S. by
Fitzhenry & Whiteside
121 Harvard Ave.
Suite 2
Allston, Massachusetts
02134

Contents

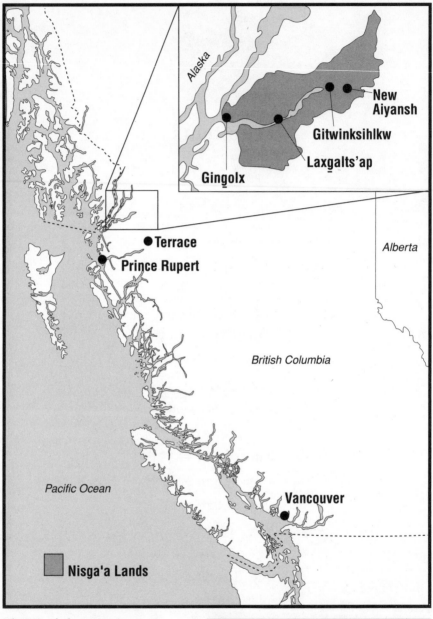

New
Aiyansh

Gitwinksihlkw

Laxgalts'ap

Gingolx

Alaska

Alberta

● Terrace
● Prince Rupert

British Columbia

Pacific Ocean

● Vancouver

Nisga'a Lands

The Nisga'a language is
constantly evolving. All Nisga'a
place names in this book are
taken from the Nisga'a Final
Agreement, Appendix F.

English	Nisga'a
Canyon City	Gitwinksihlkw
Greenville	Laxgalts'ap
Kincolith	Gingolx
New Aiyansh	New Aiyansh

Foreword

....

No ONE CAN PREJUDGE HISTORY. However, I have the sense that two of the most important accomplishments of Canadians over the last quarter century—and perhaps longer—have been the creation of Nunavut and the completion of the Nisga'a treaty.

Why? Quite simply, these two actions bring us back into the long mainstream of Canadian history. Tom Molloy and others have described the Nisga'a treaty as the mechanism that brings this people into Canada. If you take the large historical view, you could say, back into Canada.

Canada is a country constructed on a triangular foundation—aboriginal, francophone, anglophone. This is not merely a romantic formula. And it certainly has nothing to do with being politically correct. More than four hundred years ago these two groups of Europeans came to this part of the continent and began cohabiting with the aboriginal people. For at least the first 250 of those four hundred years the aboriginals either led the way or had equal power and influence. Every aspect of our civilization—from our laws to our social policies to our constitutional negotiations to our military approaches—has been marked by that long partnership.

We then slowly lost our sense of that triangular foundation, and so, in spite of many accomplishments, also lost our way. For half a century we have been trying to find our way back. As the Nisga'a and Canadian statesman Joe Gosnell has put it—"The terms of six Prime Ministers chart the years I have grown old at the negotiating table."

The story of how the Nisga'a re-entered the Canadian experiment is an important piece of our history: important for the Nisga'a; for all of those, such as Tom Molloy, who played a role; for other aboriginal peoples; and for all other Canadians. There are lessons in this story not just for the continuing process of getting us back on track, but for the way in which all Canadians see themselves living together.

One of the key lessons is that Canada really does not belong to the monolithic, linear, centralized tradition of the eighteenth/nineteenth-century nation state, as developed in Europe and the United States. From the very beginning we have been experimenting with a multi-faceted approach. You could call it the first of the postmodern nations. After all, that postmodern idea was already locked in place, legally, by the 1840s.

The linear, rational, old-fashioned approach is constantly fixed on ideas of power. Who has it? Who is in control? Who has the numbers to be in control?

Canada simply doesn't work when you think of it in those terms. It has never been a linear, logical, rational place. It has always worked on several levels at once. It has always turned its back on ideas of majority because they eliminate the idea of a country of minorities. If Canada is not rational, what is it? Perhaps the most sensible way to think of this place is as a spatial concept—the very opposite of the rather predictable linear stuff attached to the outdated nation states. Already in our triangular foundation you can see the beginnings of a spatial concept that "includes" rather than "excludes."

Some people waste time trying to apply nineteenth-century ideas of power to their interpretation of the Nunavut and Nisga'a treaties. This leads them nowhere. The originality of both agreements is that they do not follow the old exclusive monolithic models. They are inclusive spatial approaches toward society. And in that very fact you can see the return of the influence of aboriginal culture to our way of imagining and constructing Canada.

John Ralston Saul

A Note on Canadian Treaties

....

WHEN A LONG PROCESS OF INTERCULTURAL DIPLOMACY and democracy culminated in the making of the Nisga'a treaty in 1998, the world stopped to take notice. News of the deal made the front page of *The New York Times*. Reports also appeared in Switzerland, Japan, Australia, New Zealand, France, and throughout South America. In Great Britain, the journalists at the BBC and *The Economist* introduced their large global audiences to the Canadian term "First Nation." The latter characterized the tripartite agreement between the people of the Nisga'a First Nation and the governments of Canada and British Columbia as "a historic precedent." [1]

There was some truth in this characterization. For instance, the inclusion of provisions for the Nisga'a Memorial Lava Bed Park devoted to the ideals of cultural renewal and interpretation broke new ground. What the writers at *The Economist* and others failed to appreciate, however, is that the Nisga'a treaty is more about continuity than discontinuity; it is more about elaborating and projecting forward very old traditions of constitutional law than it is about breaking with our heritage in ways that lack precedent.

The Nisga'a treaty is the most recent in a long series of innovations to address legally one of the world's most pressing and pervasive human rights issues whose origins lie more in the events of 1492 than 1998. Since the beginnings of the Columbian conquests over five centuries ago, the legal minds of one European empire after another have struggled to find rationales for the overseas extension of their sovereigns' territorial claims. While one school of imperial theorists maintained that the rights and titles of the indigenous peoples on the frontiers of Europe's expansionism could be unilaterally extinguished, other voices argued otherwise.

New Spain was the first major laboratory of deliberation on what we today describe in the Canadian constitution as "existing aboriginal and treaty rights." In this milieu the debate went beyond the question of whether the aboriginal inhabitants of the colony had any right of ownership and jurisdiction in the soil beneath their feet. The question extended also to whether these aboriginal peoples could be transformed into property through the institution of slavery. The Vatican weighed into the controversy in 1537 with the *Sublimus Bull.* It stipulated that the Indians of the Americas were indeed fully human. "By no means," directed the Pope, should they be "deprived of their liberty or possession of their property, even though they be outside the Christian faith."[2]

This papal bull extended to the Americas some of the principles already fleshed out by Father Fransisco de Vitoria, a Dominican theology professor at Spain's Salamanaca University. In 1532, in a series of lectures entitled "On the Indians Lately Discovered," Vitoria described the Native Americans as "true owners" of their aboriginal lands with a "true dominion" over themselves.[3] In 1550 the proponents of aboriginal rights eventually faced in court the advocates of Indian slavery. In seminal litigation Brother Bartolomé de Las Casas made an urgent appeal to stop the murderous letting of so much Indian blood.[4] Its absorption into the soil tragically became a rite of baptism to christen the Born Again New World as an extension of Europe in what David Stannard has termed in his important book of the same name, *The American Holocaust.*[5]

Las Casas's great advocacy of human rights still reverberates across language barriers and generations. Basically he embraced the civilized heritage of First Nations in the Americas as part of humanity's commonwealth of wisdom, invention, and cultural richness. The planet Las Casas sought to enliven with his lofty literature and penetrating legal interventions was one with sufficient checks on western civilization's expansionary aggressions to afford all indigenous peoples a place of dignity and security.

Las Casas envisaged a world where First Nations could participate in, rather than be engulfed by, the forces of globalization that began in 1492. In an intellectual tradition that would be carried on in the twentieth century by the Shuswap visionary of the Fourth World, namely George Manuel, Las Casas pictured a future where indigenous peoples would have a recognized right to pass onto their progeny the adaptive ingenuity derived from their aboriginal heritages.[6] He pictured a planet where a regime of respect for aboriginal and treaty rights would establish the basis for what Richard White has characterized as a "middle ground" of compromise and co-existence between and among distinct peoples. As White would have it, Canada was, in its first incarnation, one of the continent's most important middle grounds of collaborative enterprise between Native and newcomer in the development of the French-aboriginal fur trade. The Nisga'a treaty can be pictured as yet another effort to find and hold this zone of fruitful cross-fertilization on the middle ground of an expanded, tripartite version of Canadian federalism.[7]

The history of Crown–First Nation treaty making in the English colonies, then in British North America, and then in the Dominion of Canada makes the agreement with the Nisga'a a very recent link in one of the world's oldest and most broad-ranging series of interconnected negotiations on the moving frontier of intercultural relations.[8] The early English colonies were founded in the seventeenth century on legal doctrines of "discovery" that made no provision to incorporate principles of aboriginal rights such as those articulated by Vitoria and Las Casas.

Little by little, however, some of their ideas entered New England largely by way of Holland. Roger Williams, for instance, led a small group of Protestant dissenters away from the harsh theocracy of Massachusetts. Lacking a land grant from the monarch, Williams turned to the region's Narragansett Indians to authorize a land transfer giving legal sanction to his settlement of Rhode Island. The patriarch of the Quaker colony named after William Penn also went to his aboriginal neighbours to make purchases from them to gain First Nations sanction for the establishment of Pennsylvania. Hence Williams and Penn are seminal contributors to the constitutional heritage of the tradition of Crown–First Nations treaty making that extended to Nisga'a territory in 1998.

The colonies of New Netherlands and New France provided the British imperial government with evidence that the process of colonizing British North America could be pressed forward in collaboration with First Nations through the medium of the fur trade. The officers of the Dutch colony were especially important in setting examples through their diplomacy with indigenous peoples that treaty making and gift exchanges could be instrumental in helping to extend imperial influence more deeply into Indian Country. The conquest of New Netherlands to create New York colony in 1664 and the conquest of France's colony of Canada a century later laid the groundwork for the expanding importance of imperial recognition of aboriginal and treaty rights in the expansion of British North America. The culmination of this process was the codification in 1763 of King George III's Royal Proclamation as the constitutional foundation of British imperial Canada, including the new Crown province of Quebec.

The Royal Proclamation of King George III established the constitutional foundation of British imperial Canada after the defeat of the French army in North America during the Seven Years' War. The Proclamation's formulation was hastened in 1763 when news reached the imperial capital that a confederacy of Indian peoples following Pontiac would resist the British colonization of Canada without proper provisions to recognize the collectively held title of First Nations peoples to their ancestral lands.

The Proclamation recognized that title by drawing a westerly boundary for the Anglo-American colonies. The lands to the west of this line were reserved for the Indians as their hunting grounds. The King prohibited private individuals or companies from purchasing any of the reserved land directly from Indian peoples. He stipulated that if non-aboriginals wanted to colonize this territory in the future only he and his royal heirs had the authority to conduct negotiations with the First Nations to make the appropriate adjustments in land tenure.

By asserting this power the imperial government was attempting to establish its exclusive right to regulate the westward movement of the Anglo-American settlements. Many settlers in the Thirteen Colonies resented this centralized control, and the issue became one of the major grievances of the American Revolution. The other side of the equation in this historical drama was that the Royal Proclamation helped establish a powerful tradition of alliance between First Nations and the imperial government in the interior of North America. The transcontinental fur trade, whose entrepreneurial core was the North West Company of Montreal, helped secure the economic and social basis of that alliance. In 1821 that enterprise merged with the Hudson's Bay Company, which became the Crown's primary instrument in maintaining its claim to the northwestern portion of North America until its titles were purchased by the Dominion of Canada in 1869.

The strong tradition of alliances between the First Nations, the British imperial government, and the fur-trade interests of Canada became the basis of a constitutional heritage that extends to the treaty tradition of the present day. At its most extreme, this tradition was expressed in the military alliance that was integral to the defence of Upper Canada from annexation by the United States in the War of 1812. During this conflict, more than ten thousand Native fighting men rose up in defence of their own country. In return, they expected the imperial government to support the establishment of a sovereign aboriginal dominion in the heart of North America.

That Crown protectorate was to have been governed by a council of federated Indian nations. Its purpose from the imperial government's perspective was to provide a buffer between the American republic and what remained of British North America. While this outcome was precluded by the martyrdom in 1813 of Tecumseh—the Indian confederacy's great visionary—the Indians' military alliance with the Crown in the War of 1812 was critical in preventing the absorption of Canada into the domain of the Stars and Stripes.

These large geopolitical realities established the atmosphere of friendship and alliance in which the early treaties were negotiated after the establishment of the American republic in 1783. The provisions of the Royal Proclamation were thus applied in the process of opening Upper Canada to non-aboriginal settlement. Only gradually in the first decades of the nineteenth century did these pre-Confederation treaties with First Nations come to include the establishment of Indian reserves.

In 1850 the tradition of Crown treaty-making with the First Nations was extended into the mineral-rich lands north of the Great Lakes. Some of the Anishinabek people in this region, who were mostly veterans of the War of 1812, laid the groundwork for these negotiations by closing down a small mine at Michipicoten. They did so to make the point that the Crown had never properly addressed their land rights. After Governor General Lord Elgin intervened on their behalf, two agreements were negotiated known as the Robinson-Huron and Robinson-Superior treaties. These transactions established twenty-one new Indian reserves, furthering the entrenchment of this institution into Canada's legal and territorial framework. The Robinson treaties also recognized that First Nations peoples retained hunting and fishing rights on Crown lands.

The tradition of Crown treaties with the First Nations was extended into the vast territories purchased by the Dominion of Canada from the Hudson's Bay Company in 1869. The patriotic assertions by Louis Riel and the Métis of Red River during the winter of 1870 forced Dominion officials to recognize that they needed to obtain some kind of sanction from the indigenous peoples for the imposition on their ancestral lands of the new government's jurisdiction. Accordingly, between 1871 and 1929, eleven so-called numbered treaties together with several adhesions were negotiated. Crown officials conducted negotiations with Cree, Oji-Cree, Saulteaux, Dene, Assiniboine, and Blackfoot over a vast area from the western shores of James Bay to the eastern slopes of the Rocky Mountains.

This cycle of treaty making began in 1871, just as Congress passed a law in the United States prohibiting further treaty making with Indian peoples. The persistence of the treaty tradition in Canada has many explanations, some of which go back to the importance of the alliances between First Nations and the imperial government in the era of the American Revolution and the War of 1812. That experience entrenched the legal heritage of the Royal Proclamation into the constitutional and political traditions of Canada. One small manifestation of this heritage are the red jackets of the North-West Mounted Police, a force that was brought into existence largely to conduct treaties and to enforce the reserve system on the Indian peoples of western Canada. The red jackets were to remind the First Nations of the era when their ancestors had fought side by side with the Crown's Red Coats in defending territory against the American aggressor.

The numbered treaties included promises to Indian peoples such as schools, teachers, and agricultural instructors; reserves calculated at either 160 or 640 acres per family; one-time payments and annuities of five dollars per year for every individual; medicine chests to be maintained on reserves; ploughs, breeding stock, and other agricultural implements; housing; as well as flags, medals, and buggies for the principal men. While some view the legal wording on treaty documents literally, others see these agreements as establishing general principles for relationships between peoples that are to last for as long as the sun shines and the waters flow. They see the truth of these agreements not in specific details but in more general principles that establish a framework of ongoing negotiations that must be made to adapt as Canada changes. Thus the treaty provisions for schooling, health care, economic development, policing, intergovernmental relations, etc., must constantly be reworked so that treaty First Nations can contribute effectively in the constructive transformation of the country.

On the Indian side, treaty negotiations were often understood as sacred agreements whose legitimacy was drawn more from the ceremonies that took place in the course of the negotiations than from the signatures at the bottom of legal texts. Most often these ceremonies involved the smoking of special pipes, which gave spiritual significance to the spoken words. This way of viewing these agreements places great emphasis on what was explained by translators to Indian peoples in their own languages in the course of treaty talks. Thus the contemporary interpretation of treaties requires going into the oral traditions kept alive especially by certain accomplished elders whose wisdom and learning are recognized as a primary source of continuity in the maintenance of First Nations heritages.

Except for a few treaties on Vancouver Island, British Columbia entered Confederation in 1871 outside the legal heritage of the Royal Proclamation of 1763. Since the late nineteenth century, First Nations activists in BC repeatedly argued that the provincial government was violating Crown law in opening the province for non-aboriginal exploitation and ownership without any treaties with the indigenous peoples. Finally, in 1973, some members of the Supreme Court of Canada agreed with this position in an ambivalent ruling to a legal case brought forward by the Nisga'a. The result was that in 1973 the cycle of treaty making going back to the Royal Proclamation was extended to several regions, including Canada's western-most province.

The first of these modern-day treaties was a tripartite agreement in 1975 between the governments of Canada and Quebec as well as the Cree and Inuit east of James and Hudson's Bays. In 1983 the Inuvialuit made a similar deal, which became the model for several other agreements in the western Arctic and Yukon. In 1999 Nunavut was established after the federal government and the Inuit of the eastern Arctic arrived at a complex set of compromises about how the terms of the Royal Proclamation should be applied in that vast, sparsely settled part of Canada. The previous year a tripartite agreement with the Nisga'a was formalized in a process whose substance Tom Molloy discusses in this book.

A major preoccupation of those on the aboriginal side of these modern-day treaty negotiations has been how to establish a range of new institutions to help liberate indigenous peoples from the weight of an onerous colonial system that has dominated their lives, often for many generations. The core of that colonial system has been the federal Indian Act; its primary agents have been the federal Department of Indian Affairs and Northern Development. Thus a key to advancing First Nations self-government is the development of infrastructures capable of generating some degree of economic self-sufficiency for aboriginal communities. Accordingly, many provisions in modern-day treaties put in place various means and formulae for the sharing and apportioning of natural resources along with the royalties they generate.

Many of the old treaties are sanctioned by Indian peoples with picture signatures representing the animals crests of their clans and confederacies. These pictures signify aboriginal understandings of the proper balances between society, ecology, and law. It is the juxtaposition of such representations on the same documents with legal texts in European languages that most eloquently embodies the intercultural essence of this genre of agreement between peoples.

The heritage of Crown treaties with First Nations in North America represents in its totality one of the world's oldest and most elaborate experiments in extending democratic principles across boundaries of language, culture, and ethnicity. Certainly there are aspects of this experiment that have proven tragic in the extent of their failure. But these failures are part of a larger set of problems on a planet where too often principles of power outweigh principles of justice in establishing the framework of relationships between peoples.

There is still great capacity for rectifying these inequities in Canada's continued elaboration of the principles of intercultural democracy through the enlightened extension of the Crown's alliances with First Nations through the medium of treaties. The Nisga'a treaty, despite its imperfections, projects forward a very old learning curve about humanity's ceaseless quest to find ways to share, more equitably, the good things the earth has to offer. Accordingly, Molloy's text serves to remind us that whatever lofty theory we might have about what is at issue, in the final analysis Crown–First Nation treaty making comes down to real human beings bargaining face-to-face. Theirs is pre-eminently the art of the possible in a very complex political environment. Their responsibility has been to seek out workable solutions to problems inherited from history so as to make life a little more harmonious, a little less discordant.

Anthony J. Hall
Department of Native American Studies
University of Lethbridge

Chapter One

....

IT WAS THREE O'CLOCK IN THE MORNING in a drab hotel meeting room at the Terrace Inn. There were twelve of us still at the table. We had been there for eighteen hours. Yesterday had been a typically beautiful July day in northern British Columbia. Today promised more of the same. In the room, though, the tension was like fog.

Jim Aldridge, acting for the Nisga'a, declared that it was time for all parties to lay their cards on the table. By "all parties" he meant Canada, British Columbia, and the Nisga'a Tribal Council. Of the federal negotiating team, Andrew Beynon and I were the only ones remaining at the table. The last of the five working groups that started that morning had finally wrapped things up at 1:00 AM. The other members of my team had retired for the night, their working groups having concluded their labours. Jack Ebbels, Patrick O'Rourke, Trevor Proverbs, and Boris Tyzuk represented the Province. Representing the Nisga'a were Tribal Council President Joe Gosnell, Edmund Wright, Nelson Leeson, Harry Nyce, and their lawyers, Jim Aldridge and Marcus Bartley.

At that point, the Nisga'a had been negotiating for twenty-one years. One hundred and eleven years had passed since they first approached the government of British Columbia in an attempt to settle their land claims. Now, in the early morning of July 15, 1998, all that history, all that effort, was to be put to the test. With Aldridge's announcement, suddenly the whole deal hung in the balance.

There is a moment in every negotiation—whether it is a commercial negotiation, a labour dispute, or an aboriginal land claim—when laying your cards on the table is the right thing to do. If you try it too soon, the results can be disastrous. But if you read the process and the personalities correctly, you will nearly always close the deal.

I wasn't sure this was the right time. I asked for a caucus meeting. Andrew and I retired to another cluttered meeting room, one that the Fiscal Working Group had been using until one o'clock that morning. We reviewed the list of issues under discussion and the federal position on each one.

Aldridge was right, I decided. It was time to put our cards on the table.

When we reconvened, I presented the federal position. The Province asked for a caucus, then the Nisga'a. Andrew and I spent the time reviewing their positions, knowing that they were probably changing as we did so. When we convened again, it was apparent that our points of difference had narrowed. But they were still wide enough to keep us from closure.

We needed further instructions.

At 3:30 AM we called John Watson, Regional Director General for British Columbia of the federal Department of Indian Affairs and Northern Development (DIAND). Not surprisingly, we got him out of bed. After some discussion, it became clear that more government people would need to be involved. This was problematic given the time of night, not to mention the pressure we were working under.

We returned to the table.

At 6:00 AM I asked for another caucus, and we were back on the phone to John Watson, then to Doreen Mullins, Executive Director of the Federal Treaty Negotiation Office in Vancouver. They had both been active in the background work of the negotiations for some time, as often as not defending the issues within DIAND and to their own colleagues. For meetings among the publicly acknowledged participants were only a part of the process. Behind the scenes, every government department—federal, provincial, and local, as well as numerous advisory committees—had to get involved in some way, and every bureaucrat have his or her say. Many were potentially affected by the Agreement.

We were advised that the Nisga'a and the Province were ready to meet. We weren't. It was time to get officials in Ottawa involved.

By this time, the other core members of our team had been roused. Jim Barkwell, Brian Martin, Doug Wanamaker, Fred Morris, and Maureen Parkes crowded into my hotel room with Andrew and me. The speaker phone was soon engaged as we contacted the Deputy Minister, the Justice Department, the Privy Council Office, the Prime Minister's Office, and key officials from DIAND, in addition to John Watson, Doreen Mullins, and Lorne Bownsey in Vancouver—to name a few of the more prominent participants. We presented the issues and reported the status of the negotiations.

At 11:00 AM we established a conference call across Canada, with one line into the United States where an official was travelling. The call lasted until 4:00 PM. People were added and deleted throughout the day. The internal debate continued, among departments and between people. Civil servants and deputy ministers questioned and advised, approved and disapproved, and sometimes contradicted themselves and one another. It was a necessary, if exceedingly frustrating, exercise.

Meanwhile, there were portentous activities downstairs. For some time there had been an air of expectancy hanging over the small city of Terrace, and centring on the Terrace Inn, where the negotiations were taking place. Yesterday there had been persistent rumours that the deal would close. Today, people thought, would be the day.

Nisga'a were arriving from their villages in the Nass Valley northwest of Terrace. Journalists were arriving by the handful from the rest of the province. Reporters were interviewing people on the street. Photographers and television camera operators were out capturing local colour. You could not throw a stone in any direction without hitting a print journalist or a photo journalist or a radio journalist or a television journalist. From my hotel window I could see Nisga'a dancers in their colourful blanket outfits rehearsing in the parking lot across the street. The drums were persistent and relentless. By the end of the day there were five television cameras in the hotel lobby, representing the CBC National News and other networks and their affiliates.

The arrival of the Premier of British Columbia at midday added to the tumult. Glen Clark and his entourage moved like royalty among their expectant subjects. The sense of excitement and anticipation filtered up through the floors of the hotel like a physical presence that was not entirely benevolent and that infected each of us in turn, increasing the sense of urgency and responsibility we were feeling. To say, simply, that the pressure was mounting would be to invoke a cliché that was woefully inadequate to describe the process we were struggling not only to control but to lead forward.

I dared not leave the room for fear of being recognized. The last thing I needed was to be waylaid by some eager journalist and have a microphone thrust under my chin and asked impossible questions about the delay. As

Chief Federal Negotiator my duty was clear: to stay on the job until the job was done. And I was by no means convinced that the job would be done any time soon. The phone lines remained open. Discussions were ongoing. Positions were reviewed and revised, reflected on, accepted or rejected. Legal and political opinions were sought and heard, practical considerations were weighed, and moral issues were decided on a hope and a prayer.

Each time someone left the room, he or she returned with further reports of the atmosphere downstairs: the hope, the expectancy, the incredible collective energy of a people who were convinced that generations of patience and effort were about to be rewarded in a binding agreement—in a treaty. In justice. For over a century the Nisga'a had been trying to negotiate their way into Canada, had been struggling to become full and equal citizens in a country that prided itself on being a just society. Little did they know how delicately their hopes and aspirations hung in the balance.

Sandwiches were brought in. Food was essential; the body demands fuel to fire the efforts of the mind. At the same time, it was almost irrelevant. I could have been chewing on the intestines of a mountain goat for all the difference it made to my taste buds.

The drums continued below, beating out a rhythm for our thoughts and fears. My worst fear was that now, at the ultimate moment, everything would fall apart, the deal would go down. It was a possibility that could not be ignored. During the protracted period of negotiations, of proposal and counter-proposal, of compromise and accommodation, the chance of ultimate failure had never seemed quite real. But now it was as real as the drums downstairs, beating their incessant cadence on our overtaxed minds.

What would we say to the Nisga'a people if we couldn't get a deal? What would we say to the rest of Canada? Opponents of the process—and there had never been any lack of them—would crow with delight. But that was a minor matter. Of much greater importance was how we would deal with the disappointment, even the despair, of the well-meaning and honourable men and women of the Nisga'a nation who had placed their trust in this process.

We needed to think of our press lines. It was suggested that we ask for a cooling-off period, a day or two in which we could regroup, recover our equilibrium, and perhaps even get some sleep. But no. Every report we received on the situation outside that crowded hotel room reinforced the image of a community at the very limits of tolerance. Whether the Nisga'a and their supporters erupted in excitement and celebration or exploded in anger and recrimination seemed entirely up to us. In their century-long quest for justice, the Nisga'a had not once resorted to civil disobedience or violence of any kind. Even so, I did not want to put their patience to a further test.

No, today had to be the day.

The drumming continued—not mesmerising, as drumming often is, but sharpening the edge of consciousness, flaying nerves already raw with sleeplessness and tension. The phone lines stayed open. We kept on talking, reasoning, cajoling, asking and giving advice, considering, revising, and rewriting. It was impossible to convey the sense of urgency we felt to bureaucrats on phone lines in cities as distant as Ottawa or as close as Vancouver. If they were only here, I thought, if they could only feel the tension, if they could only breathe in the heady and addictive atmosphere of expectation and excitement that surrounded us, they would set aside all their doubts and arguments and reasoned deliberations and, like minor characters in a B-movie, say, simply, "Go for it!"

But government does not work that way. The Prime Minister's Office cannot cast reason to the winds. The Department of Justice cannot bend or circumvent the principles it was created to uphold however ponderous its defence of those principles may sometimes seem. Ministers and deputy ministers must serve the interests of the democracy that justifies their existence, regardless of the mental mayhem that may be occurring in a hotel room on the ragged green edge of the continent three thousand kilometres away. And so we talked, and listened, and compromised, and refused to compromise, and the drums kept beating, and the atmosphere grew thicker and thicker with expectation and anxiety.

Just before four o'clock there was a knock on the door. To my surprise, it was Jim Aldridge. I had expected the Nisga'a and the Province to wait until we had advised them that we were ready. They wanted a meeting in the legal drafting room, he said. Was Canada ready?

"I need one more minute," I told him. Reason told me I needed hours, but emotionally I doubted if I could even last the minute. "Who should I bring?"

"Just one other person," said Aldridge.

I asked Andrew to join me. He could deal with any legal issues that might arise. I turned back to Aldridge. "I don't want to go through the lobby," I said. "The press will never let us through."

"We can take the fire escape and go in the back door."

It seemed an admirable solution. "Give us a minute," I said, and shut the door. Andrew gave me an anxious look, which I returned. He was no more certain than I was that the deal would close.

I asked the conference call participants to confirm my final instructions, then we were out the door and making for the fire escape. We made an odd trio of fugitives. I am a tall man myself. Andrew Beynon is taller, and heroically thin. I have heard Jim Aldridge described as an ageing rock star. The description hardly does him justice, as a lawyer or as a negotiator, but watching him striding along an airport concourse with his long hair flowing about his shoulders, a briefcase in one hand and his guitar in the other—he plays it in his hotel room at night to relieve stress—one can see how the description stuck.

We descended the fire escape two steps at a time, only to be brought up short by a door at the bottom and a sign to the effect that an alarm would sound if anyone tried to get out that way.

"Do you believe this sign," Aldridge asked, "or do you give a damn at this stage?"

I told him I didn't give a damn.

He opened the door. We burst through. There was no alarm.

The legal drafting room, yet another of the hotel meeting rooms we had commandeered for our purposes, was small, hot, and stuffy. It was strewn with the remnants of earlier versions of the Agreement and partly eaten meals, ketchup bottles, coffee cups, water glasses, and pop cans that had collected over the previous nineteen hours. At the moment we entered I could not have said which was more calculated to raise my anxiety level: the rancid food, the equally unpalatable evidence of previous attempts to reach an agreement, or the expressions on the faces of the Nisga'a and BC negotiators. My stomach was churning with a mixture of excitement and apprehension. A glance in Andrew's direction confirmed that he was feeling the same way. We were as prepared as we could possibly be, but somehow that didn't improve the situation. We still might fail. If we did, the repercussions would be enormous, not only across the country but in the world at large, which was watching to see if Canada, this most fortunate of nations, could or would deal justly with its indigenous peoples—peoples, in the case of the Nisga'a, who had never signed a contract or a treaty, who had never been conquered, who had never surrendered, and who had never ceded a human right or an inch of territory. If we failed, it would be proof, finally, that reasonable people cannot sit down together and settle their historical differences. Failure would follow us personally to the ends of our careers, if not to the grave.

The Nisga'a and the Province were already assembled. Andrew and I took our seats at the table. Each party put forward its final position. The Nisga'a spoke last.

And we had a deal.

It took a moment for the reality to sink in. I was shaking with emotion. Andrew and I hugged one another like excited schoolchildren.

It took another moment to realize that everyone else felt the same way. There were handshakes and hugs all around. But Andrew and I had to get back to my room. We owed it to the others to let them know what was happening. We agreed to reassemble in fifteen minutes in the Skeena Room, the main conference room of the hotel, to make the announcement.

The first person I ran into as I left the room was Premier Clark, who must have known from the din in the room that the deal had been done. He offered Andrew and me his congratulations. We accepted them hastily and departed.

The fire escape was locked. The only way back was through the lobby. We paused. On the count of three, Andrew and I rammed our way through the crowd and up the stairs. Out of breath, we burst into my room. My voice cracked as I shouted, "We have a deal!"

Pandemonium broke out. There were cheers, more handshakes and hugs. The hours and days of tension and uncertainty drained away like water. In fifteen seconds I think we all felt ten years younger. I told everyone that we had to assemble downstairs immediately.

I didn't notice at the time, but someone had disconnected the speaker phone. All the people strung out across the country on our ongoing conference call were left in the dark. They didn't know we had a deal. It was some time before they would find out.

We marched into the main room, led by a triumphant Joe Gosnell and the Nisga'a negotiators. High above his head, he held the red, three-ring binder that contained the words and phrases we had been struggling with for two and a half years: The Final Agreement of the Nisga'a People with the Government of Canada and the Province of British Columbia. The room was crowded and wild, like the committee rooms of a successful candidate on election night. Only tonight all the candidates had won. People were slapping us on the back, shaking our hands, laughing, shouting with gladness. Nisga'a dancers in their sacred colours expressed the collective joy of their people. The ubiquitous drums added to the din, no longer ominous but rejoicing.

My own mood was as high, and my emotions as deep, as anyone else's. We were in the same room, at the same tables where we had spent so much time and effort over these two and a half years to hammer out the deal. It was fitting that it should now be the scene of this celebration.

Joe Gosnell rose to speak. A man of natural eloquence and profound humility, he seemed to fill the room with his presence. "At 4:10 PM today," he said, speaking now to a hushed and solemn crowd that overflowed the large room, "negotiations with respect to the Nisga'a land question were concluded. My thoughts as I entered this room went back to 1887, when Nisga'a chiefs came down from the Nass Valley to Victoria to bring a rapid resolution to the land question. Looking around me today, July 15th, 1998, I see elders whose fathers I know were directly involved in the original negotiations. I am happy our elders could be here today."

The Province spoke, in the person of Premier Glen Clark. Then BC Aboriginal Affairs Minister Dale Lovick addressed the crowd. "This generation of British Columbians," he said, "will do that which has eluded all others before. We are going to conclude the unfinished business of an entire century." Jack Ebbels spoke for all of us when he said he could not remember when he had last had a full night's sleep. My own remarks were brief, and exceedingly difficult to deliver in that emotional moment. "This is a truly historic day," I said simply. "I trust it is the beginning of a new relationship for the Nisga'a, Canada, and the people of British Columbia."

We then surrendered ourselves to the ladies and gentlemen of the media. For they, too, were part of the process. I was interviewed and photographed until I began to believe that the microphones and the cameras—the face-pullers, as the First Nations of the interior so appropriately called them—were stealing my soul. But dealing with the press is an important part of my role, and I have come to enjoy the challenges and the excitement of it. I am no longer startled to see myself on television or to hear my voice on the radio. I no longer have to take a step back and wonder, "Who is that guy?" Some people revel in public attention. Lawyer-like, I revel in the skills I have learned over the years in saying exactly what I mean and no more. Especially that night, with emotions running so high, I had to be extremely careful of what I said, for that is how the world at large would understand the Agreement.

We answered questions into the evening, then the Premier took all three negotiating teams out for dinner. Glen Clark was in his element: elated, triumphant, and surrounded by people, many of whom trusted and admired him. After dinner, a dozen or so cigar smokers left the restaurant for the sidewalk outside to savour a box of Cubans that had been acquired by one of the BC negotiators and saved in anticipation of this moment. Though not a smoker himself, the Premier came outside to join them in conversation. I will never forget the sight of Glen Clark, wreathed in the cigar smoke of his colleagues and negotiators, the blue aromatic tendrils rising in a crown over his head and gilded by the setting sun. This was the same man who had recently launched a massive lawsuit against the tobacco companies in an attempt to recover some of the medical and social costs of smoking related illnesses. How I wished I had a camera!

At 11:20 PM I finally returned to my hotel room. It was a disaster. The detritus of the final days of work was scattered everywhere: files, briefcases, notepads, pens, pencils, cell phones, plates of partially eaten food, and half-empty bottles of ketchup. I doubted that they would ever find their rightful owners. I couldn't bring myself to care. I had not slept in forty hours. I had an early press interview, another meeting, and then a plane to catch at 9:55 the following morning.

To everything there is a season, the preacher said, and a time for every purpose under heaven. Twenty-four hours earlier I might have argued with him. But now, at least for the moment, the time for negotiation was over.

It was finally time for sleep.

Chapter Two

....

IT WAS IN 1887 that a group of Nisga'a chiefs first journeyed from the distant Nass Valley to Victoria to meet with the Premier of British Columbia, William Smithe. They came to ask the government of the new province to recognize their title to ancestral lands, and to negotiate treaties. Premier Smithe barred them from the legislature. "When the whites first came among you," he said, "you were little better than wild beasts of the field."[1]

Smithe was following in the tradition of Sir Joseph William Trutch, former Chief Commissioner of Lands and Works in the colony of British Columbia, and subsequently the first lieutenant-governor of the province. In 1867, the year of Canadian Confederation, Trutch had written:

The Indians really have no right to the lands they claim, nor are they of any actual value or utility to them, and I cannot see why they should either retain these lands to the prejudice of the general interests of the Colony, or be allowed to make a market of them either to the Government or to Individuals.[2]

Sir Joseph's version of reality was at considerable variance from the one recorded by Hudson's Bay Company traders who arrived in the Nass Valley in 1832 and found the Nisga'a living in "two storey wooden houses the equal of any in Europe." At the time of contact, their population was nearly thirty thousand. They had been living in communities along the Nass River for generations, governing themselves according to *Ayuukhl Nisga'a*, their ancient code of civil order, property ownership, and succession.

Since that first humiliating voyage to Victoria's inner harbour in 1887, the journey of the Nisga'a has taken them to the British Cabinet and Privy Council, to the Supreme Court of Canada, and ultimately to the Canadian Parliament. Their perseverance was founded in their own traditions as a self-governing people and in the Royal Proclamation of 1763, which established British primacy over aboriginal territories in the expanding British Empire. The Proclamation reads, in part:

> Whereas it is just and reasonable and essential to our Interest, and the Security of our Colonies, that the several Nations or Tribes of natives with whom We are connected, and who live under our Protection, should not be molested or disturbed in the Possession of such parts of Our Dominions and Territories as, not having been ceded to purchase by Us, are reserved to them . . .

British colonial law thus dictated that aboriginal lands not ceded to the Crown through negotiation and purchase remained, in fact, aboriginal lands. To the Nisga'a, the issue was much simpler: they had a right to live where they had always lived, and to own and control the land they lived on.

The official view of the day, both in the Canadian government and the British Colonial Office, seemed to hold that the Royal Proclamation of 1763 had never applied either in Rupert's Land or to points west and north of Rupert's Land. Hence, few would have regarded the Proclamation as restricting his or her actions in British Columbia in the nineteenth century. The Nisga'a saw things otherwise. Indeed, as Paul Tennant has written, the contents of the Proclamation "were an inspiration" to British Columbia Indians once the document became generally known among them:

> For many Indians it was a moving revelation to discover that the British monarch, already seen as a symbol of justice, was the very one to have long since proclaimed the very principles that British Columbia Indians had been pursuing, seemingly alone. Knowledge of the proclamation gave a powerful boost to pan-Indian sentiments. Each Indian could see his or her tribal group as one of the "nations or tribes" recognized and promised justice by the proclamation but denied it by the actions of provincial officials.[4]

With the appointment of Joseph Trutch as Chief Commissioner of Lands and Works in the 1860s, the Proclamation, whatever its intent, was explicitly ignored. Surveying parties were sent throughout the colony to subdivide the land into manageable segments for Canadian and European settlers. Early surveyors sent into Nisga'a territory were banished by the chief, Israel Sgat'iin, but with the sanction of the government in Victoria they soon returned. The practice continued long after British Columbia became a province in 1871.

Following in Trutch's footsteps, Premier Smithe, who came to office in 1883, initiated the "Great Potlatch" era, so called because of the policies of successive provincial governments of making generous grants of Crown-owned resources to private entrepreneurs. Ironically, the Potlatch, the traditional feasting ceremony of west coast First Nations, was banned in 1884 by an amendment of the Indian Act.

The Nisga'a had few friends in either Victoria or Ottawa. In 1888 Edward Blake, who has the distinction of being the only federal Liberal leader in Canadian history never to have been prime minister, characterized the aboriginal societies of Canada as "an inferior race, and in an inferior state of civilization."[5] His successor, Sir Wilfrid Laurier, journeyed to Prince Rupert in 1910 in an attempt to settle the land question, but little came of it but confusion. Sir Wilfrid advised the Nisga'a to petition the British Privy Council. No doubt he meant the Judicial Committee of the British Privy Council, which at that time was Canada's highest court. The Privy Council itself is a large and catholic group of advisers to the Crown that meets as a body only "to sign the proclamation of the accession of a new sovereign, and when a sovereign announces an intention to marry."[6]

Whatever Sir Wilfrid meant, or said, the Nisga'a proceeded to act on it. Their petition was addressed to "the King's Most Excellent Majesty in Council" with a covering letter to the Secretary of State for the Colonies. "The petition was thus intended for the cabinet or government of the day," according to Paul Tennant, "but it was addressed to the Privy Council, the formal entity of which the cabinet is only the active part. The petition was not addressed to the Judicial Committee of the Privy Council, the highest Imperial court, as Canadian officials at the time, and scholars later, assumed."[7]

Clearly, however, the Nisga'a regarded the Privy Council as a real and active body that could effect change in British Columbia and bring about justice. In 1913 the Nisga'a Land Committee, which had been active since 1890, sent a delegation of chiefs to Britain to request that Nisga'a land ownership be respected according to the Royal Proclamation of 1763. Their carefully respectful petition ran to some two thousand words, almost half of which comprised excerpts from the Proclamation. "We are not opposed to the coming of the white people into our territory," they wrote,

> provided this be carried out justly and in accordance with the British principles embodied in the Royal Proclamation. If therefore as we expect the aboriginal rights which we claim should be established by the decision of His Majesty's Privy Council, we would be prepared to take a moderate and reasonable position. In that event, while claiming the right to decide for ourselves, the terms upon which we would deal with our territory, we would be willing that all matters outstanding between the province and ourselves should be finally adjusted by some equitable method to be agreed upon which should include representation of the Indian Tribes upon any Commission which might then be appointed.[8]

The confusion over whom the petition actually addressed had multiple and often contradictory effects in Canada. In the first instance, it lent the Nisga'a and other aboriginal peoples in British Columbia a sense of purpose and hope that, once the injustice they were suffering had been brought to the attention of the highest Imperial authority, Britain would of course act to rectify the situation. Canadian Government officials, on the other hand, knew that most general references to the "privy council" in fact referred to the Judicial Committee of the Privy Council, which *was* a real and active body, but which normally acted on an internal Canadian matter only on appeal from a Canadian court. As long as no one launched a court action, therefore, there was little chance that the Nisga'a petition would ever land on the desk of anyone who might be moved to do anything about it. There was "the outside possibility," again according to Paul Tennant, "that the British cabinet might refer the matter to the Judicial Committee," but "Canadian officials, devoutly hoping that it would not do so, did not admit this possibility in their dealings with the British Columbia Indians."[9] This policy of concealment, if not deception, raised problems of its own, as the continuing belief that their petition was before the highest authority in the Empire had the inconvenient effect of keeping Nisga'a political aspirations alive, and thus hindered their assimilation into the larger society.

It was in 1913 that Duncan Campbell Scott became Deputy Superintendent of Indian Affairs. Generations of Canadian students recognize Scott's name as one of the Confederation poets they were forced to study in high school. The ubiquitous *A Book of Good Poems,* which is still in use in high schools today, contains four of Scott's best efforts. Two of them— "At Gull Lake; August, 1810," and "The Forsaken"—deal explicitly with Native themes. In the biographical notes at the back of the book we are told that Scott spent fifty-two years in the Department of Indian Affairs, eighteen of them as head, for which he was awarded the Companion of the Order of St. Michael and St. George by King George V in 1934. "His knowledge of Indians," the editor avers, "is the background for austere and quietly powerful poems."[10] What readers are not told is that Scott spent the major energies of his career not in writing poetry to vex future generations, but in trying "to get rid of the Indian problem."

"Our objective," he declared, "is to continue until there is not a single Indian in Canada that has not been absorbed into the body politic, and there is no Indian question, and no Indian Department . . ."[11]

One of his earliest efforts was to undermine the Nisga'a petition and deflect Native attention in general from political action. He was largely, if only temporarily, successful. Canada and British Columbia then undertook to address the land question with a Royal Commission.

The Royal Commission on Indian Affairs for the Province of British Columbia was appointed on March 31, 1913. The McKenna-McBride Commission, as it came to be known, travelled throughout the province for three years, until 1915. The commissioners interviewed hundreds of Indians, as well as non-aboriginal people—farmers, representatives of local governments, railway officials—whose interests might reasonably be expected not to coincide with those of the Indians. In addressing the situation of the Nisga'a, the commission recommended that they be allotted seventy-six square kilometres of reserve land. Ottawa concurred.

This came as no great surprise to the Nisga'a, for the federal government had passed the first of several incarnations of what became known as the Indian Act in 1876. Among other things, the Act denied First Nations citizens the right to vote. An amendment in 1884 outlawed the traditional feasting ceremonies, which for the Nisga'a were the Native equivalent of title deeds and acts of succession. Just as the eldest child of a reigning monarch cannot succeed to the British throne without the sanction of the law, neither could the succession of a Nisga'a chief be recognized without the feasting cere-mony—neither, indeed, could the transfer of property or of territory be accomplished. A comparable act might be if the federal government simul-taneously shut down all the courts and land title offices throughout the country and then proceeded to declare itself illegal.

In 1927, Parliament again amended the Indian Act, this time to prohibit First Nations from organizing or raising money to pursue aboriginal land claims without the permission of the Indian Affairs Department.

In 1951 this legislation was repealed.

In 1960 First Nations were granted the right to vote in federal elections.

In 1967 the Nisga'a Tribal Council, under the leadership of then-President Frank Calder, instructed Vancouver lawyer Thomas R. Berger, QC, to initiate legal proceedings against the government of British Columbia to obtain recognition of their aboriginal title. In what became known as the *Calder* case,[12] the courts were asked to declare that the Nisga'a had neither surren-dered nor lost title to their traditional territories.

They lost. Berger took the case to the Appeal Court of British Columbia, where they lost again. The Nisga'a Tribal Council prevailed upon Berger to pursue the case to the Supreme Court of Canada.

In 1969, Prime Minister Pierre Trudeau, speaking in Vancouver, asserted that "We can't recognize aboriginal rights because no society can be built on historical 'might have beens.'"[13] Nevertheless, in November 1971 the Supreme Court agreed to hear the case, rendering its decision fourteen months later. In January 1973, the Court admitted the possibility that abo-riginal title to the traditional territory of the Nisga'a in the Nass Valley might not have been extinguished.

Historically, there are three principal ways in which aboriginal title can be ceded or extinguished. The first and more accepted means involves the surrender of aboriginal rights to lands and resources in exchange for rights granted in a treaty. The second is by war and conquest. The third is a longer process, in that prior to the Constitution Act, 1982, the Crown could exercise its sovereignty in a manner that, by the fact of its governing, could erase abo-riginal title. In its arguments before the Supreme Court in 1973, British Columbia claimed that aboriginal title to the traditional territory of the Nisga'a had been extinguished by virtue of the way in which the Province had governed the territory.

The Court was divided. Although six of the seven justices found that the

Nisga'a had held title originally, three ruled that they retained title still, while three ruled that aboriginal title had been lost. The seventh justice ruled against the Nisga'a on a technicality, observing that they had violated a relic of British parliamentary law by not first obtaining a fiat to sue the Crown— i.e., obtaining permission from the Crown to sue the Crown.

The decision, though legally inconclusive, influenced Pierre Trudeau's thinking to the extent that he reconsidered the legitimacy of aboriginal title and declared that the land question was an issue to be settled through negotiation. In effect, a prime minister of Canada had finally heard the voices of those elders who had journeyed to Victoria harbour eighty-six years earlier.

In 1976 the Government of Canada opened negotiations with the Nisga'a Tribal Council. British Columbia first took part as an observer only, but eventually recognized that issues of land and resources, which fall under provincial jurisdiction, could not be decided without its full participation.

On March 20, 1991, at New Aiyansh, Nisga'a Tribal Council President Alvin McKay and five other chiefs signed a Framework Agreement with the Honourable Jack Weisgerber, BC Minister of Aboriginal Affairs in the Social Credit government of Premier Bill Vander Zalm, and the Honourable Tom Siddon, federal Minister of Indian Affairs and Northern Development. A news release issued jointly by the Government of Canada, the Province of British Columbia, and the Nisga'a Tribal Council read, in part:

> The framework agreement marks the beginning of a two-year period of negotiations leading to an agreement-in-principle. Topics for negotiation include lands, renewable and non-renewable resources, environmental issues and economic development. An important provision is a commitment to a co-operative program of communication, consultation and public awareness.
>
> During the ceremony, Chief McKay said, "The Nisga'a are glad that the framework agreement is officially signed. Now the three parties can activate the agreement and substantive negotiations can begin in earnest. One of the major highlights for the Nisga'a Tribal Council is that there is now a formal, official commitment by each of the three parties to negotiate."
>
> Mr. Siddon noted, "The Nisga'a have played an historically significant role in addressing the issue of land claims and they are proof that negotiation is the best route to go. Signing this framework today

is a positive and encouraging step toward a land claim settlement. This historic event marks the first time a tripartite agreement has been reached in this province to commit all parties to the negotiation process."

Mr. Weisgerber said, "The Province of British Columbia entered negotiations with the Nisga'a and the federal Government because we believed that it was the right thing to do. We remain convinced that the just and equitable resolution of outstanding Native concerns through negotiation in good faith is in the best interests of all British Columbians. With the signing of this framework agreement, I am pleased to have the opportunity to demonstrate the Government of British Columbia's continuing commitment to the process."[14]

Sadly, Alvin McKay would not live to see the Final Agreement ratified; he died in late December 1999.

In British Columbia, the negotiation process became considerably less complex following the "Report of the British Columbia Claims Task Force" of June 28, 1991,[15] and the subsequent British Columbia Treaty Commission (BCTC) Agreement of September 21, 1992; the BCTC is an independent body of five commissioners appointed by British Columbia, Canada, and an umbrella organization known as the First Nations Summit. Canada and British Columbia each passed legislation to give effect to the Agreement. For all First Nations in British Columbia—except the Nisga'a—it changed the criteria for entering into negotiations and established the process to be followed. First Nations were no longer required, as the Nisga'a had been, to provide detailed information and evidence concerning the use and occupancy of traditional lands.

Since the BCTC Agreement of 1992, treaty negotiations in British Columbia have occurred in six stages. The first is a Statement of Intent: a First Nation or its representatives submit a document to the British Columbia Treaty Commission, providing a map of their traditional territory and indicating their intention to negotiate a treaty. In the second stage, the readiness of all parties to enter the negotiations is established. According to the Agreement,

7.1 The Commission shall:

(f) Assess the readiness of the Parties to commence negotiation of a framework agreement in accordance with the following criteria:

(i) Each Party has:

A. appointed a negotiator;

B. confirmed that it has given the negotiator a comprehensive and clear mandate;

C. sufficient resources to carry out the procedure;

D. adopted a ratification procedure; and

E. identified the substantive and procedural matters to be negotiated.

(ii) In the case of a First Nation:

A. has identified and begun to address any overlapping territorial issues with neighbouring First Nations.

(iii) In the case of Canada and British Columbia respectively:

A. has obtained background information on the communities, people and interests likely to be affected by negotiations; and

B. has established mechanisms for consultation with non-aboriginal interests.[16]

The third stage is the Framework Agreement, which identifies the topics and objectives of the negotiations, and establishes procedural arrangements and a timetable. The fourth stage, the Agreement in Principle (AIP) establishes the major points of agreement among the parties; although it is non-binding and its provisions may change during the negotiation process, it is generally taken as the basis for the eventual treaty. The fifth stage is the Final Agreement, which embodies the principles set forth in the AIP and brings them to their final form. It does not actually become a treaty, however, until it has been ratified by all parties: the British Columbia Legislature, the Parliament of Canada, and the First Nation in question. Finally, in the Implementation phase of this six-stage process, the terms and commitments that have been articulated in the treaty are put into effect.

The Nisga'a, having commenced negotiations before this process was in place, had to meet much more stringent criteria. They entered into negotiations with Canada based on the 1973 policy that was initiated following the

Calder case.[17] *Calder* did not require the government to change its policy and begin to negotiate treaties, but it did call into question the ownership of lands and resources across the country where treaties had not yet been negotiated. The Office of Native Claims was established in 1974 to represent the Minister of the Department of Indian Affairs and Northern Development (DIAND) and the federal government for the purposes of negotiating and settling land claims. They were known as comprehensive claims because they covered a broad range of issues, such as the protection of hunting, fishing, and trapping rights, land titles, and money and other benefits. First Nations that filed claims with the government, including the Nisga'a, had to provide extremely detailed information and evidence concerning their current and historical use and occupancy of traditional lands. This information was then reviewed for historical accuracy and legal merit—the Department of Justice was also involved—and the Minister of DIAND would issue a formal response on behalf of Canada.

In 1981 the federal government published *In All Fairness: A Native Claim Policy*, outlining an amended policy on claims negotiations. It noted in an appendix:

> In British Columbia, the potential for negotiating the Nisga'a
> claim is tenuous due primarily to the apprehension with which the
> provincial government approaches the possibility of unextinguished
> Native title within the province, and the doubt which the province
> has as to whether it should accept any responsibility to compensate
> native people for the loss of use and occupancy of
> traditional lands. Nevertheless in June of this year a full-time chief
> government negotiator was appointed by the Minister to negotiate a
> settlement and the province has agreed to participate in the
> negotiations. Preliminary negotiations with the Nisga'a Tribal
> Council got underway earlier this fall.[18]

In 1976, when the federal government accepted the Nisga'a claim for negotiation, the parties would generally begin substantive negotiations toward an Agreement in Principle immediately. It was only later that the treaty negotiating process required the parties to enter into a Framework Agreement before proceeding to the AIP. This explains why the original Framework Agreement between the Nisga'a and Canada was not dated until

September 12, 1989. Following October 3, 1990, when British Columbia became a party to the negotiations, a new Framework Agreement was negotiated and signed on March 20, 1991.

In a press release dated February 15, 1996, Canada, British Columbia, and the Nisga'a Tribal Council announced that they had reached an Agreement in Principle in British Columbia's first modern treaty. The Agreement in Principle was a two-hundred-page document that would form the basis of the Final Agreement negotiations. As detailed in the press release, it contained

> provisions on fisheries, lands and resources, access to lands, environmental assessment and protection, Nisga'a government, taxation, financial transfers and cultural artefacts.
>
> In essence, the agreement calls for a cash payment to the Nisga'a of $190 million and the establishment of a Nisga'a Central Government with ownership of and self-government over 1,900 square kilometres of land in the Nass River Valley. It also outlines the Nisga'a ownership of surface and subsurface resources on Nisga'a lands and spells out entitlements to Nass River salmon stocks and wildlife harvests.[19]

"Today we make history," Ronald Irwin declared. As Minister of Indian Affairs and Northern Development, he spoke for Canada. Joseph Gosnell, President of the Nisga'a Tribal Council, described the document as "a hard-fought compromise," and spoke of "a generation of Nisga'a growing old at the negotiating table." But he stressed that they were "making that compromise in order to become full and active participants in the social, political, and economic life of this country." BC Aboriginal Affairs Minister John Cashore spoke of the broader interests of British Columbians, and felt "very comfortable taking this back to the public for discussion."[20]

These heady words expressed the hope and the confidence, and perhaps the relief, that after more than a century of effort the journey of the Nisga'a was almost over. For me, however, the journey had just begun.

I was assigned to the negotiations on May 24, 1996. My appointment had been in the works for nearly five months. I was not reluctant to assume the challenge, *per se*, but I knew it would involve a great deal of travel, days and weeks away from my home and family in Saskatoon, and my personal life at the time needed to be considered with particular care. My wife, Alice, diagnosed twelve years before, had finally succumbed to cancer in late February of that year. Our four daughters were feeling the loss as deeply as I was. Though young adults, they and a granddaughter were all living at home.

I knew from experience that the work would be all consuming. I had been a Chief Negotiator for the Government of Canada in British Columbia since 1993, but had been working on land settlements as a Chief Negotiator since March 1982 when I left an established practice as a labour negotiator to begin talks with the Inuit of the Eastern Arctic, which eventually led to the Nunavut land claims settlement and the creation of Nunavut. My explicit mandate as a Chief Negotiator, as my press biography states, is:

> to advise on the preparation and approach regarding negotiations in British Columbia; to assess and co-ordinate the federal government's preparation for the initial meetings with First Nations and British Columbia; and to represent the Minister of Indian Affairs and Northern Development in the initial and other meetings convened by the British Columbia Treaty Commission with First Nations and British Columbia.

In this role, I have met with more than thirty First Nations as they entered the treaty process, and I have represented the federal government at numerous workshops and regional meetings aimed at explaining the British Columbia treaty process and the role of the federal government in it. I have also negotiated framework agreements with the Gitanyow, the Gitksan, the Haisla, and the Wet'suwet'en. So I had a fair idea what would be involved in the Nisga'a negotiations. Especially in the Final Agreement stage, when pressure is mounting on all sides, the demands on a negotiator's time and energy can be overwhelming. Suddenly you have no personal life, and sometimes it seems you have no family, either. When you do get home, you are completely exhausted, and your children's rightful claims on your time can be only partially fulfilled. I have always been fortunate in having a supportive family, but I am not unaware of the sacrifices I have asked of them in order to pursue my work. Of course, the same sacrifices were asked of all the negotiators' families, whether they represented the Nisga'a, British Columbia, or Canada.

At the time of my appointment to the Nisga'a file, I was concurrently involved in several other negotiations in British Columbia, which I would leave to take over the Nisga'a negotiations, and with the Inuit of northern Quebec. I was also finalizing the report of the Western Grain Marketing Panel, of which I was the chair. Even after the Final Report was delivered on July 1, 1996, there was clean-up and media work to be done to bring the process to a conclusion.

So it wasn't as if I needed the Nisga'a negotiations to round out a half-filled itinerary. Rather, I felt it was something that needed to be done, and I was deeply honoured to be asked to do it. Unlike labour negotiations, treaties are not based on a legal duty to negotiate an agreement. Governments have accepted the responsibility as good public policy, based on social, legal, economic, and political reasons. More than that, the Crown has a moral obligation to address the concerns and, where possible, redress the grievances of aboriginal peoples living under its protection. This is true of all citizens, of course, but in the case of aboriginal citizens it needs to be said aloud. It was in that spirit, then, that I accepted the challenge.

As Chief Federal Negotiator, my job was to represent the Government of Canada on behalf of the Minister of Indian Affairs and Northern Development in negotiations with the Nisga'a Tribal Council and the Province of British Columbia. Broadly speaking, I was responsible for all negotiations and consultations as they applied to the federal position. More specifically, I was to assist and direct the federal negotiating team in interpreting federal government policies and translating them into suitable bargaining strategies. As a team, we were to negotiate, within the mandate approved by the federal Cabinet and subject to ministerial instructions, all documents that would ultimately comprise the settlement package that would be recommended to the Minister for approval.

Jim Barkwell was responsible for the internal management and operations of the core team. The core team reported to Jim, and together we carried out the day-to-day activities of the team. The core team also participated in developing negotiation strategies, advising and informing the working groups, composing briefing notes to the Minister and senior department officials on "hot topics and issues," responding to the many letters received by the Minister and the department, drafting and redrafting memoranda to Cabinet, and liaising with the department on negotiation positions, internal meetings, and frequent presentations to third parties and advisory committees, as well as attending main table and working group meetings.

The structure and method of the negotiations had already been established. The core federal team included Florence Roberge as Associate Chief Negotiator, and Jim Barkwell as Senior Negotiator. Jim worked tirelessly within the system, always questioning and prodding when the federal answer to one of our questions or requests was "no"; I imagine they grew to despise him in Ottawa, which made him all the more valuable in our eyes. Andrew Beynon, another member of the core team, was someone I had worked with on other negotiations in British Columbia; I had tremendous confidence in his legal skills and his approach to issues. The team was rounded out by the quietly competent Maureen Parkes from the Department of Justice; Brian Martin from the Federal Treaty Negotiation Office, whose primary role, aside from wine-maker and connoisseur, was in fish and wildlife; and the pipe-smoking Doug Wanamaker, whose expertise was in lands and resources. I had the good fortune to have worked with Doug in the Nunavut land selection negotiations, and was accustomed to his bad jokes. Kalia Rothkop, our Program Assistant, co-ordinated support services, including travel and accommodation, and engaging secretaries when necessary. Even in the most frantic periods of the negotiations, she maintained her sense of humour and managed to make sure we were always where we needed to be when we needed to be there, and that what we required was there, too.

The others at that time were strangers to me, as I was to them. In time we would develop the confidence in one another that is critical to negotiations. Each of us brought different skills to the task at hand, and we worked effectively as a team.

I immediately began work with the core team on organizing our resources and being brought up to speed on issues to be dealt with at the main negotiating table and among the various working groups. As many as seventeen working groups and committees existed during the negotiation period, with names as formidable as the tasks that had been set them: Legal Drafting, Tax, Fiscal, Lands, Right of Way and Indemnities. Each had a vital role to play in the overall process.

At the beginning and throughout my tenure as Chief Federal Negotiator, I sought direction from government departments—at one time or another every one of them was involved in the Nisga'a treaty—and as often as not tried to reconcile their sometimes conflicting demands with what I thought would be possible, given our resources and the time frame we had been given. The government was looking at twelve months to the Final

Agreement. I could not be so optimistic. It is impossible to assess the time necessary to do something when it is not yet apparent what details need to be worked out at the negotiating table. One thing I did know from experience was that the legal drafting of the Agreement and the development of an implementation plan would be extraordinarily time consuming. I had no real confidence that we would be finished in twelve months.

For one thing, it soon became apparent that the Agreement in Principle was not as detailed as others with which I was familiar. Many homeowners will sympathize with the metaphor that struck me as we peeled off the temporary wallpaper of the Agreement in Principle to apply the permanent paint of the Final Agreement, only to find gaping holes in the wall itself. They had merely been papered over. This is not to be critical of the drafters of the Agreement; there is no magic formula as to what an Agreement in Principle must contain, and this one was obviously something with which all parties had been satisfied. But it led others outside the process to a certain lack of appreciation for the amount of work still required, and no doubt contributed to rising pressure for a quick closing.

On June 19, 1996, I held my first meeting as Chief Federal Negotiator with representatives from the Province and the Nisga'a Tribal Council. The purpose of the meeting was simply to review the numerous issues to be addressed, to look at dates and deadlines, and to develop a working plan. Once these details had been decided, negotiations on the Final Agreement would begin in earnest.

The first substantive meeting of those negotiations opened routinely. A Nisga'a elder offered a prayer, and each session thereafter was opened the same way. This was followed by a few brief opening remarks of welcome, then we moved to the business at hand. I was reassured by the ordinariness of it, and by the attitude of a people who did not separate their faith lives and traditions from the mundane tasks of everyday existence. Other than that, it was business as usual, or so I assumed.

I was soon disabused of the notion. The meeting proved to be anything but routine. Having taken over the file from another Chief Negotiator—who had left under circumstances about which I knew, and asked, nothing—I was expecting a certain amount of unease, even hostility, from those who had been involved in the process for months and years already. I was not disappointed. Nor was I particularly surprised at the suspicion and mistrust accorded me as a new player entering the talks at this advanced stage and at such a senior level. It was not my mandate to be popular, or even liked, among those I would be facing across the table. It was essential, however, that I be trusted, and building that trust proved more difficult than I had anticipated.

The task was not made any easier when I had to present some hard lines at that first meeting. One had to do with the Openness Protocol. In British Columbia, this is a document negotiated among the three parties to an agreement—the three parties being, again, the Province, the federal government, and the First Nation seeking a treaty—that makes provision for public involvement in the process. It may include open sessions at the table, inviting the media to observe and report on the proceedings, or releasing tabled documents to the public. For the Nisga'a negotiations, the federal position was that the Openness Protocol must reflect the positions of other openness protocols in the province. Hardly a controversial proposal, one might have thought. But, as with all relationships, whether among individuals or among governments, this issue had a history.

Nearly two years before, on September 19, 1994, the provincial government had issued a written *Instruction on Open Negotiations* for treaties.[21] To ensure that lasting arrangements were negotiated with the First Nations of British Columbia, the Province felt that local governments, third parties that might be affected by a proposed treaty, and the public at large must have confidence in the negotiating process. Ideally, the process, if not the individual participants in the process, would enjoy the support of all the diverse communities of British Columbia.

For the Province and the federal government alike, this was a departure from previous policy, but it is worth remembering that British Columbia was breaking new ground here. The *Calder* case had opened the door for the Nisga'a to begin negotiations in 1976. With the advent of the BCTC process in 1992 the way was open to every First Nation in the province that was prepared to file a Statement of Intent, and there were many. The *Instruction on Open Negotiations* was therefore aimed at insuring that the interests and concerns of all British Columbians would be taken into account throughout any treaty negotiation. As spelled out in the *Instruction*, the manner in which any given negotiations were to be open was delineated in the Openness Protocol negotiated among the representatives appointed by the First Nation, the Province, and the federal government. These protocols, further, were to be subject to express principles that were outlined in the *Instruction* under such headings as "Open Negotiations," "Voices of All British Columbians," "Information Sharing," "Province Wide Mandates," and "Ratification by the Legislative Assembly."

Shortly after the *Instruction on Open Negotiations* was issued, Anna Terrana, MP, speaking to the Treaty Negotiations Advisory Committee (TNAC) on behalf of the federal minister and government, confirmed Canada's commitment to a more open treaty negotiating process:

> Canada recognizes that a well-informed public and an effective consultation process are essential to the success of the treaty negotiation process in BC. Our challenge is to satisfy the public's desire for openness without jeopardizing the effective negotiation of new treaties.
>
> People and organizations want to be involved, and they want a consultation process which meets their communities' expectations. Negotiators are seeking to accommodate these concerns, while keeping in mind the purpose and intention of third party consultation.[22]

A communiqué released with Mrs. Terrana's speech explained that Canada's approach would be guided by the following considerations:

◆ Canada will invite members of local third-party advisory committees to work directly with and have access to federal departments, and to provide comments on options being developed for discussion at the negotiating table.

◆ Agreements-in-principle among the federal and provincial governments and First Nations will be publicly explained and discussed before ratification.

◆ Canada will continue to seek effective and innovative means of information sharing—including the widest possible sharing of documents.[23]

Mrs. Terrana's speech and the accompanying press release were rightly taken as a commitment on the part of the federal government to the principles expressed in the *Instruction on Open Negotiations*. Its intent has been honoured in every treaty negotiation since.

The Nisga'a negotiations, however, had commenced before either government changed its policy, and consequently operated in a more closed environment. They were by no means secret, as opponents of the Final Agreement have since tried to suggest. Consultations with regional advisory committees, treaty advisory committees, sectorial advisory committees, and TNAC were well established and ongoing. Still, the federal position I enunciated in that first meeting required that the Openness Protocol be addressed. It was as much a provincial issue as a federal one, but I took the flack for it. While respecting the confidentiality of the proceedings, I don't think I will be giving much away by chronicling some of the concerns of my fellow negotiators.

Broadly speaking, the feeling was that I had been foisted upon them from elsewhere and wanted to change a process that had already resulted in a very good Agreement in Principle. I could not expect everyone else just to accept my ideas. This process had worked extremely well until I arrived. Why should they change it? Was I suggesting that everyone there, including my predecessor, had been ineffective in their consultations, that they had not been keeping the public informed? I was reminded that it was Canada, in the person of my predecessor, who had stressed that no major deal could be successfully negotiated in public. Third parties would simply use the information to undermine the process. Was that what Canada wanted?

There was a good deal of personal abuse as well, much of it impugning my motives and my honesty. It was nothing I had not heard in other words and at other tables. Jim Aldridge, one of several speakers who took the occasion to express his concern, was particularly eloquent. One never becomes entirely inured to such things, but it helps to remember that what seem to be bitter personal attacks across the negotiating table are rarely either bitter or personal. Many of us at the Nisga'a table were lawyers, and lawyers, perhaps alone among modern professionals, are trained in argument and rhetoric. This goes a long way toward explaining why there are so many of us in government—and why many of us end up facing each other across negotiating tables. It seems to be our natural element, and while a casual observer might have been embarrassed, incensed, or outraged by the words that flew across the table, I recognized—and could not help but admire—that Aldridge is an extremely good lawyer.

It did not stop with the Openness Protocol. For I brought other "good news" to the table in that first session: specifically, Canada was not prepared to be legally bound by the Interim Protection Measures (IPM) Agreement.

According to the Province's own definition, interim protection measures are

> formal agreements between Canada, the Province and a
> First Nation, which are undertaken in the later stages of a treaty
> negotiation. The agreement may include carefully defined limits
> on the development or alienation of a specific area of land in order
> to protect what has been agreed to in the negotiations. Interim
> protection measures require agreement among all parties to the
> treaty and must be approved by the Provincial Cabinet.[24]

Typically, interim protection measures might preclude the sale or development of land by the Crown or by individuals in an area being claimed as traditional territory by a First Nation while negotiations are ongoing. In the case of the Nisga'a negotiations, the IPM Agreement had expired with the initialling of the Agreement in Principle in February 1996. Another one was in the works, as a new IPM Agreement is necessary at every major stage in the negotiations, but Canada was not prepared to regard it as a binding contract. The federal position was that negotiations are voluntary, and there are no binding agreements except for the treaty itself.

In addition, the new IPM Agreement contained a clause that committed the federal government to "use best efforts to conclude the treaty by January 31, 1997." I could not sign such a document. The term "best efforts" put a heavy onus on the government, and despite the fact that the Nisga'a had committed to that date, I believed it was unrealistic.

Both the Province and the Nisga'a were less than happy about this. And I wasn't finished yet. Two other issues I had to raise before the day was over had to do with the environmental chapter of the Agreement in Principle and Nisga'a citizenship. That pushed them to the edge.

Were previous understandings to be breached now that I was Chief Federal Negotiator? Had I been appointed simply to impede negotiations? Once again I was reminded that this table had a process that worked, and I couldn't just show up with my past and impose new processes and ideas at the whim of the federal government or as an exercise in personal aggrandisement.

I wondered offhandedly how I could be expected to show up anywhere and not bring my past with me. Who was I, if not the sum of my experiences? And surely those experiences had some bearing on my appointment as Chief Federal Negotiator. At one point, in fact, I was asked to explain something— based on my experience.

I did.

Point made: experience counts for something after all.

When the meeting broke up, it simply ended. There were no handshakes, no smiles, no expressions of good will. I was feeling drained and weary. Still, I had survived my baptism of fire—for such I assumed it was.

Welcome to Nisga'a.

Chapter Three

....

I WAS INVOLVED IN MANY LABOUR NEGOTIATIONS before becoming a full-time treaty negotiator. Once, during talks with the Steelworkers' Union in Saskatoon, my opposite number somehow received the impression that I had called him a liar.

"Are you calling me a liar?" he demanded. "Is that how I'm supposed to take that?"

"You can take it any way you want to," I told him.

He became livid, and invited me in adolescent macho fashion to "take this outside." I understood his position, if not his response. Losing face at the negotiating table can be as damaging as showing your hand too soon. He had to show me—and, more important, his own bargaining team—that he would not tolerate accusations against his honesty as a negotiator.

Leaving aside for the moment the question of whether the accusation might have been justified, I found myself in an impossible position. As an adult, a lawyer, and a professional negotiator, I could hardly accept his invitation to settle the matter with violence. On the other hand, I would weaken my own position irreparably if I just sat there, or gave the impression that I was afraid of him. In the end I made a gesture that I hoped did not betray my deep unease and followed him out of the meeting room.

The talks had been taking place in the basement of a downtown hotel. We emerged into a concourse of glass-fronted shops that was anything but deserted in the middle of a busy day. Curiosity and alarm were plain on the faces of the business owners and their customers as my fellow negotiator lit into me. To my everlasting relief, he had the sense to use insult and invective rather than his fists.

"You bastard!" he shouted. "You son of a bitch! Don't you *ever* call me a liar in front of my team! Don't you *ever* accuse me of deliberately misrepresenting an issue! Don't you *ever*—"

And on it went. After listening for a moment or two, I suggested that if all he was going to do was yell at me he could do it just as well inside. I turned my back to him and hurriedly returned to the meeting room. Moments later we were all back at the table, and negotiations proceeded, if not amicably, then at least with mutual respect.

The point is I went outside. Had I not shown myself willing to do so, I doubt we could have closed the deal as soon as we did.

It is rare that such moments arise in negotiations, but when they do, negotiators must show themselves willing, at least metaphorically, to "take it outside." Reason, argument, and compromise—the basis of any successful negotiations—are only truly effective when they are not seen to proceed from a position of weakness. People on both sides of the negotiating table must believe that what they are doing is right and just and true if the resultant agreement is to withstand public scrutiny and the test of time. They must have courage, if you like—the courage of their convictions, the courage to carry on in the face of exhaustion, delays, and often-contradictory instructions from departmental bureaucrats, and the courage to stand up to constant criticism from those outside the process who have no real grasp of the process itself or of the issues at stake.

Some might call it stubbornness rather than courage. If so, it is stubbornness with a purpose, and it is especially important in treaty negotiations.

While there are many similarities between bargaining toward a collective agreement and negotiating toward a treaty, the differences are profound. Certainly, one brings the same skills to each table, the same attitude, the same commitment to a just and reasonable settlement. In each case, too, negotiators must be responsible to the principals they represent. They must each have a mandate that is clear, yet flexible enough to allow them to compromise where necessary in order to resolve contentious issues.

Chuck Connaghan, a former Chief Commissioner of the British Columbia Treaty Commission, used to advise, "There are three important steps to any successful negotiation: preparation, preparation, and preparation!" Preparation is essential in both labour and treaty negotiations. Participants must have a genuine understanding of the issues, and each must be willing to listen to what the other party is saying—even, sometimes, while appearing not to. A key objective of labour agreements and treaties is to provide a framework for a relationship that will be long lasting, and both will provide a broad range of mechanisms for resolving disputes. In each case, too, negotiators are bargaining for collective rights that will largely be exercised by individuals.

Unlike a collective agreement, however, a treaty is forever. The parties will not be able to revisit its provisions in two or three years. There are no labour relations boards to act as adjudicators, no amendments except in accordance with strict provisions that must themselves be negotiated. A treaty is a compromise between expectations and reality. No one party ever gets everything it wants. It must be fair, it must be equitable, and it must represent the best efforts of all involved because it will endure well beyond the lifetimes of those who negotiated it.

Another major difference between labour and treaty negotiations, in British Columbia at least, is the tripartite nature of the exercise. With three participants, each negotiating team is dealing with two others, not just one. This does not merely create a third more work for everybody. The relationship between the number of participants and the effort demanded from each seems to be geometric rather than arithmetic, and the complexity of the negotiations can become overwhelming, especially when Canada and British Columbia, or British Columbia and the Nisga'a, or Canada and the Nisga'a, while all wishing to achieve the same goal, bring fundamentally different approaches to the table. This contributes to the length of time it takes to conclude an agreement. A collective agreement may take days, weeks, or even months; a treaty will take years.

The first year of the Nisga'a negotiations toward a Final Agreement proceeded much as I had expected: with animosity, frustration, and mutual distrust, tempered by a shared sense that we were all involved in something much greater than our individual desires and ambitions, and occasionally— just occasionally—a small step forward.

In late August 1996, three months after I was assigned to the file, representatives of the Nisga'a Tribal Council journeyed to Ottawa to meet with various officials and discuss the progress—I use the term advisedly—of the negotiations. I wanted to be part of it for several reasons. The trip provided me with the first opportunity I'd had since my appointment to meet with key senior officials, including Scott Serson, Deputy Minister in DIAND. I was able to brief him on outstanding issues, review strategies, and receive direction on policy and procedures. I came away from the meeting with a general idea of who would need to be involved in facilitating certain decisions. Scott Serson's intimate knowledge of the workings of government, his acquaintance with most of the major players at the deputy minister level, his commitment to a treaty, and most of all his advice, freely offered and gratefully accepted, proved invaluable to me in the subsequent conduct of the negotiations. As with many things in life, but especially in government, knowing who to talk to is at least as important as knowing what to say.

This was the first of several occasions that the Nisga'a met with officials from the Minister's office during the Final Agreement negotiations. In my experience, such meetings can be helpful if they focus on one or two key areas of difference—there is little profit, at this stage, in talking about things everyone agrees on, or bringing in a laundry list of grievances—but they should not be too frequent, otherwise they tend to undermine the role of the federal negotiation team. For this reason, too, it is important that the Chief Federal Negotiator or a key member of the team be present, so that subsequent statements made at the negotiating table about what was said or promised by the Deputy Minister or other ministerial officials can be verified or challenged with the authority of first-hand knowledge.

It was not until the following month that I had my first opportunity for a face-to-face discussion on the Nisga'a file with the Honourable Ron Irwin, the Minister of DIAND, who had overall responsibility for the negotiations. While ministers are continually receiving briefings and briefing notes from departmental officials and are generally familiar with the issues, personal meetings are always helpful.

The Minister was in Vancouver for several reasons, and the Nisga'a negotiations were not the only subject on the agenda. Even so, we managed to discuss the status of the negotiations, and the capacity of the Province and the Nisga'a to negotiate in a timely manner. We reviewed the outstanding issues that were the responsibility of DIAND, such as certainty, self-government, and fiscal matters, and others, including fishery concerns, that crossed departmental jurisdictions and might necessitate minister-to-minister consultations.

Members of the Minister's staff attended, as well as Assistant Deputy Minister John Sinclair, Greg Gauld, John Watson, and Doreen Mullins, all of whom I would be working with closely in the months to come. It was interesting to observe the dynamics of their relationship with the Minister, to see how each of them responded to him, and to assess his response in turn. A negotiator learns to observe relationships among people, to categorize personalities and situations, much as an actor will study various people in order to bring fidelity to a role. Humankind is of prodigious variety, and one can never have enough information about them. Knowing what to say at the negotiating table, knowing what to expect, knowing how to read the others around you is largely a matter of applied experience.

Experience, of course, is ever expanding and constantly useful, and the Nisga'a negotiations provided a rich new source of knowledge. The Nisga'a themselves were no small part of this.

In late September, after my meeting with the Minister, we held our first negotiating session in Terrace, the small city at the junction of the Skeena and Kitsumkalum Rivers in northwestern British Columbia. For practical reasons, the bulk of the negotiations took place in Vancouver, and occasionally Victoria, but for equally practical reasons we also met on a regular basis in Terrace and the slightly larger city of Prince Rupert, 140 kilometres to the west at the mouth of the Skeena River, and from time to time in New Aiyansh and other Nisga'a communities. These changes of venue were critical in providing the federal and provincial negotiating teams with an opportunity to experience first-hand the culture and territory that formed such a large part of our discussions at the table. They allowed us to meet with other members of the Nisga'a community, to talk with elders, and to gain a deeper sense of the issues at stake and the historical importance of the exercise we were privileged to be carrying forward. Equally important, perhaps, meeting in traditional Nisga'a territory allowed the beneficiaries of the treaty, particularly the elders, to attend the negotiating sessions and in some sense take ownership of the process. They had been at it since 1887. If anyone deserved a share in the hope that the efforts of more than a century were finally bearing fruit, it was the progeny of those who had first journeyed to Victoria Harbour so many years before.

In many ways, these trips north, though problematic and sometimes dangerous in winter, were stimulating, even inspiring. I believe they contributed directly to the ultimate success of the whole enterprise. At the very least, they gave everyone a perspective on the negotiations that we might never have had if we had stayed holed up in Vancouver.

On a more practical level, they gave the negotiating teams a better understanding of third-party interests. Third parties are defined as people and groups outside governments and First Nations who have an interest in the treaty. The interest might be practical or economic. Someone might own land within the boundaries of a First Nation's traditional territory; a corporation might hold a logging or a mining lease in or near the proposed territory; a town or a city might be concerned about the possible impact on the local economy. Our regular trips north allowed us to meet with third parties, to hear and observe how they might be affected both positively and negatively by the treaty, and to obtain their advice and suggestions on the matters under negotiation.

Third-party concerns were of much greater importance to the federal and provincial governments than many third parties realized. While in Terrace and Prince Rupert, the federal and provincial teams spoke to the local press, gave briefings and interviews, met with local politicians and community leaders, heard their concerns, and, more important, began to seek ways of addressing them. We also met with the various advisory committees with whom we would be consulting more and more frequently in the coming months. Our first meetings were with the Kitimat-Stikine Regional Advisory Committee in Terrace and the Bulkley-Skeena Regional Advisory Committee in Telkwa. Both organizations represented a broad range of citizens and interests. We discussed the status and nature of the Nisga'a negotiations, reviewed outstanding issues, and touched on the possible strategies and directions our respective governments were liable to follow. We sought their advice and direction on all issues. As negotiations progressed, the federal and provincial negotiating teams met with these and other committees many more times, often reviewing treaty chapters with them clause by clause.

In Vancouver, meanwhile, problems were developing more rapidly than we could solve them. By early October 1996, a work plan had been established that outlined the issues and topics that would take us to the spring of 1997. But the devil, as they say, was in the details. It was becoming increasingly apparent that the schedules and deadlines established at the main negotiating table, though useful in keeping our energies focused, had more to do with wishes than reality. It mattered little what we wanted to accomplish or how soon we wanted to accomplish it, the wheels of the bureaucratic process were ponderous, and they turned exceedingly slowly. This was less true at the provincial level than the federal, but in both cases, systems were in place, and if we were to make any progress at all, they would have to be respected.

Our own system at the main table was comparatively simple. Negotiations could involve as few as eight people or as many as forty, depending on the issues under discussion. The shape and size of the table varied accordingly. Generally, it was rectangular or triangular, with each team occupying its allotted position. Refreshments were available at all times: water, coffee, tea, juices, pastries, and fruit were provided by the host team every day—another essential point of negotiation—and they were much appreciated.

Daily sessions began with a prayer led by one of the Nisga'a elders, followed by statements from the Chief Negotiators. Sessions were chaired by a member of one of the negotiating teams, rotating weekly among Canada, the Nisga'a, and British Columbia. The chair was responsible for calling the session to order, recognizing speakers, following (sometimes enforcing) the agenda, and adjourning for breaks and lunches or when one or more of the parties requested a caucus.

Because these were Final Agreement negotiations, the main table worked from the text of the two-hundred-page Agreement in Principle. The schedule of chapters to be discussed was decided in advance, as members of all three negotiating teams frequently had other commitments related to the negotiations and would have to arrange their schedules to attend main table negotiations when their presence was required.

In most cases, at the main table or during legal drafting sessions, the text under discussion would be projected onto a screen from Jim Aldridge's computer, and negotiations would proceed on a clause-by-clause basis. As one clause was agreed upon, the focus shifted to the next, and the next. All sides expected that once a clause was accepted at the main table it would be accepted by all three negotiating teams, subject ultimately to our principals' review and acceptance, our principals being the governments of Canada and British Columbia and the Nisga'a Tribal Council.

Sit down, talk, work things out; it sounds simple enough. If we had been left to ourselves, it probably would have been. It might also have been a recipe for disaster. Much as we sometimes might have liked to, no one can negotiate in a vacuum.

The federal consultation and decision-making process involved a number of key committees. Our primary point of contact was with the Ottawa

Federal Caucus, a vast body comprising all government departments and agencies. Most often, representatives met on an "as needed" basis to consult with the negotiating team on chapters, policy issues, and memoranda to Cabinet. The British Columbia Federal Caucus, made up of all federal departments represented in the province, provided advice at the provincial level. Wherever it was located, each department maintained and guarded its own jurisdiction. It was at this level that problem-solving initiatives were put in train and consensus was sought on wide-ranging issues.

The Senior Policy Committee, which is internal to DIAND, was chaired by the Deputy Minister and made up of the Associate Deputy Minister, Assistant Deputy Ministers, and other senior officials. This committee approved all policy initiatives within the Department and all memoranda to Cabinet before passing them on to the next level. The federal team looked to the Senior Policy Committee for direction in interpreting government policies.

The Federal Steering Committee on Comprehensive Claims is an interdepartmental body made up of Assistant Deputy Ministers. Normally, issues identified or put forward by the negotiating team in British Columbia would begin to be resolved at the Federal Caucus level before being passed on to the Senior Policy Committee for refinement and approval—or sometimes disapproval—and then handed up once again to the Federal Steering Committee. From there they would be referred to the Minister, who would refer them to the relevant Cabinet committee, when required, or directly to the Cabinet.

To the average citizen, the system may appear needlessly complex. This is to ignore the historical reality that all government systems are needlessly complex, and no one in Ottawa saw any reason the Nisga'a negotiations should be any different. In theory, the process was designed to resolve a given issue at the lower levels, so that by the time it worked its way through the system it would be narrowly defined and all departments would be supportive of it. In reality, virtually every form of inter- and intra-departmental communications and consultation had to be invoked in order to bring closure on any specific issue or point of contention. Members of the federal core negotiating team who were obliged to take part in departmental consultations and attend their meetings, either in person or by telephone, found themselves perpetually arguing, cajoling, and pleading in and among departments to arrive at a simple clarification of policy. Half the time, it seemed to me, we were negotiating not with the Nisga'a or British Columbia but with the various and labyrinthine departments of our own government.

For the core team in Vancouver, the Nisga'a negotiations were the centre of the universe, the ultimate priority. We had agreed on our timetables with the Province and the Nisga'a. We had set our deadlines . . . and more often than not failed to meet them. To the other parties at the table, such behaviour was seen as deliberate, almost conspiratorial. Some even saw Canada's unconscionable foot-dragging as a calculated attempt to scuttle the treaty. This put enormous pressure on the core team, and additional strain on already strained relationships around the table. What the Nisga'a and the Province could not, or would not, see was the weight of the bureaucratic burden that had been placed on us. The federal government put tremendous emphasis on these negotiations, but the cogs and wheels of the system that served it often appeared utterly indifferent.

The changing priorities and workloads of every government department will have a substantial impact on the government's ability to advance any particular issue. Our Minister might have wished to push the Nisga'a negotiations forward with the highest priority, but the system as a whole could not place the same degree of urgency on a single matter when it was concurrently dealing with hundreds of others: national and international crises, domestic policy, prairie farmers, the Atlantic fishery, the economy, the Armed Forces, the situation in Rwanda, the CBC, the National Film Board, the separatists in Quebec, and the myriad of issues within DIAND involving other First Nations in British Columbia and across Canada. The Nisga'a negotiations occupied just one more place in the queue.

Understanding this did not lessen the frustration of those of us who stood next to the blaze while the fire chiefs debated the size of the hose they should give us to put it out. It was always difficult to balance the needs of the table with the realities of other government and departmental activities and priorities.

Equally frustrating were my continual attempts to convince my colleagues across the table that the Minister was neither omniscient nor omnipotent. While Ron Irwin, Jane Stewart, and Bob Nault, successively, were responsible within the federal system for conducting the negotiations and obtaining ratification, neither they nor the Department had the jurisdiction and the authority to deal with all of the issues being negotiated, and neither did the Prime Minister. Under the federal government, it is through legislation that ministers are granted specific authority and responsibility in their areas of jurisdiction, and legislation cannot be changed by a policy to negotiate treaties. Topics under negotiation frequently crossed jurisdictional boundaries. Access to Nisga'a lands, for example, was a topic of interest to all departments, but it was particularly important to the Department of National Defence, the Department of Transport, the Department of Fisheries and Oceans, DIAND, and Natural Resources Canada, while the Department of Finance, the Treasury Board, the Privy Council Office, and the Department of Justice had an overarching interest in all areas. The range of issues covered by the Nisga'a treaty touched on virtually every ministry of the Canadian government at some point in the negotiations.

As chapters of the treaty came up for negotiation, members of the core team were obliged to meet with the affected department or agency in advance to review the draft chapter, identify the issues that needed to be dealt with, and elaborate a strategy for doing so. More than one meeting was required, as frequently there were differences of approach among departments and between the negotiators and the departments. At best, it was time consuming. At worst, it was like pulling teeth to reach a consensus and develop a response that could be brought to the table. But the support of individual departments was critical to the ultimate success of the negotiations, and every member of the negotiating team knew it. Unfortunately, so did every department. Without the support of the departments that had jurisdiction over the issues being negotiated, it would be difficult, if not impossible, to obtain Cabinet approval. Consequently, we attended numerous difficult and frustrating meetings. The paper on which we drafted and redrafted successive chapters and provisions would have eaten up a small forest, and I'm sure I racked up enough air fares between Vancouver and Ottawa and my home in Saskatoon to keep at least one airline out of financial trouble!

Government policies and internal directives are continually subject to review owing to changing circumstances, in response to legal decisions, or simply because it's time for another departmental review. Policy reviews, much like treaty negotiations, are notorious for their longevity and missed deadlines. As the Nisga'a talks were taking place over years rather than weeks or days, it was inevitable that we would one day collide with a departmental review. In fact, we hit several, and each time it proved extraordinarily difficult to secure any guidance over a provision or a chapter that impinged on the department's jurisdiction. Officials were unwilling, I suppose, to step out in advance of a new direction.

To be fair, the concerns of the various government departments and agencies over the Nisga'a negotiations were rarely trivial. Despite the popular, and in some cases justified, view of politicians as unprincipled opportunists who care only for short-term policies that will keep them in power, I found the federal ministers, to be, for the most part, dedicated men and women who cared passionately not only for the process we were following but for the long-term consequences of that process—consequences that by their nature would only be felt long after they had retired from public service and passed on the frustrations and responsibilities of governing this maddening, eclectic nation to future generations.

Indeed, the ministers to whom we were directly responsible in DIAND brought a commitment to the Nisga'a negotiations that was critical to the eventual success of the enterprise. Aware that we were not only following a process but in many ways defining it as we went, each felt acutely his or her responsibility to posterity. They each brought different skills and talents to the issues that culminated in the treaty. Ron Irwin steered the Agreement in Principle through Cabinet and secured our mandate to conclude the final negotiations. He also began the process for a new approach to certainty. Jane Stewart concluded the certainty process, achieved the support of her colleagues for the treaty, and concluded the work on the legislation to eventually move it to Parliament. Bob Nault steered the contentious legislation through the parliamentary process, and would be responsible for beginning its implementation.

Still, the bureaucratic mind is beguiled by detail, by possibilities, by what-might-be or what-might-have-been. Chief among departmental concerns was the possibility—indeed, the certainty—that what we were doing would have consequences for other land claims not only in British Columbia but in other parts of Canada where treaty negotiations were being conducted. Responses and positions had to be carefully nuanced to minimize possible prejudice in future negotiations.

Treaty provisions were reviewed not only in the light of government policies and programs, but with an eye toward proposed changes in those policies and programs. Policy statements were deliberately vague, as if to invite a number of interpretations. More than once we were caught in the awkward position of having negotiated provisions according to previously acceptable government policy, only to find that they were no longer acceptable because policy had changed, or was about to change, or changes were being contemplated. In these circumstances our relations with DIAND, Justice, Fisheries, Environment, the Privy Council Office, Finance, and every other department whose fiefdom was impinged upon by the proposed provisions of the treaty were often fractious and argumentative. The reality was that we were at the table with the Province and the Nisga'a, dealing with real issues in real time, with very real constrictions on us and the process we were struggling to carry forward, whereas departmental Ottawa was, metaphorically speaking, at the table with the entire country, had no discernible timetable and, indeed, no apparent sense of time. We were concerned with immediate effects in our immediate vicinity, especially the impact any change in policy might have on the Province or the Nisga'a. Ottawa was concerned with potential effects across the country. I understood this, but from time to time, I admit, an image of thousands of civil servants with their heads in the sand rose unbidden to my mind.

It took a tremendous amount of time and effort to find solutions that would be acceptable to both sides—both sides being the federal negotiating team and the army of the civil service in Ottawa. Negotiations were no longer tripartite: a fourth participant seemed to have snuck in the back way. That we were, in effect, arguing against ourselves was a continual frustration. It was energy that we could have employed to much better effect at the main table or in the working groups. Compromise was the order of the day, and it was not always gracious compromise. Still, federal departments were sometimes forced to allow things to go forward that were not entirely to their liking. They did not always get what they wanted. Sometimes they, too, had to compromise, but in the end we had their support.

It was a requirement of our mandate that we meet from time to time with the Federal Caucus in Ottawa. Consequently, October 16 found us in the nation's capital, briefing them on our plans and progress and reviewing some of the major outstanding issues. For despite the endless internal consultations, the arguments, and the often contradictory instructions we received from bureaucrats, the one area that was left entirely up to the Chief Negotiator working with the core federal team was the conduct and strategy of the negotiations themselves. We alone determined how issues would be handled at the table. We alone decided who would attend the sessions on behalf of the federal government, even when departmental representatives from Ottawa sat in at the table or one of the working groups to provide practical information and technical advice. And we alone dictated the timing, subject to necessary responses from the ministries involved. In this instance, my aim was to provide the Caucus with an explanation of the role it would be expected to play as we moved toward the Final Agreement. Every Chief Negotiator has a different approach to the role of the Caucus, and I wanted to make sure they understood the cooperative line we preferred to take in the Nisga'a negotiations.

In this we were fairly successful, and we managed to reach an understanding of what we, the Province, and the Nisga'a referred to as a "handshake agreement." It was our first major goal in the final negotiations. It meant simply that we had a written agreement on all major issues, but there were still i's and t's to be dotted and crossed, and the document was subject to review by the principals.

Later that month we were in Prince Rupert, which afforded us an opportunity to meet with the Nisga'a Fisheries Advisory Committee. Fish are the traditional mainstay of the Nisga'a diet and economy, and, not surprisingly, they figure largely in tribal art and mythology. The Nass River supports five species of Pacific salmon, the fish that Frank Calder has called "the most important currency we have ever known."[1] In addition to the salmon, there are oolichan, also known as candlefish because the oil content of their flesh is so high that they can be dried and lighted like candles. These finger-sized members of the smelt family have fed the Nisga'a and provided them with oil for centuries. They have also attracted predators to the Nass—seals, porpoises, orcas, sea lions—to be hunted, in turn, by the Nisga'a. Fish were also of major economic concern to third parties and the region. Little wonder, then, that fish and fisheries were the subject of a good deal of consideration and contention during the Final Agreement negotiations.

I did not attend many meetings of the Fisheries Advisory Committee, as they tended to focus on technical matters. At the time there were major differences between the committee and the two governments that confounded all discussion. The issue of a commercial fish allocation for the Nisga'a, in fact, would never go away, and eventually resulted in one of the legal actions that was brought against the Final Agreement. For the moment, it was helpful to put the major policy issues to one side and focus on technical matters.

By November we needed something to celebrate. It came with an invitation to attend the formal signing ceremony of a Memorandum of

Understanding between the Nisga'a Nation and the Tsimshian Nation concerning their overlapping territories. The event took place during the Tsimshian Annual General Meeting in Prince Rupert on November 7. It lasted nearly six hours. More than two thousand people crowded into the Prince Rupert Civic Centre, including the Chief Negotiators for Canada, British Columbia, and the Nisga'a. The Tsimshian negotiators were also there, of course, along with five hundred Tsimshian and Nisga'a in traditional attire, the omnipresent drummers and dancers, and elders from both nations.

While the term "overlap" may have a number of meanings, in this case it refers to a territory or a resource that is occupied or used by more than one First Nation. An overlap agreement spells out how the First Nations' use of the shared territory or resource will be accommodated. Canada's preferred approach in negotiating modern treaties has been one of non-interference: First Nations should resolve such issues among themselves. But the ideal, at times, has proven difficult to achieve. In these instances the Chief Federal Negotiator has been mandated to assist the parties by such means as seem appropriate and timely to arrive at an agreement. If this, too, fails, Canada would still be prepared to conclude a treaty if three conditions had been met: the First Nation in question had negotiated with its neighbours in good faith, steps taken to resolve the impasse had proven to be unsuccessful, and the treaty contained an explicit statement that it would not affect any aboriginal or treaty rights of any other First Nation.[2]

The decision to proceed in the absence of an overlap agreement is not lightly taken. The situation is constantly monitored by DIAND, and any decision to proceed ultimately must follow the same tedious process as any other policy decision, ultimately to be considered by the Cabinet as part of the approval process for the Final Agreement. It is an issue that concerns not just our Minister and Department, but Justice, the Privy Council Office, Treasury Board, and others. The Nisga'a-Gitanyow overlap issue went through the same rigorous process to ensure that all three conditions had been met.

The Nisga'a had some time earlier reached an overlap arrangement with the Tahltan Nation, and while it appeared that overlaps existed with the Gitanyow and Gitksan, the agreement between the Nisga'a and the Tsimshian had been achieved without federal intervention. The Memorandum of Understanding the two parties signed on November 7, 1996, defined the relationship between the Nisga'a and the Tsimshian regarding boundary definitions, access to natural resources, and common development activities, and detailed the processes to be followed in future negotiations.

The signing ceremony in Prince Rupert was described to us as an extremely significant event in cultural terms, the equivalent in English law of signing and sealing a document, though with a good deal more celebration than is generally seen in lawyers' offices. Each side brought their elders, chiefs, and citizens together to hear the terms and bear witness to the agreement. Among the speakers at the ceremony were Robert Hill, President of the Tsimshian Tribal Council, and Chief Joe Gosnell of the Nisga'a, who described it as the completion of another important task in the treaty-making process. I remember thinking that life in Ottawa might be substantially more interesting and rewarding if politicians and civil servants could have experienced a portion of the joy and satisfaction that I witnessed in Prince Rupert that day.

Following the signing ceremony, we returned to Vancouver and business as usual, or as usual as business can get considering the task we had set ourselves. Winter was advancing: rain and fog in the south, rain and fog and snow and ice in the north. On our next trip to Terrace the airport was fogged in—again, business as usual—so we landed in Prince Rupert and arranged for buses to take us the 140 kilometres to Terrace. Evening had turned to night, and the damp and the cold promised to accompany us all the way. It would be extremely late by the time we got there; there might just be time enough to unpack or read a few paragraphs of the documents to be discussed tomorrow before falling into bed. The Province and the Nisga'a suggested that a preparatory visit to a wine and beer store might help lighten the journey.

There are few less formal venues than a bus, unless it's a bus with wine on board. Drunkenness has no place in treaty negotiations, but the occasional loosening of professional inhibitions in an informal setting can be invaluable. I had been working with these people for six months, but that bus ride from Prince Rupert to Terrace provided the first opportunity I'd had to talk with Jim Aldridge and some of the provincial and Nisga'a negotiators not as ciphers at a negotiating table but as people who shared a common humanity. My conversation with Jim was especially valuable, in that it allowed us to drop our adversarial postures and begin to establish a relationship based on shared experiences and training and a not-dissimilar past. It was at this point, I think, that the other negotiators recognized that I shared a common purpose with them, and though there were many, many rough days ahead, they were made easier by a sense of mutual trust and respect that I sensed had not been there before.

Perhaps as an immediate consequence of that bus trip, we were able to issue a joint press release the following day, December 5, 1996:

NISGA'A NEGOTIATIONS OPENNESS PROTOCOL SIGNED

TERRACE—Negotiators for the Nisga'a Tribal Council and the federal and provincial governments signed an openness protocol at the first Nisga'a open negotiating session today as the three parties began formal negotiations toward a final treaty.

"This protocol achieves the balance between practical and effective negotiations, and public information and consultation," said Indian Affairs Minister Ron Irwin. "I will ensure that the draft final agreement is made available for consultation purposes, in accordance with the terms of the openness protocol."

"Our government's endorsement of the protocol reconfirms our commitment to openness," said BC Aboriginal Affairs Minister John Cashore. "We are pleased that from now on the public will be invited to observe open treaty negotiations sessions, just like in all 46 sets of negotiations under the BC Treaty Commission process."

"The details of the Nisga'a negotiations have been widely communicated, discussed and debated since we signed our agreement-in-principle last March," said Nisga'a Tribal Council president Joseph Gosnell, Sr. "This new initiative is another way to ensure that the general public and all interested parties can learn more about our treaty. We welcome it. And we welcome them."

The public, media and stakeholders will all benefit from the establishment of the formal openness protocol that provides for:
♦ continued consultations with the public
♦ access to the negotiation table
♦ the public release of documents, and
♦ public information activities.

The negotiators also signed a new interim protection measures agreement to replace the one that expired with the initialling of the agreement-in-principle in February. It will provide certainty for all

parties' interests in lands and resources while a final treaty is
being negotiated. All existing licences, permits and tenures will be
honoured and public access to recreational areas ensured. Since the
signing of the agreement-in-principle, details of the new Interim
Protection Measures have been discussed with Nisga'a third-party
advisory groups.[3]

Not bad for a day's work, I thought. Still, the list of tasks yet to be accomplished seemed endless. At the same meeting in Terrace we reviewed scheduling plans and reports from all the working groups. None of the latter were able to give any indication of when information on specific topics would be available, beyond vague references to "spring" and "soon" and "consultant hired for the New Year." The end was still nowhere in sight.

On December 6, Canada and British Columbia met in Vancouver to discuss issues of mutual concern. It was one of many bilateral meetings we held throughout the negotiations. We did not exclude the Nisga'a by any means, but there were certain issues, such as third-party consultation and compensation, cost-sharing, and certainty, that the provincial and federal teams could attempt to resolve apart from the Nisga'a to allow the negotiations at the main table to move forward.

That same month, Trevor Proverbs was named Chief Negotiator for the Province, replacing Jack Ebbels who had been appointed Deputy Minister of Aboriginal Affairs in Victoria.

On December 11, during a negotiation session in Victoria, the British Columbia team hosted an informal gathering for all the negotiators at Patrick O'Rourke's home before the Christmas break. Everyone helped out with food and refreshments. The provincial Minister and the new Deputy Minister attended, and Jack received a gift from his former provincial colleagues.

On December 12 the working groups and the main table shut down for Christmas, but an endless stream of meetings kept the federal team occupied. We held internal consultations about self-government and certainty. We met with members of the Federal Caucus and with the Senior Policy Committee in Ottawa. On December 16 we met with our Deputy Minister and senior officials, and again on December 19 by telephone.

All three parties were busy charting their plans for the New Year, which arrived much faster than anyone had anticipated. In early January we were in Terrace again or at least trying to get there. According to anecdotal accounts, Air BC had a better record than Canadian Airlines for landing in Terrace. The type of plane they flew could land with a lower ceiling. We took Air BC, but could not land in Terrace. Canadian landed with no difficulty. In Prince Rupert we learned that snow slides had closed the highway. It looked as if we would be heading back to Vancouver. In the meantime, we would have to wait for a flight.

Hours passed.

The highway was open again before a flight became available, so we boarded a bus for Terrace, then travelled onward by car to Nass Camp, the site of a former logging operation. Begun as seven houses along one street in 1961, the population of Nass Camp peaked in the early 1970s with three hundred employees occupying eighteen houses and more than forty trailers. It had a ski lift, a skating rink, and all the equipment necessary for a bowling alley. The bowling alley was never built, but the rink is the only one in the Nass Valley, and it remains open for anyone who wants to use it.

The next day the phones were out at Nass Camp and Gitwinksihlkw. It rained to ensure that the roads would be treacherous. Even so, I was looking forward to visiting Gitwinksihlkw, a village on the west bank of the Nass River that, until recently, was accessible only on foot by suspension bridge. It was our first negotiation session in a Nisga'a community. The elders and residents made us feel welcome.

Gitwinksihlkw is a modest community of frame buildings and the occasional satellite dish, surrounded by forest and river except where the lava beds reach southward to the sacred mountain known to the Nisga'a as Xhlawit and to the Euro-Canadian, rather more prosaically, as Vetter Peak. A few years before, a pts'aan, or totem pole, had been carved and raised in the community for the first time in one hundred years.

The weather improved, and it was a pretty drive back to Terrace. We saw wolves, eagles, swans, and a set of antlers sticking up through the ice of the frozen river. The Nisga'a told me that a bull moose had plunged through a crack in the ice, and it had frozen over him before his antlers went under. I don't know how they can tell such stories and keep a straight face.

The plane was hours late leaving Terrace. It was after 1:00 AM when I finally arrived at my hotel room in Vancouver. The conclusion of another typical northern winter trip.

And welcome to 1997.

Chapter Four

....

THERE CAN BE FEW TALES MORE DRAMATIC or compelling than the modern struggle for aboriginal rights in Canada. True, those who seek tales of individual valour or villainy will be disappointed. We have no Sitting Bulls, no Crazy Horses, no General Custers or Geronimos. The closest we can come to that kind of notoriety is Louis Riel, the visionary, Sulpician-educated Métis leader who exhausted all avenues of diplomacy before he finally, reluctantly, took up arms in defence of his culture. That he and his Saskatchewan lieutenant, Gabriel Dumont, could cause such trouble—albeit short-lived—for the British Empire still amazes us. More telling, perhaps, that a half-caste, largely illiterate society could throw up two leaders of undoubted genius in a single generation was more than Canadian society could contemplate at the time.

And yet, Riel's struggle was in many ways the crucible of modern aboriginal land claims. From his first confident dispatches to the Canadian Government in 1869 to his final, desperate pleas in 1885, he sought not to exclude British and Canadian society from the wealth and promise of his birthright, but only to welcome settlers and newcomers in a manner that would respect the rights and traditions of his people. With very few exceptions, aboriginal society in Canada has followed his first choice ever since, seeking redress not through confrontation but through diplomacy and the law.

I am an Irish Catholic, born and raised in Saskatchewan. My traditions are as ancient and venerable as those of any nation. When the ancestors of the Nisga'a were developing *Ayuukhl Nisga'a*, my ancestors were listening to St. Patrick expounding the mysteries of the Trinity with the aid of a shamrock. And yet, much of my identity today is bound up with the cultures and languages of the people who were here ten thousand years before I arrived. Saskatoon, Saskatchewan, Assiniboia, Manitou, Pasqua: these place names are more familiar to me, and dearer, than Dublin or Derry or Limerick or Cork. Molloy may be one of the most common names in Ireland, but Saskatchewan—an Algonquian word meaning "the big angry water" or "swiftly flowing water," depending on the translation—is where I belong. I am content with this definition of myself, not because it is Irish or British or Algonquian, but because it is quintessentially Canadian. And if we are seeking model citizens for what the broadcaster Laurier LaPierre has called "this magnificent experiment called Canada,"[1] we need look no further than the First Nations who lived and died here long before Europe dreamed of their existence. The First Nations of Canada define us in a way we have yet to appreciate or understand.

A treaty, by definition, is an agreement between nations. A treaty in Canada is unique in that it is an agreement between the conquerors and the unconquered. We come to the table as equals, neither having ceded or surrendered anything that names us or defines us or makes the future possible. Our major task, then, is to explicate and elaborate the terms under which we may peacefully, cooperatively, and reasonably join together in unity. No First Nation has ever tried to negotiate its way out of Canada. Rather, they have each, in their individual ways, sought to belong.

The Nisga'a are no different. Since 1887 and before, their chief desire has been to negotiate their way into Canada, as citizens with appropriate rights and privileges, with mastery over their future, and with the same control over their traditional territory in the Nass Valley as I enjoy over my house and lot in Saskatoon. It is as simple as that—and as complicated. For if I were forced, suddenly, to demonstrate my right to that house and lot without reference to the traditions and laws that have governed my society for generations, I would run into a few snags. Indeed, my ancestors ran into those same snags some eight hundred years ago when the English invaded Ireland and claimed for themselves land that had been farmed and hunted by the indigenous population for thousands of years. It was no good saying, "We are who we are. We have always been who we are. We have always lived here." We had no proof of it but our own history and traditions, a unique language and culture, and a relationship with God that our conquerors could not tolerate.

The scenario is disturbingly familiar to the original inhabitants of Canada.

Luckily, in eight hundred years the Crown learned a thing or two. One of the most valuable is something that we, as Canadians, have picked up only in the last quarter century. But at least now when people tell us, "We are who we are. We have always been who we are. We have always lived here," we know we have a responsibility to listen. And if the listening is fruitful, we now have the means to act. This is what makes the tale so dramatic and compelling: it is proof that reasonable adults can sit down together and negotiate and compromise, separate the possible from the impossible, and arrive at an agreement that everyone can live with. It is not as exciting as warfare and genocide, perhaps, but it leaves more of us alive. And there is just as much opportunity for valour and villainy: valour among those who literally pour out their lives for the duration of the process, and villainy among those who wilfully distort that process to serve their own political ends.

Of course, it is easier to distort a complex process than a simple one, and treaty making can be as complex as it gets. Because of this, it is necessary that the work be divided and apportioned according to expertise. It was the task of the core team to grasp and direct the entire strategy and design of the process—a process that dealt with literally thousands of issues and resulted in a document of some fifteen hundred pages—but much of the technical and detailed work of the Nisga'a negotiations was done by working groups and committees, where discussion focussed on practical rather than positional issues. These groups and committees were created and mandated by the main table, and their work was approved by the main table, but it made little sense, for example, to bring to the Chief Negotiators a section-by-section review of the Indian Act to determine what transition provisions were required in the Final Agreement. Similarly, the tedious work of drafting the replacement tenures was not a task for the main table. This type of work was done at the committee level, and the process worked extremely well. Indeed, leaving the experts to discuss the issues often brought about practical solutions to problems that had seemed insurmountable to the negotiators at the main table. The working groups also performed the necessary task of narrowing the issues to determine which ones needed to be brought to the main table for direction, instruction, or approval.

The size and composition of the working groups and committees varied throughout the negotiations. Each of the parties brought its experts and technicians to committee meetings, which were generally also attended by one of the core team and a legal representative from each party, plus representatives of the departments and agencies of the federal and provincial governments who had jurisdiction. As Chief Federal Negotiator, I participated in working groups depending on the topic under discussion, as did the Chief Negotiators from the Nisga'a and the Province. Trying to juggle working group and main table responsibilities added another layer of complexity to an already complex process.

The working groups and committees pored through volumes of technical, legal, and scientific data on a myriad of issues and government acts so that the main table could discuss them intelligently and draw reasonable conclusions from the information we had. The ultimate success of the Final Agreement was due in large part to the knowledge and expertise we were able to draw on from these groups that laboured day after day throughout the negotiations, even up to the final hours. Five working groups were still meeting on the last day and the last of those finally wrapped things up at 1:00 in the morning.

The Certainty Working Group was a bilateral Canada/British Columbia committee whose task was to establish a legal technique for achieving certainty in the Nisga'a Final Agreement without requiring the surrender of aboriginal rights and title. It was one of the most important working groups, since it found a way to achieve certainty as no other process or negotiations had. The term "certainty," though perhaps employed unconventionally in this context, can be defined as any standard dictionary would define it: undoubted, a thing that may be relied on. As the Preamble to the Final Agreement states, "The Parties intend that this Agreement will provide certainty with respect to ownership and use of lands and resources, and the relationship of laws, within the Nass Area." Indeed, as an information sheet produced by the Federal Treaty Negotiation Office in Vancouver makes clear, the Final Agreement "provides all Canadians with certainty as it relates to lands and resources originally claimed by the Nisga'a and to the relationship between federal, provincial and future Nisga'a laws."

"Certainty," the communiqué elaborates, "is a central thread woven through the Nisga'a Final Agreement," which sets out all the rights that the Nisga'a have under section 35 of the Constitution Act, 1982, the area over which they apply and the limitations to those rights. It does so by modifying any Aboriginal rights the Nisga'a may have and by clearly defining any other rights the Parties have agreed the Nisga'a should exercise.

In addition, through the Final Agreement, the Nisga'a agree not to pursue any claims they may have arising from past infringements of Aboriginal rights.

And finally, as a precaution, the Final Agreement contains an agreement by the Nisga'a to release any Aboriginal rights the Nisga'a may be found to have, to the extent that those rights are different from the rights set out in the Final Agreement.

In short, the Federal Treaty Negotiation Office assures us, there is "no vagueness about the Nisga'a Final Agreement." It is "a full and final settlement of Nisga'a Aboriginal Rights."[2] The Cultural Artifacts Committee was charged with a task not quite so triumphal, but perhaps equally important to the Nisga'a: identifying and listing the cultural artifacts that were to be repatriated to the Nisga'a from the Canadian Museum of Civilization in Hull and the Royal British Columbia Museum in Victoria. The relevant chapter of the Final Agreement specifies that the museums will return a portion of their collections of Nisga'a artifacts to the Nisga'a—who will build a facility in the Nass Valley for their preservation and display—while retaining others for public exhibitions. The committee was also responsible for formulating the custodial arrangements governing the care, maintenance, and preservation of Nisga'a artifacts remaining in the two museums, including such items as masks, charms, soul catchers, rattles, sculptures, neck rings, aprons, and headdresses, to name only a few of the items listed in the exhaustive documentation of this committee. One thing the committee did not address was the historical circumstances whereby these artifacts came to be lodged in museums thousands of kilometres outside Nisga'a territory in the first place.

The Existing Interests Committee identified such things as transmission lines, BC Hydro lines, and the RCMP transmission tower that already existed within the boundaries of Nisga'a territory, and developed agreements to protect or replace them. It was during the drafting of the replacement tenures, when the federal and provincial negotiators talked about the need to "grandfather" certain provisions, that we were gently reminded by the Nisga'a negotiators that, as they were a matriarchal society, the more appropriate word would be "grandmother." The term stuck.

The Fisheries Committee was responsible for all technical details relating to the drafting of the fisheries chapter in the Final Agreement, developing the Harvest Agreement, and creating the Lisims Fisheries Conservation Trust to affirm the stewardship role of the Nisga'a for Nass River fisheries (*Lisims* is the Nisga'a name for the Nass River). It was an enormous task, considering the importance of the fishery not only to the Nisga'a but to the larger economy of the entire northwest of the province. As spelled out in the Agreement in Principle, the conservation of fish stocks was the primary consideration. The relevant chapter in the Final Agreement runs to 117 paragraphs.

The Forestry Committee was to develop the annual allowable cut for Nisga'a lands, review the Forest Practices Code, and develop transition measures where required. The forestry has been of special concern to the Nisga'a since the late 1800s when loggers first arrived in the Nass Valley. The lower Nass watershed was the first to be cut. Since the 1950s, according to Nisga'a assessments, harvesting has continually outstripped recovery and reforestation. In 1986 the provincial government embarked on a policy of liquidation of the old-growth forest in the upper Nass watershed. Consequently, the Nisga'a saw it as critical that they manage the forestry on Nisga'a lands.

The Land Titles Committee also had a critical task, as the Nisga'a territory was to undergo a fundamental legal redefinition in light of the provisions of the Final Agreement. The committee reviewed the entire British Columbia Land Titles Act, clause by clause, and determined the manner and method of bringing Nisga'a lands into the provincial land titles system while simultaneously maintaining the integrity of the system and identifying possible amendments to the Act that might become necessary.

The Land and Mapping Committee was charged with the task of providing a mapped boundary of all Nisga'a lands, and with developing a complete legal description of the boundary capable of being surveyed, as well as the various parcels and interests that were to be excluded. Each party had its own views as to how this could be achieved.

The Legal Working Group ensured the legal integrity of the text, the internal consistency of words and phrases, and the accuracy of cross-referencing schedules and appendices. But its primary mandate was to ensure that the Final Agreement accurately reflected, in legal form, the intention of the parties. The group—Andrew Beynon, Jim Aldridge, Marcus Bartley, Boris Tyzuk, Patrick O'Rourke, Jack Ebbels, and myself—had one of the more onerous responsibilities. Because of the tripartite nature of the group, we dealt with many contentious issues, and lawyers, as anyone will tell you, have different opinions. We worked extremely long hours, especially through the final months of negotiations, and it didn't end on the handshake or the initialling, but continued to the final signing. There was much work that remained that would continue to require the time and talents, not to mention the patience, of my colleagues.

The Nisga'a Government Committee developed transition provisions to convert existing band institutions into Nisga'a government institutions. The committee had to refine the authorities and jurisdictions of the proposed Nisga'a government and to deal with the matter of which law would apply in areas of concurrent jurisdiction. This was the first treaty to be negotiated under the federal Aboriginal Self-Government Policy of 1995, and, as would subsequently become clear, a whole new dynamic of seemingly eternal internal consultation was spawned. As the concept of aboriginal self-government is controversial among Natives and non-Natives alike across Canada—a timely article in *The Globe and Mail* referred to "those conservative Canadians who are queasy with the concept of native self-government"[3]— the work of the Nisga'a Government Committee was particularly sensitive and complex, as reflected in the 142 paragraphs and countless subparagraphs of Chapter 11, the Nisga'a government chapter, in the Final Agreement.

The Parks and Ecological Reserves Committee, whose task was to confirm the descriptions of the boundaries, review issues relating to access, and resolve management issues, necessarily had overlapping concerns with the other land committees.

One of the most interesting tasks of the Place Names Committee was to identify and agree on geographic features in the Nisga'a language, for the complex and poetic rhythms of the language grew as much out of the landscape as the lived experience of the nation. When the Nisga'a refer to X̲hlawit or K'ipmat'iskw, they are not just naming a mountain; implicit in the name itself is a lesson in history and theology. The committee's commission was to identify geographic features that would be set out in the treaty and recorded in the British Columbia Geographical Names database in the Nisga'a name with its historic background. This committee also identified sites of cultural and historic significance to the Nisga'a outside Nisga'a lands to be designated provincial historic sites.

The Regional District Committee developed the manner and means whereby the Nisga'a would relate to and participate in other local and regional governments.

The Roads Committee identified and described the various classes of roads on Nisga'a lands, from the provincial Nisga'a highway that runs through the Nass Valley from Laxgalts'ap to north of Nass Camp to the complex of secondary highways and forestry access roads that twist and braid the valley. The committee elaborated right-of-way agreements for secondary provincial roads and drafted the technical provisions related to the relevant chapter of the Final Agreement.

The Taxation and Fiscal Committee, to no one's surprise, was preoccupied with money—not so much with how to get it, as one might expect, but with what to do with it. Fiscal in this sense simply means pertaining to public revenue. The cash component of the committee's deliberations included details of the actual amounts of capital transfer payments and schedules with respect to the provincial and federal treasuries, as well as loan repayment schedules, for the Nisga'a had borrowed money to enable them to conduct the negotiations. Details also had to be worked out concerning the manner in which the new Nisga'a government's own revenue would be taken into account in the calculation of transfer payments from the federal and provincial governments. As Nisga'a revenues increase over time, their reliance on federal and provincial financial transfers will be reduced.

The first fiscal financing agreement dealt with the transfer of revenues to the Nisga'a government for program delivery, and had to be worked initially at the committee level based on the principles set out in the Agreement in Principle. Procedures also had to be established for the negotiation of subsequent financial agreements, as well as for mechanisms to transfer funds and programs. In all, the Taxation Agreement, the Fiscal Financing Agreement, the Own Source Revenue Agreement, Remission Orders, the schedule of Capital and Transfer Payments, and the Loan Repayment Schedule were all developed and drafted by the Taxation and Fiscal Committee. The group had the additional task of undertaking a technical review of various tax acts in drafting the taxation chapter of the Final Agreement.

The Third Party Compensation Working Group, another bilateral

Canada/British Columbia committee, was charged with developing satisfactory approaches to compensation for third parties whose interests were affected by the forestry and fish licence buy-back program mandated in the Final Agreement.

The Water Committee examined the economic and technical details related to the water provisions in the treaty. This committee was primarily interested in things such as volumes, flow, licences, and reservation of water for domestic, industrial, and agricultural purposes. The traditional uses of the water and the Nisga'a attitude toward it formed no part of this committee's deliberations. Even so, their work encompassed another area of particular sensitivity to the Nisga'a, to whom the water is as sacrosanct as the land, both in a practical and a metaphysical sense. The river is a highway linking communities. It is a hunting ground for sea mammals, and of course a rich fishing ground as well. In the past it was the means of migration from summer to winter villages, for trade amongst themselves, and for access to the larger world. They also derived—and continue to derive—an enormous variety of minor benefits from the water, including a multiplicity of shellfish and fish eggs. As with the land committees, the water and fisheries committees had numerous overlapping concerns that were reflected in the Final Agreement.

The Wildlife Committee was responsible for the technical details relating to the drafting of the wildlife and migratory birds chapter of the Final Agreement, which covers a range of issues and concerns, including hunting allocations, trapping, conservation requirements, the cooperative management of wildlife resources, and the bartering of wildlife among the Nisga'a and other aboriginal communities.

The Implementation Plan Committee was concerned with developing strategies to implement all the provisions of the Final Agreement for the first ten years following ratification. Previous experience told me that the work of this committee, along with legal drafting, would be among the most time consuming of the whole exercise, and would likely not be finished until the very last minute. Coincidentally, or perhaps not, it was Daniel Watson, the Implementation Negotiator for British Columbia, who had brought the box of Cuban cigars the night Premier Glen Clark took all the negotiators out to dinner. No doubt he felt the labour had been long and intense.

The Commercial Recreation Tenure Committee was charged with developing the terms, conditions, and locations of the commercial recreation tenure provided for in the Final Agreement. A tenure, in this sense, consists of non-exclusive access to provincial Crown lands to carry on commercial recreational activities, such as eco-tourism.

The Indian Act Transition Committee reviewed the Indian Act and the provisions of the Final Agreement clause by clause to ensure an effective and expedient transition from one to the other. As it is currently constituted, the Indian Act governs the daily existence of every First Nations person in Canada who falls under its provisions. On the effective date of the treaty, however, the Act ceases to apply to the Nisga'a. It was this committee's task to ensure that items and issues currently covered by the Act would not be orphaned once the treaty came into effect.

The Legislative Consultation Committee was created so that the Province and Canada could consult with one another and with the Nisga'a on proposals for legislation to ratify the treaty. As the legislative approaches of British Columbia and Canada were at variance, and the Nisga'a did not necessarily agree with either, the work of this committee was difficult and time-consuming; they were in session up to the eleventh hour. Technically, it was a consultative exercise and the agreement of all parties was not mandatory, but it would have been difficult to imagine either Canada or British Columbia introducing legislation that any one of the parties could not substantively support.

The French Translation Working Group, formed after the Final Agreement was concluded, was tasked with translating the main document, the appendices, and other agreements into French. Each party had its own approach, and, being a tripartite exercise, all three parties had to agree on the translation. It was tedious and contentious work, and extremely time-consuming.

All our main table negotiations, committees, and working groups were internal to the negotiations, which were conducted on a "without prejudice" basis, a concept that has led to a good deal of misunderstanding among opponents of the process. Briefly stated, there were no recording or broadcasting devices used in any negotiating session, and most sessions were closed to the public; in Terrace and the Nisga'a villages, and occasionally in Prince Rupert, Nisga'a elders and other members of the Nisga'a community were invited to attend. The text of chapters dealt with each day at the main table was distributed among the parties. Differences of opinion on provisions within the draft chapters were identified with square brackets, underscoring, or footnotes according to drafting protocols that were developed and agreed to throughout the negotiations. Formal minutes of each session were not taken. All three parties maintained their own records of discussions.

But this was only half the story—the half that many opponents of the Final Agreement have chosen to dwell on to the virtual exclusion of the truth. The accusations of secrecy and lack of consultation that have dogged the Nisga'a negotiations since the Agreement in Principle was released in 1996 are utterly without foundation. It is a matter of public record that more than five hundred consultation and public information meetings were held with third parties during and after the Agreement-in-Principle negotiations. That alone should dispel any notion that shadowy figures were meeting behind closed doors with intentions obnoxious to the public. Sceptically, I have often wondered if all the accusations of secrecy are simply third-party code for "We didn't get everything we wanted."

Of course you didn't. Neither did the Nisga'a. Neither did British Columbia. Neither did Canada. The process isn't perfect. But the Nisga'a negotiations were unlike any other in Canada to that point. I had hoped that the extensive third-party consultations that were an essential part of the process would have the effect of bringing diverse interests together in a common understanding of the necessity of compromise. This was not always the case.

Of all the modern treaties that Canada has negotiated, the Nisga'a consultations were the most extensive. In public meeting after public meeting following the conclusion of the Final Agreement, I have challenged people to show me one provision in the Nisga'a treaty that took them by surprise. "Can you show me one phrase or paragraph that surprises you?" I have never received an answer. Certainly, the Final Agreement is not perfect, but it represents a fair and reasonable settlement in the eyes of all parties.

The federal negotiators were aware that public acceptance of the treaty was critical to its successful ratification. Consequently, we were in a continual balancing act with the desires of third parties, the often conflicting views of government departments (both internally *and* with third parties) and the Province, and the desires and aspirations of the Nisga'a. Difficult decisions had to be made daily by all parties in order to achieve the essential balance that would result in agreement at the main table.

Third parties have habitually claimed that the balance was not tilted in their favour. Leaving aside for the moment the question of why it should have been, it must be stated that third parties had a substantial impact on the process and achieved significant changes in the Final Agreement, especially in regard to replacement tenures, forestry transition provisions, access rights, fee-simple ownership of Nisga'a lands, provincial ownership of the Nisga'a highway, non-exclusive shellfish harvesting, and the commercial fisheries licence retirement plan, not to mention the certainty model that in many ways informed the whole process. Without exception, these were issues of major concern to third parties, and in each case they involved substantial compromises on the part of government, both provincial and federal.

The nature of consultation changed from pre-AIP to post-AIP. Working toward an Agreement in Principle, the parties sought a consensus on the basic parameters of the Final Agreement in sufficient detail to allow for the effective negotiation and drafting of a treaty. The federal government solicited advice from its respective advisory committees on the development of federal policies and positions. The purpose of consultation groups at this stage was to ensure that economic, environmental, labour, resource, and social interests were understood by the parties and taken into account during treaty negotiations. Groups were given a public forum to exchange information among local interests and federal and provincial negotiators, as well as to proffer advice on the issue or issues being negotiated. Equally important was that the public be acquainted with the government's own interests and positions. Negotiators provided background information on the issues under discussion and regular briefings to the consultation groups on the status of the negotiations. They solicited advice on how various interests might be affected by those issues, and then reported back to the members of the consultation group on how the group's advice was applied. During the Agreement-in-Principle negotiations from 1991 until their conclusion, more than two hundred meetings were held with third parties and the public.

The nature of consultation changed in the Final Agreement stage. It was not the obligation or the responsibility of the parties to reopen or renegotiate the terms and conditions of the Agreement in Principle. Our task now was to look at the legal and technical consequences of the provisions being negotiated. It is an important distinction, and one we tried to clarify in each of our first meetings with the consultation groups. Nevertheless, we did manage to accommodate many third-party concerns during the final negotiations, and, because of the preliminary nature of many of the provisions of the AIP, we thought it wise to revisit some of the processes outlined above.

Six advisory committees were consulted during the AIP and final negotiations.

The Kitimat-Stikine Regional Advisory Committee (KS RAC) was made up of a broad range of community, local government, wildlife, fisheries, environmental, business, resource-sector, and labour interests. Meetings with this group were held in Terrace, and occasionally Prince Rupert.

The Nisga'a Fisheries Committee was a broadly based group of commercial and sport fishing interests. Provincially and locally in Prince Rupert, trawlers, gill-netters, seiners, fish processors, and unions were represented on the committee. The sport fishing interests originated from Terrace. Again, most meetings were held in Terrace and Prince Rupert.

Membership on the Nisga'a Forestry Advisory Committee was equally broad-based, with local forestry companies, the Council of Forest Industry, licensees, truckers, and union representatives. Most meetings were held in Terrace.

The Nass Valley Residents' Association was made up of the existing property owners and residents of the Nass Valley. Meetings took place in Nass Camp or in one of the members' homes.

The Skeena Treaty Advisory Committee (TAC) was comprised of representatives from local municipal governments and the two regional governments of Skeena–Queen Charlotte and Kitimat-Stikine. TAC appointed one member to the provincial negotiating team—George Thom, a long-time resident and businessperson in the region whose opinions were widely respected—and consultation was generally conducted throughout the Province.

The Treaty Negotiation Advisory Committee (TNAC) was established in 1993 as a federal-provincial body of thirty-one ministerially appointed organizations. Constituted simultaneously were four sectoral committees: Governance, Fisheries, Lands/Forests/Wildlife, and Compensation. We met with the committee and its sectoral committees in Vancouver, and occasionally in Victoria.

A separate Certainty Working Group was established at the request of the TNAC to bring some of its members and their legal counsel to review and discuss approaches to certainty. There was some overlap of membership between this tripartite group and the federal-provincial working group previously mentioned, but their functions were quite separate. Why no one thought to give it a different name is one of those mysteries that will likely never be solved, but its very existence is clear proof of the widely consultative nature of the treaty negotiation process.

Aside from these six advisory committees with whom we met regularly, we also briefed and took advice from the Bulkley-Skeena Regional Advisory Committee and the BC Utilities Committee. The latter was primarily interested in access for utility companies and their replacement tenures. (A replacement tenure is a negotiated transfer from one jurisdiction to another; a company that held a lease under provincial jurisdiction, for example, would be granted another from the Nisga'a government.) Members of the committee who had interests on Nisga'a lands were regularly consulted on replacement tenures and, on occasion, participated in drafting the legal documents for the tenures in the relevant working group.

Prior to April 1998, the main table and the working groups observed standard business hours, though there were frequent exceptions, and a great deal of research and preparatory work had to be done in the evening and early morning. Because members of the core team were attending either a working group or the main table every day, internal consultation, brainstorming, and decision-making were extremely difficult, so breakfast, lunch, and supper were invariably given over to work as well. At times, even in the beginning, it seemed you couldn't get away from it.

As the process moved inexorably into 1997, members of the core team began to feel the frustration of endless deadlines and never-ending negotiations. We took no holidays, but continued to push the system and ourselves to accommodate an increasingly demanding schedule. The three-hour time difference with Ottawa both aided and confounded the situation. I and other members of the federal team were daily vexed by the fact that 9:00 AM in Ottawa is 6:00 AM in Vancouver, and while the Deputy Minister may have been at his desk and solving the nation's problems for an hour already, the person on the other end of the telephone line may have just been awakened from the only three hours of sleep he or she was likely to get in the twenty-four. As a rule, though, we were up before 6:00 for a conference call at 6:30 or 7:00. Despite the horrific hours, it was advantageous for us to speak with Ottawa at the beginning of their working day. Key people were more likely to be at their desks at that time, and it did not interrupt the working day of the Province and the Nisga'a in Vancouver. It was not uncommon for us to meet in advance of the daily session to review the work that needed to be done, and again afterwards for a post mortem and to strategize for the next day.

Out-of-town meetings, whether for negotiating sessions or conferences with the various advisory committees, invariably meant that work dominated the entire day, including travelling time and meals. A few fortunate souls might find time to exercise, or in some other way pay brief homage to the ideal of a healthy lifestyle. Jogging was rare, though: you not only had to change your clothes beforehand but wash yourself afterwards, and most people could not find the requisite twenty minutes in a day to do so. Walking was dangerous: you might get outside and take in a little fresh air, but someone from one of the teams usually spotted you, and you invariably ended up discussing work. Jim Aldridge had his guitar, but I suspect that most evenings it stayed in its case in his hotel room.

The one advantage of travelling under these circumstances was that it forced you into a social relationship with the other negotiators. At the end of a long day, it was not uncommon to share a meal and a tale or two with people you might have been arguing with ferociously only a couple of hours before. "Do as adversaries do in law," Shakespeare advised. "Strive mightily, but eat and drink as friends."[4] Indeed, shared effort and shared exhaustion lead to a certain intimacy among people, even—or perhaps especially— when you have been defined under other circumstances as opponents.

It is often at such times that humour rears its welcome head. In the complex and sometimes bewildering process of the negotiations, we frequently reminded one another of the acronym "KISS," meaning "Keep It Simple Stupid." One of the Nisga'a negotiators, having heard this several times, was moved to remark that there was a similar saying in his own culture: "KISS— Keep It Simple *Sim'oogit*."[5]

I guess you had to be there.

Chapter Five

....

BETWEEN JANUARY 15 and the beginning of May 1997, I flew to Ottawa five times, not to mention Victoria, Vancouver, Terrace, Montreal, Gitwinksihlkw, New Aiyansh, and home to Saskatoon when I could manage it. I hesitate to add up the kilometres I have travelled, or to estimate the hours, even days I have spent ten thousand metres above the earth. Sometimes it seemed I would never get home. Home is in the mind, it is true—or where the heart is, to invoke the tired cliché—but if the mind is overwhelmed by things of greater urgency, it can play havoc with the heart.

Travellers frequently report the phenomenon of waking up in a hotel room and not knowing where they are. The moment is fleeting, but disorienting. More disorienting, like a lucid dream, is waking up at home and not knowing where you are. Or waking in a panic because the part of your mind that is supposed to take care of day-to-day living has just informed you that you forgot to order a cab for your early morning flight. Or that you'll have to spend the week in Ottawa in your pyjamas because you forgot to pack and now there isn't time (logic plays no part in horror). Sometimes you're up and across the room, one hand on the phone and the other pulling things at random out of the closet before the rational part of memory overrides the random and informs you that it is Sunday, and you're at home, and you don't have to go anywhere until tomorrow. But by then the unforgiving adrenalin has prepared you to slay dragons, and further sleep is impossible.

One of my worst moments occurred in Vancouver. I was staying at the Four Seasons Hotel on West Georgia. I decided to go out for supper. Dining alone is one of the benefits of frequent travel—or one of the trials, depending how you look at it. Making your way through strange cities at odd hours belongs in the same category of experience. At the very least, one gets used to it. At best, one learns to enjoy it; cities and restaurants alike are a constant source of information and stimulation.

One can even come to enjoy the rain in Vancouver, I've found, if you accept that there is nothing you can do about it. It was no surprise that it was raining as I stepped out of the hotel. West Georgia Street runs southeast through central Vancouver. I followed the traffic for two blocks, then cut through the Hotel Vancouver to get out of the rain. Emerging onto Robson Street, I was heading for Earl's Restaurant when I heard the familiar, importunate summons of the cell phone in my coat pocket. It is not a ring so much as a whine. I was resigned to taking up the endless business of the day once more as I retrieved the instrument and put it to my ear. To my delight, it was my daughter Alison. As was our custom, I told her I would find a pay phone and call her back, thus avoiding exorbitant cellular charges. The Hotel Vancouver was the handiest place. I retraced my steps and made my call, and it was with a lighter heart that I subsequently ate my dinner and returned to the hotel.

When I got off on my floor, though, it seemed different. In the same price range, of course, one hotel is very much like another. But the lighting and the colour scheme were definitely wrong. Then I noticed that I was on the "Gold Key" floor. Abashed, I returned to the elevator and pushed the correct number. I was glad there had been no one in the hallway to recognize me or see my mistake.

"Wasn't that Tom Molloy, the Chief Federal Negotiator? Doesn't he even know what floor he's on?"

It was worse than that, for the elevator door immediately opened again at the same floor. In confusion, I stepped out again and looked around. Then it struck me with the force of a physical blow that I was not only on the wrong floor; I was in the wrong hotel. I had inadvertently returned to the Hotel Vancouver instead of the Four Seasons. Where was my mind? I wondered. Was my brain finally giving up the struggle and slipping into dementia? It is difficult to convey how truly unnerving I found this incident. But at least when I got to the right hotel, I didn't have to ask at the desk which floor I was on.

I was not the only one who suffered such lapses as negotiations progressed and tensions escalated. All of us, from time to time, became so wrapped up in the days and nights at the table, so consumed by the issues, that we lost sight of the rest of the world. But events have a way of bringing one back to reality. It might be as naturally disorienting as losing your way in the wrong hotel, or it might be a phone call informing you that your daughter and granddaughter have been involved in a horrific traffic accident.

It was a Sunday evening, about 7:30 in Terrace. I was at the table when I heard the familiar summons of the cell phone. It was Corinne, my eldest daughter. She was extremely upset. She and Hanna had been hit broadside on the driver's door by a car going through a stop sign. My heart gave a jolt. My chest was suddenly hollow. Everyone else in the room faded into insignificance. There was only Corinne and me and the telephone. My immediate concern was for her and Hanna. But Corinne seemed more upset about the car. It was my car she had been driving, and it had been "totalled," according to the insurance company's euphemism. Both Corinne and Hanna, miraculously, were unharmed. It took a moment for my heart to settle down to a reasonable pace, and for me to accept that a tragedy had been averted. And later, it made me wonder when was the last time I had seen them.

On another occasion, a lawyer for the Province received a phone call late one night informing him that his mother had suffered a heart attack. He left the next morning, only to find that it was a false alarm. He returned the following day. At other times in the course of the negotiations, Jim Barkwell broke his hand playing hockey, Brian Martin walked through a glass door and required surgery to remove particles of glass, and numerous people became ill from one cause or another.

But if some events occasionally forced us back into reality, others carried us onward as if they had a life of their own. Negotiations continued with slight regard for the families and friends of those involved. What made it doubly vexing was our apparent lack of progress both in the working groups and at the main table. Forward movement was agonizingly slow. Then Premier Glen Clark arrived home from the Asian Team Canada trip early in 1997 and, for reasons known only to himself, announced that he and the Prime Minister were committed to concluding the treaty before the end of June. The Province had previously indicated a late fall date.

It might have been a blessing in disguise, for it struck me that the elaborate bureaucratic apparatus that had been created to serve the treaty negotiations had somehow got itself turned around, and the negotiations were now serving the system. It needed a jolt like that to shock it into consciousness. Still, I rather wished they had told us earlier.

We revved up the federal system. Which meant more meetings. We held internal meetings to prepare a list of the major issues and devise strategies to deal with them, over and above what was already in place. We held meetings with the Province, and with the Province and the Nisga'a, to find out who was waiting on whom. We wrestled with the major issues: lands, forestry, fish, wildlife, certainty, fiscal arrangements, dispute resolution, implementation, specific claims, and local and regional government relationships.

On February 12 we went to Ottawa for a meeting with all relevant DIAND personnel, from Assistant Deputy Minister John Sinclair down. We discussed the involvement of the Minister, the Deputy Minister, and the Associate Deputy Minister, and tried to explain the urgency of getting cooperation from other government departments. We briefed the Deputy Minister on the major issues; the list had hardly diminished since my report to the Kitimat-Stikine Regional Advisory Committee (KS RAC) shortly after I took over the file in the spring of 1996. Some progress had been made, but hardly enough to reward the amount of work we had done.

February 19 was my first opportunity to brief the Treaty Negotiation Advisory Committee on the Nisga'a negotiations. Once again I reviewed the outstanding issues—fish, forestry, lands, overlap, and certainty, among many others—but nothing to advance the process was immediately accomplished.

A journal entry of the period reflects my frustration:

The negotiation schedule and time frame is very much a concern, everybody "talks the talk" but nobody seems to "walk the walk" (to use an old expression)—even the Feds—we are 13 weeks from our target and we are really no further advanced than we were 6–8 weeks ago—our schedule over the next number of negotiating sessions will not advance us substantially . . . there is no closure on any topic at the moment and there is a very large number of issues on which major work remains. 13 weeks and not one chapter anywhere near conclusion.

On March 4, 1997, we were back in Ottawa for a meeting with the Deputy Minister and other officials on the perennial and critical topics of self-government and certainty. It was at this time that we instituted the "ADM weekly conference call." Chaired by John Sinclair, Assistant Deputy Minister (ADM) of Claims and Self Government in DIAND, the regular communication was to provide an opportunity to review the outstanding issues and the progress, if any, being made in resolving them. Even outside the conference calls, John Sinclair was always available to us, and his expertise was invaluable in guiding things through the bureaucracy.

On March 10 the federal negotiating team filed a lengthy written submission to the Select Standing Committee on Aboriginal Affairs, and were once again reminded of the ponderousness of the system we were up against whenever we tried to expedite matters. For the government moves at the government's pace, provincially or federally, and we were but one cog in the vast machine. The Standing Committee was another cog, and this was not the first time we had ground against it.

Seven months earlier, on August 8, 1996, the British Columbia Legislature had authorized the all-party Select Standing Committee on Aboriginal Affairs to "examine, inquire into, and make recommendations on":

1. the application of key issues arising out of the Nisga'a agreement-in-principle to treaty negotiations throughout BC, and
2. how progress can be made towards treaty settlements with aboriginal people beneficial to all British Columbians.[1]

The government, concerned about what appeared to be growing opposition to the treaty and the treaty process, further authorized the committee to provide opportunities for all citizens of British Columbia, aboriginal and non-aboriginal alike, to express their views on these matters.

The twelve-member committee held thirty-one hearings in twenty-seven communities throughout British Columbia before issuing its report, entitled "Towards Reconciliation: Nisga'a Agreement-in-Principle and British Columbia Treaty Process,"[2] on July 3, 1997, five months after we had last appeared before it. A news release issued by the Legislative Assembly summarized the committee's findings:

SELECT STANDING COMMITTEE ON ABORIGINAL AFFAIRS BACKS
SETTLING ABORIGINAL CLAIMS SETTLEMENT THROUGH TREATY PROCESS

The B.C. Legislature's Select Standing Committee on Aboriginal Affairs has concluded that there is widespread public support in British Columbia for settling aboriginal claims through the treaty process.

These conclusions are contained in the committee's final report, which is being released today with 72 recommendations, most of which have the unanimous support of the committee's members from the NDP, B.C. Liberal and B.C. Reform parties.

The committee received nearly 800 written submissions and oral presentations from aboriginals and non-aboriginals about the treaty making process in British Columbia. For the first time in B.C., many of the committee's 31 hearings in 27 communities across the province were broadcast by cable operators in 10 different communities.

The committee reached the following conclusions:

◆ There is widespread public support for settling aboriginal claims.

◆ The treaty process is overwhelmingly viewed as the best option for settlement.

◆ Treaty negotiations must be streamlined, but at the same time they should include more input from communities affected by land claims settlements.

◆ Governments must make a major commitment to establishing clear mandates for its negotiators, and provide the necessary resources to carry them out.

The majority report contains 72 recommendations aimed at addressing concerns arising from the aboriginal claims negotiations and improving the treaty making process. They include the following, which have unanimous consent:

◆ Replace the Indian Act with a system of aboriginal self-government which must operate within the context of the Canadian Constitution, and respect the Criminal Code and the Charter of Rights.

◆ Eliminate tax-exempt status for Status Indians.

◆ To promote closure on past injustices and to move
forward, the Crown should offer an apology to
aboriginal people.[3]

Several Reform and Liberal opposition members of the committee, notwithstanding the findings of the committee as a whole, issued a partially dissenting report, concluding that the Nisga'a treaty should not be brought to the
legislature for debate until a majority of British Columbian voters had given
their approval through a province-wide referendum. Treaties, they said,
should not include the constitutional protection of a "third order of government," and commercial fishery entitlement should not form any part of any
treaty, including the Nisga'a treaty.

The report, including the dissenting report, received little attention at the
time, though some of the major points of contention would later emerge as
key issues on which debate over the Final Agreement would focus. For our
part, we had been given assurances that the committee's deliberations would
not interfere with our work at the negotiation table. While it is true that
negotiations were never interrupted as a direct result of the committee's
work, that work did prove to be a major distraction, requiring time to attend
hearings and make presentations as well as prepare and file an extensive
brief. Canada, British Columbia, and the Nisga'a had all attended before the
committee on September 17 and 18, 1996, to brief the members on the
Nisga'a Agreement in Principle. We had appeared again on February 17,
1997, and then filed our written submission on March 10. For a time there
was some apprehension that the Province might put the negotiations on
hold pending the committee's final report. Thankfully, that fear never materialized, and negotiations proceeded more-or-less uninterrupted.

Overlap continued to be a major issue. Although the Nisga'a had signed
a Memorandum of Understanding with the Tsimshian the previous year, and
had also entered into an agreement with the Tahltan, there remained outstanding claims with the Gitanyow and Gitksan. The overlap with the
Gitanyow had been discussed on numerous occasions internally, bilaterally,
and at the negotiating table. A meeting among Canada, British Columbia,
and the Gitanyow negotiating team had failed to resolve the issue. On April
14 the Province, Canada, the Gitanyow, and the Nisga'a met. Follow-up
meetings between the Gitanyow and the Nisga'a were planned for later in
April and May. Our efforts to resolve the issue would not end there, but

would continue throughout the negotiations and even beyond.

On April 15 we held an open negotiating session in Terrace. Six people showed up, plus the press. In the evening we had another briefing session with KS RAC. On April 16, following the negotiating session, we met with the Forestry Advisory Committee. On April 18, TNAC was brought up to date.

The week of April 28 was the fortieth Annual Convention of the Nisga'a Nation. High on the agenda, as in previous years, was the status of the negotiations. Several days were devoted to the treaty, affording the membership an opportunity to express their views and to affirm their negotiators' continuing mandate. I attended the convention, along with DIAND Regional Director General John Watson. Minister Ron Irwin was also there with his assistant, Ron French, despite the fact that there was a federal election campaign under way. The Minister himself was not running for re-election, but neither was he pushing for a quick finish to win votes for the Liberal Party. Later quoted in the Victoria *Times Colonist* of May 2, he said there were too many outstanding issues for a quick wrap-up of the talks. In the same article, Premier Glen Clark said that a final deal was likely a long way away: "It looks like within the next three or four months, there is a reasonable chance of getting a treaty with the Nisga'a."[4]

The Annual Convention was also the venue for electing the Nisga'a Tribal Council. No one was surprised that Chief Joe Gosnell was re-elected president, or that other members of the current executive who allowed their names to stand retained their seats. It was Chief Gosnell's third victory. In the Calgary *Herald* of May 5, 1997, he was quoted as saying that the election was "a validation of unity regarding the historic Nisga'a Agreement in Principle reached with the province last year."[5]

Following the convention, it was back to business as usual. During a routine planning meeting we came to the conclusion that the legal drafting of the Final Agreement would take much longer than even I had anticipated. Then, in mid-May, the first lawsuit was initiated against the treaty. Two dissident members of the Nisga'a community, Frank Barton and James Robinson, commenced an action to have the Agreement in Principle set aside on the grounds that there had been a lack of proper notice for the ratification meeting. They wanted to stall any final agreement until the Agreement in Principle had been ratified according to their own criteria. They also wanted to have the Nisga'a Tribal Council wound up. Dissent is to be expected in any complex, long-lasting negotiations, but this action came as a surprise to the Nisga'a as well as to the provincial and federal negotiating teams. It was the first of what would become a series of legal actions against the treaty, none of which, fortunately, affected the mood of the negotiations. Our concern was to get the job done, and done well enough that the very fabric of the document we produced would forestall future legal challenges.

During the first week of June, the Nisga'a Tribal Council, all the band councils, and the governing and social institutions of the Nisga'a held a three-day meeting to review the status of the negotiations. A concurrent review of the chapters by the federal team revealed that some progress was now being made. The definitions chapter was complete, subject to final inclusions, and listed precise meanings for words and terms used in the agreement, beginning with "adjusted total allowable catch" and ending some fourteen pages later with the single word "year." The preamble was written. The general provisions chapter was complete, except for certainty. The land and resources chapter was substantially complete. The chapters on access, fisheries, wildlife and migratory birds, environmental assessment and protection, Nisga'a government, and local and regional government relationships were becoming more complete—or at least less incomplete. There remained substantial work to be done on legal drafting, the implementation plan, fiscal management, replacement tenures, and most of the appendices.

On June 10 and 11, while we were in Prince Rupert for negotiations, the newly re-elected Prime Minister Chrétien announced the new federal Cabinet. Our Minister was Jane Stewart from Brantford, Ontario. Her Parliamentary Secretary was to be David Iftody, MP for Provencher, Manitoba (the name of the seat once held by Louis Riel). A new round of briefings would have to begin.

From June through to the end of August the working groups and main table met as required, mostly in Vancouver but occasionally in Terrace and Prince Rupert. The Nisga'a took the week of August 4 to go to Ottawa. During this period our internal systems carried on, including the ADM conference calls. Several difficulties had arisen over converting the language of the Agreement in Principle to that of the Final Agreement. Unfortunately, I had taken part in neither the negotiations that led to the AIP nor its approval. It had evidently met the needs of those who negotiated it, but in many cases their intentions had to be interpreted in light of subsequent positions and decisions, and the document left a good deal of work to be done.

In addition, we were discovering a lack of documentation in our own system to tell us how certain problems the federal team had encountered in the earlier negotiations had been resolved—or not resolved, as the case may be. By early summer it was apparent that we could not bring closure to the negotiations until October at the earliest. This, I knew, would make many people unhappy. Including me.

During this period, we met with KS RAC and the Nisga'a Forestry Advisory Committee. We also held an open forum in Terrace. It attracted some eight people who were not involved in the negotiations and two members of the press—not an impressive turnout, given the subsequent accusations of secrecy levelled against the negotiations. It would be fair to say that none of the issues raised at the meeting were new, and many predated the Agreement in Principle: the nature of self-government; the district and its relationship to any future Nisga'a government; wildlife management; third-party compensation; dispute resolution; the status of off-reserve members of the Nisga'a Nation; the establishment of harvesting quotas, particularly on moose and mountain goats; Nisga'a citizenship, and who determines it; certainty; overlap; ratification; and will Nisga'a citizens be Canadians?

We met once with the Ottawa Federal Caucus, and on July 31 we had our first opportunity to brief the new Minister face to face. She appeared to be a quick study, and her understanding of both the issues and the process impressed me. She would have received departmental briefing along with written briefing materials before meeting me, and she had evidently read them and grasped them. I also attended the following day when she met with the Nisga'a Tribal Council and reviewed the status of key issues such as timing and certainty. There were no tripartite meetings scheduled for the first week of September, so Florence Roberge, Jim Barkwell, and I took the opportunity to hold a series of meetings in Ottawa over the course of several days. We met once again with the Deputy Minister, Associate Deputy Minister Gary Wouters, and the Federal Caucus, this time with bad news: while we had hoped for a fall closing, it was becoming increasingly apparent that the lack of significant progress over the past three months was making this a faint hope, at best. Everyone agreed with my assessment that we had to move from a negotiating mode to a closing mode. Several chapters were substantially complete, but there remained work to be done on all of them.

We set out a work schedule between the other two parties that took us to the end of October.

On September 15, there was a briefing meeting with the British Columbia Federal Liberal Caucus, consisting of BC Liberal Members of Parliament and Senators. The Honourable David Anderson, then Minister of Fisheries and Oceans, chaired the meeting.

On September 16, a Tuesday, we were in Gitwinksihlkw for negotiations. On the 17th we were briefing officials of the Privy Council Office. Through to the end of October, negotiations were held in Vancouver, New Aiyansh, and Prince Rupert. We were also in Ottawa for a meeting with the Deputy Minister and the Associate Deputy Minister. In this period we met twice with TNAC, KS RAC, and the Nass Valley Residents' Association. The working groups continued as usual.

By mid-November I had to conclude that, while we had continued to meet—*ad nauseam*, it seemed—in the past months, none of the major outstanding issues had been dealt with and we hadn't made any significant progress. Our respective governments, federal and provincial, were simply not making the decisions necessary to carry the negotiations forward. Reviewing where we were and what was left to do, we came to the conclusion that March 1998 was a much more realistic closing date, provided there were commitments on all sides to get decisions from our respective principals.

The date was worrisome, in that even if we did manage to close by then it was unlikely that the Province would be able to take the deal to the spring session of the legislature for ratification.

We needn't have worried.

Chapter Six

....

I HAVE FOUR DAUGHTERS, ranging in age from twenty-eight to twenty-one: Corinne, Jennifer, Alison, and Kathryn. They are beautiful, intelligent, graceful individuals, and I am frequently overcome with gratitude that I had some hand in bringing them into the world. Like any father with more than one daughter, however, I occasionally feel beleaguered. There are more of them than there are of me, and they have passed their skills and knowledge down to one another over the years. By the time Kathryn was born she stood to inherit some fifteen or sixteen years of collective experience from her elder siblings. At five years old, she knew better than perhaps anyone else how to get something out of her father.

One weekend she decided to apply her skills. I had just returned from a long session of labour negotiations, and I wanted nothing more than to enjoy a quiet weekend at home with my family. I cannot remember exactly what it was Kathryn wanted, but she was persistent. I was equally determined that she was not going to get it.

"Please, Daddy?"

"No."

"Can I?"

"No."

"Come on, Dad."

"No."

Finally, with the deep disdain that five-year-olds reserve for fathers who have erred, she said, "You call yourself a negotiator, but all you do is sit there and say no!"

It was not the first time something of the sort had been said to me, though it was the first time I had heard it from the mouth of a child. Kathryn's disdain, in fact, though temporary, was more articulate than much of the condemnation and denunciation that greeted the process and the product of our negotiations with the Nisga'a some years later.

It was in the summer of 1997 that opposition to the treaty emerged in a formal way for the first time. True, a group calling itself BC F.I.R.E. (BC Foundation for Individual Rights and Equality) had been active for some time, but it was poorly organized and largely ineffectual. It mostly urged people to form "Stakeholders Groups," write to their elected representatives, and read *Our Home or Native Land?* by Mel Smith, "the leading constitutional expert in the province."[1] But in July a self-proclaimed citizens' group calling itself The Citizens' Voice on Native Claims ran advertisements in a number of BC newspapers under the headlines "The big fib" and "Before aboriginal treaties are set in stone." Martyn Brown, communication director of the British Columbia Reform Party before moving to the provincial Liberal offices, was the executive director of the new organization. Its abiding philosophy was later articulated by Liberal Leader Gordon Campbell in an article that appeared in the Vancouver *Sun* on April 8, 1998: "Indeed, the only thing worse than no treaties are [sic] seriously flawed treaties imposed against the wishes of most British Columbians."[2]

It was the Citizens' Voice on Native Claims that first demanded a referendum on the Agreement in Principle, a call that was later taken up by the provincial opposition, and then by the federal Reform Party when the Final Agreement went to Parliament for ratification. The campaign also raised the issue of race-based government, which no one with any sense of history or a modicum of political knowledge can take seriously. To be sure, it is the function of the opposition to oppose, but to be ignorant in opposition is tantamount to being wilfully illiterate. Nevertheless, the Citizens' Voice claimed to have raised over $200,000 in four months, and it managed to sow the seeds of several contentious issues before eventually disappearing from the scene.

A second attack was launched in November. While not aimed specifically at the treaty, it drew opposition focus onto the provincial government. Under British Columbia law, a petition signed by 40 percent of the voters in a constituency within eighteen months following an election can force the recall of a member of the Legislative Assembly. The campaign affected Helmut Giesbrecht of Skeena and Education Minister Paul Ramsey in Prince George. Had either effort been successful, it would have seriously threatened the ability of the government to govern, as the NDP had only a three-seat majority. Other constituencies were subsequently targeted, with the same result. The following year, organizers spoke of recalling every NDP MLA in the province, but the campaign was never launched owing to a lack of funds.

Between the newspaper campaign in July and the recall campaign in November, I booked a tour of Nisga'a territory to familiarize myself with the land and customs of the people with whom I had become so politically intimate. I felt badly that it had taken me so long to do this, for I have always felt it is important for negotiators to get a genuine sense of the history and territory of the First Nations with whom they are working. Individual First Nations are just that—individual, with individual histories, cultures, geographies, languages, customs, and political structures.

One of the purposes of treaty making across this country is to forge new relationships among aboriginal and non-aboriginal peoples and communities. But we must first understand and appreciate existing relationships. We must come to the table with a clear and realistic view not only of the physical landscape of the First Nations we are working with, but of the other factors that make up their cultural landscape, the things that make them who they are. We must also recognize that the cultural landscape of the First Nations in Canada has been indelibly marked by the history of colonization.

In negotiating a land claim agreement, two different cultures set out to achieve a common understanding, and then come to an agreement over that understanding. Any resolution will demand a huge commitment of time and effort, which, in turn, must be founded in a well-developed sense of cultural awareness and trust. Both sides must appreciate the differences that separate them. Mutual respect can only develop through an appreciation of the cultural implications of one another's interests. Until these factors are accorded appropriate respect, any possibility of an expeditious or mutually satisfactory resolution across a formal negotiation table is, at best, remote.

It was with anticipation and a certain humility, then, that I asked the Nisga'a to arrange a tour of their territory for me on the weekend of September 12, 1997. Typically, they were both gracious and generous. I took along my good friend Eli Bornstein, the prominent Canadian artist. The Nisga'a arranged a very full three-day program for us.

Friday morning we spent in New Aiyansh (*Sii Aẏans* in the Nisga'a language). Although the Nisga'a have lived in villages along the Nass River since Brian Boru was High King of Ireland, New Aiyansh is what its name suggests: new. The original Aiyansh (meaning "fertile valley") was founded in 1883 by one J. B. McCullough, a Christian missionary who undertook to erect a Victorian village six kilometres downriver from the old and thriving community of Gitlaxt'aamiks. With its charming picket fences and wooden sidewalks, a new school and sawmill, a printing press, an Anglican church, and a community hall, Aiyansh had attracted most of the Gitlaxt'aamiks people by 1900. In 1906 a devastating flood persuaded the residents that the Reverend McCullough's site was not as ideal as they had imagined, so they dismantled their buildings and rafted them piece by piece back up the river to the original site of Gitlaxt'aamiks, where they rebuilt the village. After two more floods—one in 1936 and another in 1961—the community decided to move to higher ground, and New Aiyansh was constructed on a low hill on the opposite side of the river. The first families moved to the site in 1963, and a Department of Indian Affairs school opened the following year.

In 1977 the Unity Pole was erected in New Aiyansh, the first pts'aan to be raised in the Nass Valley in over a century. The significance of this event as a reclamation of history and culture cannot be overstated, though the significance of the pts'aan, or totem pole, was utterly lost on the missionaries who first came to the Nass Valley in the latter part of the eighteenth century. Fearing them as symbols of idolatry, or statues of pagan gods, they exhorted the Nisga'a to chop them down as a condition of their accepting Christianity. Many were burned. Some were shipped to museums in other parts of the world. Others were put to severely practical uses. Chief Joe Gosnell remembers, as a small child, being stared at by mute figures as he and his brothers played in the canoe stored beneath their grandfather's house. Only later, on returning from residential school, did he realize that the footings of his grandfather's house were chopped up and recycled totem poles, and the mute figures staring at him as he played were, in fact, his inheritance.[3]

Far from being a symbol of idolatry, every pts'aan is a catalogue of crests that tells the history of a family and its property. Raising a pts'aan is a sign of wealth, as feasting and gift giving are integral to the ceremony. The carvers must be lavishly thanked, and the pole raising and accompanying feast are major events for the whole community. One need look no further than wills and title deeds to find a parallel to the totem pole in common law. One would need to look considerably further afield, however, to find a similar sense of celebration and gratitude among those who compile such documents.

Eli and I spent the morning with Edward Allen, who briefed us on the structure of Nisga'a organizations. A lawyer by training, Edward practised law in the Nass Valley before assuming the position of Chief Executive Officer of the Tribal Council. New Aiyansh is the seat of the Tribal Council and the site of Wilp Wilxo'oskuhl Nisga'a (Nisga'a House of Learning), a college affiliated with the University of Northern British Columbia in Prince George. We visited School District No. 92, the first Native-run school district in British Columbia and one of the few in Canada. The Nisga'a Elementary Secondary school opened in 1975, and twenty years later it could boast a forty-three-piece school band, computers, industrial shops, a community library, and a population of some 450 students, 95 percent of whom are Nisga'a. The Nisga'a language, compulsory from kindergarten to grade seven and an elective thereafter, is an accredited second language in British Columbia colleges and universities.[4]

We also visited the Nisga'a Fisheries office, the Nisga'a Language and Cultural Centre, the band government offices, Nisga'a Economic Enterprises Incorporated, and the James Gosnell Memorial Health Centre, named in honour of Joe Gosnell's brother, a highly respected previous president of the Nisga'a Tribal Council. This centre, with an annual budget of $3 million, was opened in 1986, with satellite clinics in two neighbouring villages. The Nisga'a Valley Health Board employs doctors, nurses, community health workers, alcohol and drug abuse counsellors, and a psychologist, as well as various support staff. Nisga'a elders are becoming increasingly involved in the work of the clinic, developing programs that are consistent with Nisga'a values and traditional culture.[5]

At noon we enjoyed a lunch that had been prepared for us by the Anglican Church Women. Following that we toured Gitwinksihlkw, another relatively new settlement if one is speaking in terms of æons. Floods and volcanic eruptions have been a constant threat to Nisga'a settlements since time immemorial, so any modern village along the Nass River will have a history of moving and rebuilding. The history of Gitwinksihlkw includes flood and fire and lava, and a long period of abandonment before being resettled in 1917. In 1927 a Major Carruthers of the Salvation Army saw fit to rename the village Canyon City, no doubt because the syllables were easier on the anglophone tongue. In 1989 the residents officially changed the name back to Gitwinksihlkw. It was shortly after that, in 1993, that the first pts'aan carved in the village in a hundred years was raised in front of the community hall.

Eli and I visited the Ts'oohl Ts'ap Memorial Hall (*ts'oohl ts'ap* means "behind the village," and refers to a previous move the community was forced to make years ago) and the local medical clinic. We walked across the famous suspension bridge, the community's only means of access on foot, and marvelled at the pts'aan on the new bridge and in front of the community centre and school.

Later that afternoon we toured Laxgalts'ap, another village farther downriver. *Laxgalts'ap* means "village on village," as it was erected on the site of a much older settlement that had been abandoned a generation or two earlier. Indeed, the first village on this site has been dated to the fifteenth century AD. For years Laxgalts'ap was called Greenville, after a local missionary, Alfred Eli Green. It was said that the Reverend Green preferred the Nisga'a name, but when the government opened a post office on the site it named it after him regardless. It was some years before the name reverted to its Nisga'a origin. Here, too, as in the other villages we visited that day, there had been a hundred-year gap in the raising of totem poles. It was not until 1989 that the first pts'aan raised in over a century was erected in Laxgalts'ap.

On Saturday morning we took part in a moose-tracking excursion by helicopter with Nisga'a resources negotiator Harry Nyce Sr. High above the valley, one could not help but be moved by the beauty of that sublime vista. An immense forested landscape drapes itself like a vast blanket over the coastal mountains. The river and its tributaries cut deep into the landscape, creating an intricate shoreline of shoals and bays and islands that can be measured only in thousands of kilometres, while vast and forbidding lava beds stretching south and west from New Aiyansh and Gitwinksihlkw are a stark memorial to the two thousand people who perished when the volcano erupted two centuries ago. It was easy to conceive of the vision those Nisga'a chiefs took with them to Victoria in 1887, and why a generation has since grown old at the negotiating table. Had this been my birthright, I thought, I too would have been willing to expend my life preserving it for my children and my children's children.

We had a pleasant and informative lunch at the Nyces's home. Harry and his wife, Deanna, and daughter, Allison, an anthropology graduate, all have an abiding interest in culture. Harry was active in the treaty negotiations on matters of culture and heritage, while Deanna is president of Wilp Wilxo'oskuhl Nisga'a. We talked of the Nass Valley, and of Nisga'a history and traditions as they and their daughter served us a variety of types and preparations of salmon, oolichan, and oolichan grease. The latter is not so unappetizing as its name might suggest to those with a delicate palate. Squeezing fish to get its oil out is not so far removed in intention or result from squeezing a cow's udder to get milk. Congealed, oolichan grease spreads like butter on bread and toast, and is at least as palatable as butter. Perhaps if we referred to butter as cow grease, or milk grease, we might think differently about it ourselves.

Later that day Eli and I took a long hike to the top of the volcano cone, accompanied by our Nisga'a guide who regaled us with traditional *adaawaks*, or stories, and local history. The adaawak of the volcano is a cautionary tale not unlike many biblical stories.

The children of several villages, it seems, had been tormenting the fish in the river for their own amusement. At night they tore bark from the trees, rolled it into strips, and set fire to it. They then stuck the blazing strips of bark into the backs of the fish, and the surface of the water came alive with moving lights. The elders and the chiefs warned them against this practice; they were not only being cruel, but disrespectful. But the children continued, delighted with the effects of the burning bark on the backs of the fish. Remembering an earlier time, when K'amligihahlhaahl, the Creator and Supreme Being, had punished the irresponsible killing and maiming of animals with a great flood that covered the earth, the elders lived in dread of the catastrophe that they knew must come. The Creator would use either fire or water to kill them all, they warned. But still the children persisted in their folly. The chiefs set watchers in the valley day and night, so that the community might have some warning of K'amligihahlhaahl's inescapable punishment. When the watchers heard the sounds of many great drums in the distance, they knew it had finally come. Lava roiled down from the upper valley, burying two villages and swallowing everything that lay in its path. The eruption literally swept the river aside. It was only through the intervention of a supernatural bird that extended its beak across the valley, blocking the flow of lava, that total devastation was averted. Even so, the resulting lava bed covers forty square kilometres. It is now a provincial park, and a memorial to the two thousand people who died there.

A priest aboard the Spanish ship, the *Sonora*, which was passing down the coast in August 1775, noted in his diary that flames lit up the sky, and the sailors on board suffered from the heat of them. The priest made no mention of a supernatural bird, but it is ironic that this tragic event coincided with the first European sight of Nisga'a lands.

As for me, I felt the distinct weight of history as I climbed to the cone. In the evening the Nyces joined us for a meal of halibut, seaweed, oolichan, and various types of salmon. Our discussion of Nisga'a history and culture continued.

On Sunday we took a driving tour of the Nass Valley, visiting a variety of fish and stream operations, including road deactivation and stream restoration projects. Later in the day, we went up in the helicopter again for an aerial tour of Kincolith, or Gingolx in the Nisga'a language. We saw the Nisga'a highway under construction below us, joining the communities in the valley to themselves and the outside world. Later, touring the village on foot, we were shown some of the projects the community wished to undertake, and Eli met a fellow artist who had recently completed a carved boat.

Kincolith was the first Christian village in the Nass Valley. In 1867 a missionary named Doolan had found his flock growing to such an extent that they decided to form their own community, so they built a raft and began floating themselves and their belongings downriver toward Iceberg Bay. As they approached the coast, the story goes, a mighty wind blew up and grounded them at the place called Gingolx. Taking it as a sign from God, they unloaded the raft and founded their village where the wind had blown them ashore. One hundred and thirty years later the village is still thriving, and the Christian church has become one of the strongest and most vocal allies in the struggle for aboriginal rights in the Nass Valley. All in all, it seemed a suitable place to complete an incredible weekend. The beauty of the territory, the rich history of the Nisga'a people, the breadth and diversity of their institutions and activities would remain with me, I knew, long after our negotiations had come to a conclusion.

In the meantime, though, negotiations were ongoing, and duty and a renewed sense of purpose brought me back to the table. By the middle of September 1997, three chapters had been concluded: administration of justice, environmental assessment and protection, and cultural artifacts and heritage. Progress was being made on fisheries and wildlife issues, while work continued on lands and resources, access, governance, fiscal matters, regional government relationships, dispute resolutions, eligibility and enrolment, ratification, and the implementation plan. The ineffectual and time-wasting recall campaign launched later that fall—dubbed "Total Recall" by the organizers, perhaps in honour of the Arnold Schwarzenegger movie—did nothing to ease anyone's anxieties about timelines and deadlines.

In November, Minister Jane Stewart and her provincial counterpart, John Cashore, met over dinner to discuss bilateral issues. Around the same time, the provincial Deputy Minister, DIAND Regional Director General John Watson, Associate Chief Negotiator Florence Roberge, and I met to review the perennially outstanding issues. We decided to aim for January 31, 1998, as our closing date. I agreed to it—what was the point of disagreeing?—but I was skeptical of our ability to be finished by then. In the meantime, our ADM conference calls continued, as we still needed answers from the federal system, particularly on certainty. We continued to meet with the Province on cost-sharing matters. The main table met in Vancouver, Terrace, and Victoria until mid-December.

I took my daughter Kathryn to the Victoria negotiations and to the Province's annual Christmas party. Her opinion of her father's negotiating skills had improved somewhat since she was five, but I wanted to give her a chance to observe first-hand what was involved in treaty negotiations. I have always found it difficult to describe what I do, so I take advantage of every opportunity to have my daughters see for themselves. Corinne was with me in Iqaluit when we settled the contentious portion of the boundary during the Nunavut negotiations. All of them had been to the eastern Arctic, and to the Nass Valley before the Nisga'a agreement was ratified. The opportunity to be exposed to and observe other cultures is a unique learning experience, and helpful in building bridges between communities.

During a discussion with John Cashore at the party, he mentioned how important it was to get the Nisga'a deal finished soon. I agreed, of course, but I stressed that the government would have to make some difficult decisions rather quickly if we were going to reach a Final Agreement within the time frame required by the Province. In a subsequent conversation with Trevor Jones, Cashore's executive assistant, he told me that the dinner meeting between his Minister and Jane Stewart had been productive, in that they both acknowledged that they needed to make some tough decisions. Despite Cashore's commitment, though, the issue would inevitably require the Premier's attention, and it was critical to get it as soon as possible if we were not to miss yet another deadline.

In my remarks—apparently Chief Negotiators are expected to speak at parties as well as press conferences—I referenced the season of hope and joy, in that we hoped we would soon have the joy of closure, but the only way that could be accomplished was if all parties focused internally and made the tough decisions that each needed to make within the shortest time possible.

John Cashore spoke of the momentum he sensed building, much as it had developed and grown when the negotiations toward the Agreement in Principle were coming to a close. Speaking generally but fervently about the importance of the Nisga'a treaty, he stated that the parties were now moving into closing mode.

I was not sure I agreed—a feeling that was confirmed at our next negotiating session. Again, a passage from my journal reflects my frustration:

> I gather several people took the opportunity to talk to Ebbels and the Minister about the Province needing to make decisions. Today at the table they indicated that on two major issues in wildlife, they could not respond until next week—despite a commitment by all parties that each would come to the table with an ability to close—same old story. The Nisga'a have a meeting with Cashore tonight. Hopefully, they can make some progress.

The last session before Christmas was held on December 17. On December 11, however, the Supreme Court of Canada had handed down its decision in the *Delgamuukw* case.[6] Initiated by the Gitksan and Wet'suwet'en First Nations in 1984, it was the latest of a number of cases in which the Supreme Court interpreted the issue of aboriginal rights in Canada. The Gitksan and Wet'suwet'en had claimed both jurisdiction and ownership over some 58,000 square kilometres of land in northwestern British Columbia, arguing that tribal law should prevail over provincial law within the territory whenever the two conflicted. The subsequent decision of the Supreme Court has been seen as a turning point in treaty negotiations in Canada, affirming not only that aboriginal title does exist in British Columbia, but that it includes a right to the land itself, not just the right to use the land for traditional purposes.

The *Delgamuukw* case represented the first time the Court had focused on aboriginal title as a distinct aboriginal right. It defined aboriginal title in a manner that granted the right to exclusive use and occupation of the land for a variety of purposes that were not necessarily limited to traditional ones. However, it also dealt with the limits on how First Nations can use their land; they cannot, for example, strip mine territory that had traditionally been used for hunting, or in any way use the land in a manner that would be irreconcilable with the nature of their traditional occupation of it. *Delgamuukw* also addressed the requirement to prove occupation, the limits on extinguishment and infringement of title, the requirements for infringement, and the acceptance of old histories. The Court held, finally, that aboriginal rights and title fall under federal jurisdiction.[7]

Though welcome in many respects, as it clarified issues that had been in question for years, the decision had the immediate effect of forcing all three parties as well as many third parties to begin working out the implications of the decision and how it would affect future negotiations with the Nisga'a. In the end, *Delgamuukw* turned out to be a tempest in a teapot for the Nisga'a table. But we were not to know that when the decision came down. In the meantime, it ensured that we would be fully occupied over the Christmas season until negotiations resumed in Terrace on January 6, 1998.

We were all hopeful that this would be the last New Year of negotiations.

Chapter Seven

....

ONE EVENING, AFTER A DAY OF NEGOTIATIONS followed by a caucus, the federal team retired to the lounge at the Coast Inn of the West in Terrace. Three of us ordered beer. Doug Wanamaker told the server that he would have coffee, "if it's fresh." Florence Roberge, our Associate Chief Negotiator, also ordered coffee. The server returned shortly with three glasses of beer and one cup of coffee. She placed the latter in front of Florence.

"Your coffee," she said to Doug, "should be ready in a couple of minutes."

Florence gazed askance at the cup that had been placed before her. "So what does that make my coffee?" she asked.

The server looked at her as if to say, "You get what you order at the Coast Inn of the West."

It was one of those moments that can feed the discontent of someone who has been working too hard for too long, or that can dissolve into laughter. Florence chose to laugh, and soon we were all caught up in the general hilarity of the exchange, though I suspect our server could not quite fathom what was so funny.

In a hotel lounge or at the negotiating table, humour can be a powerful ally. It releases tension, dissolves self-importance, and reduces pedantry to a caricature of itself, usually with the would-be pedant's willing collaboration. I daresay there was not a moment in the negotiations when any one of us was not aware of the complexity of the task we had been set, but even under such conditions it does not do to take oneself too seriously. A good joke, well timed—as in all good comedy—can set negotiations back on track more surely than a handful of briefs from a working group or even the personal intervention of a minister.

Humour can also be an effective tool in convincing one side or another how unsaleable their position is. A simple phrase such as "Keep it simple, stupid," and the Nisga'a rejoinder, "Keep it simple, Sim'oogit," can break an impasse and remind negotiators that they are all human, after all, and working toward a common goal. We were doubly fortunate at the Nisga'a table, first because there always seemed to be someone who could sense when a carefully timed joke would be appropriate without being offensive, and second because, regardless of how heated the argument or how delicate the issue, our internal humour was always respectful of the party on the receiving end, be it Canada, the Nisga'a, or British Columbia. All of us knew from experience that if you can't make or take a joke, long-term negotiations will seem to go on forever. I have been told that I have a good sense of humour; it has certainly served me well in the nineteen years I have been associated with DIAND.

All negotiations develop their own terminology. At the Nisga'a table, we not only "grandmothered" certain provisions, we also put "hats" and "shoes" on them. Many sections of the treaty begin with an introductory statement, followed by subsections, and then concluding sentences. An introductory statement became known in our discussions as a *chapeau*, while the concluding sentences were the *soulier*—the hat and the shoe. Thus, one would hear at the negotiating table, "The *chapeau* should read as follows," or "We'll have to rewrite the *soulier*."

As humour is a tool in negotiations, so is silence. My father, George, who spent many years negotiating collective agreements in the separate school system, taught me the value of occasional muteness at the table. As Boccaccio wrote, "By this silence, no shame redounded to him or her, whereas prating must needs be the publisher of open infamie."[1] In my own experience, it is always better to be asked why you did not speak than why you did. I have been at several tables where "prating" led to "open infamie" when silence would have been the more appropriate tactic. Sometimes a position expressed by the other side is so fundamentally opposed to your own that no other civilized response is possible. On the other hand, I never cease to be amazed at how such a calming thing as silence can provoke people into imprudent revelations. More than once I have listened in gratified surprise as the party across the table revealed previously unsuspected areas of flexibility in an attempt to fill the void. It is not so much a case of trying to take advantage of the other parties, I am convinced, as of identifying areas where there is more room to move than they have previously stated.

Of course, wit and silence count for little in the absence of skill. When it comes down to it, it is the craft and expertise of the negotiators that ultimately carry the process forward. In this, too, we were fortunate at the Nisga'a table. Florence Roberge, for example, was a valuable member of the federal team, not only for her wit and humour—it was she who developed the term *soulier*—but also for her legal skills. She had been working on the file for approximately a year as legal counsel before my appointment. Having an associate Chief Negotiator was a new experience for me, but we worked well together, dividing the topics between us with the understanding that I had overall responsibility and decision-making authority, and that she would not exceed our mandate or breach departmental guidelines without discussing it with me. We made good progress on her topics during her tenure on the federal team, and it was difficult to say goodbye to her. I tried to persuade her to stay on, but my negotiating skills did not extend so far: she had made a commitment to her family to leave at the end of 1997. I had to respect her decision, but it meant that we were missing an important resource as we moved into the new year.

Florence's departure emphasized a problem we had been experiencing since the talks began but which became more acute—and more annoying— as we moved toward closure. In any long-term process such as treaty negotiations, people will come and go, from politicians and bureaucrats to secretaries and clerks, and those who replace them do not always have an appreciation of what has gone before. A new bureaucrat, freshly appointed, will often be eager to put his or her stamp on a provision without any real sense of its history. The same is true of many politicians. An extreme example is the 471 amendments to the Final Agreement that the Reform Party tried to force through Parliament when the document came up for ratification in the final month of the twentieth century. Not one of the amendments was passed during the forty-two-hour voting session in the House of Commons—no one seriously expected one to—but the attitude that would bring such a disruption to the business of the nation in the first place is indicative of a fundamental lack of historical and technical knowledge regarding a process that had been going on for more than two decades and to which many people had devoted a good part of their lives.

But long before December 1999, people at every level of government and the civil service were proposing changes and amendments to provisions that had been decided long ago, often with considerable compromise and metaphorical bloodletting. It was as if our long hours at the negotiating table had merely resulted at some distant desk in Ottawa in a shrug and a "Yes, but what if we try . . . " as if we hadn't tried it already and failed.

Early in 1998 we began hearing suggestions that several issues needed to be revisited. It struck me that what was lacking in Ottawa was both a sense of history and a sense of what negotiations are really about. New people in old positions, and even old people in new positions, were looking at clauses solely from their own perspective and concluding that certain provisions needed to be "tidied-up," with no appreciation that every clause—sometimes every word—was the product of negotiation and compromise. There was a sense that anything could be changed, and an expectation that we should "go to the wall" on everything. Would some people *never* understand the complexity of these arrangements? I wondered. When many of these positions were revisited at the table, I knew, the atmosphere would be poisoned.

In the first week of the new year we met with the Kitimat-Stikine Regional Advisory Committee (KS RAC), then on January 8 the Nisga'a met with the Gitanyow, accompanied by federal, provincial, and First Nations negotiators from all sides. On January 13, we met with the Fisheries and Wildlife Committee of Treaty Negotiations Advisory Committee (TNAC). In February we met in Vancouver, Prince Rupert, and Terrace. We met with the KS RAC again while we were in Prince Rupert.

How I wish that opponents of the treaty who would later make preposterous accusations about the clandestine nature of the exercise and how the Final Agreement had been foisted upon the Canadian public without warning or consultation could have accompanied us on some of these trips, if only to share our collective exhaustion. Indeed, there were days when it was almost impossible to get out of bed, and harder still to imagine going to the table yet again. Your body aches from weariness. The constant pushing and prodding, not only at the main table but also in the working groups and the bureaucracy, the continual debates in the public forum—all these things combine from time to time to render the immediate future intolerable. The certain knowledge that you have felt this way before and got over it, or that *tædium vitæ*[2] is something that most negotiators experience at one time or another, somehow doesn't help when you're staring at the ceiling of yet another hotel room in yet another city with yet another day of negotiations and consultations ahead of you.

"Some mornings it's very hard to get out of bed," Joe Gosnell once told me. "Your body is so full of arrows."

Still, the human animal is largely self-healing. If you can just force yourself out of bed, you know the weariness will eventually pass. Often by the end of a good hot shower, in fact, a miracle has overtaken the day and you're raring to go.

One of the things that made this morning resurrection possible was the character of the negotiators, not only on my own team but also on the Nisga'a and the provincial team as well. The stamina and dedication they brought to their work never failed to amaze me. Indeed, there were times when we seemed to feed on one another's energy, and the work flowed at a pace none of us could have sustained otherwise. We had our differences, of course, but always, in the end, we worked things out. A major contributing factor, I am convinced, was that we felt comfortable enough with the work and with one another that we could hold discussions over a meal or a beer as well as across the negotiating table.

It was over a beer with the provincial negotiators early in the new year that we discussed the legal drafting of the document, which was taking a tremendous amount of time, and other outstanding issues such as certainty that we had yet to address. At the same time we had to begin thinking about more mundane practical matters, such as when the parties would get together in public for the handshake and signing, what type of ceremony should be planned, what media briefings would be necessary, and how we could get a federal minister and a provincial premier in the same place at the same time on relatively short notice. On each of these issues, three parties expressed three opinions, and as we moved toward closure these questions proved to be both contentious and time consuming. In January 1998, however, much of that was still ahead of us. Assuming we did come to a Final Agreement, Trevor Proverbs, the Province's Chief Negotiator, believed it would take us to May or June. I said at least June. At that, I was still a month out.

In February the Province appointed Dale Lovick as its new Minister of Aboriginal Affairs. Provincial politicians were talking glibly of an end-of-March closing. We agreed to meet until the middle of March and then adjourn for a week.

The perennial problem of obtaining certainty was by no means resolved. As we have seen, certainty provides that once a treaty is signed, it constitutes a full and final settlement. The First Nation signatory cannot return with further demands related to past grievances. Possible future claims to lands held by third parties and governments are eliminated. Negotiations are over. Without certainty, issues such as property ownership, commercial development, hunting and fishing rights, wildlife and forestry concerns, governance, and a myriad of larger and smaller issues will remain unresolved. First Nations cannot effectively develop industry and employment opportunities on their land if the ownership of the land is in dispute. Similarly, third parties will be hesitant to make commercial deals with First Nations if they are uncertain whether the latter have the legal authority to do so. Certainty, as federal Minister Jane Stewart said, "is one of the most important by-products or results of the treaty process."[3]

But certainty is also one of the most contentious issues facing modern claims negotiators, and the phrase "cede, release, and surrender" is at the very heart of it. The land claims policy approved by Brian Mulroney's Conservative government in 1986 stated that the primary purpose of settlement was to provide certainty of rights and title to the use of lands and resources for First Nations, governments, and third parties. Certainty was seen as a benefit to aboriginal peoples, as their rights to lands and resources would be explicitly defined, and the treaties that defined them enjoyed constitutional protection under section 35 of the Constitution Act, 1982. However, the policy provided only two options to achieve certainty: on coming to an agreement, the aboriginal group would cede, release, and surrender all rights and claims to lands and resources throughout Canada, or it would cede, release, and surrender all rights to lands and resources throughout Canada while retaining any aboriginal rights and title that existed in specified or reserved areas. In short, treaties offered a straightforward exchange: undefined aboriginal rights to lands and resources for rights, benefits, lands, and financial benefits outlined in a given treaty. This method of achieving certainty was often referred to as "extinguishment." The policy was not a blanket extinguishment of aboriginal rights, but pertained only to lands and resources.

Aboriginal leaders have long argued that this approach is offensive. "Cede, release, and surrender" connotes a loss, a giving up, as if to an enemy. They see it as an attempt to cut off their past; it severs them from their history, their culture, and their spiritual links to that history and culture. Many groups refused to negotiate because of this policy.

In 1993, the Liberal Party platform included a pamphlet, "The Aboriginal Peoples of Canada,"[4] which asserted that the government would no longer require blanket extinguishment for land claims based on aboriginal title. The *Red Book*,[5] at the same time, insisted that any change to the policy must provide certainty with respect to land rights for aboriginal people and for natural resource industries. This commitment was reiterated in the next election in *Our Future Together: Preparing Canada for the 21st Century*,[6] in which the government once again stated that the policy must provide certainty with respect to land rights for both aboriginal people and for the resource industry.

Following the Liberals' election in 1993, the Standing Committee on Indian Affairs and Northern Development was tasked to study the issue. On June 23, 1994, it recommended that the Minister of DIAND "consider the feasibility of not requiring a blanket extinguishment of Aboriginal rights or title in future land claims agreements." In response, Minister Ron Irwin promised to appoint a "fact finder." This he did on December 22, 1994, naming Mr. Justice A. C. Hamilton as a fact finder with respect to surrender and certainty issues affecting the negotiation of land claim agreements. For six months, Mr. Justice Hamilton met with aboriginal peoples across Canada, as well as provincial and territorial government representatives, third parties, and members of the public, both in open meetings and in written presentations.

In the meantime, an interim report from the Royal Commission on Aboriginal Peoples (RCAP) was tabled in the House of Commons on March 23, 1995.[7] Established in August 1991, the RCAP had been given the job of examining a broad range of issues relevant to the relationship between aboriginal and non-aboriginal peoples in Canada. The interim report recommended that aboriginal peoples no longer be required to accept the blanket extinguishment of their land rights in exchange for rights or other benefits delineated in land claim settlements. The Royal Commission saw this as a precondition to negotiations.

Mr. Justice Hamilton's report, *Canada and Aboriginal Peoples: A New Partnership*,[8] was delivered to the minister on June 16, 1995. It, too, recommended an alternative to surrender provisions.

Consequent on all this activity, DIAND developed a set of principles to serve as a basis for a new legal technique for achieving certainty, an approach that would eliminate the requirement for a clause surrendering aboriginal rights but at the same time provide the certainty required by federal and provincial governments, aboriginal peoples, and third parties. Once approved within the federal system, the Minister circulated the proposed principles for consultation. From August 1996 until April 1997, DIAND and the Department of Justice carried on further consultations with aboriginal groups, provincial and territorial governments, and other interested parties. The five-volume *Final Report of the Royal Commission on Aboriginal Peoples*[9] had been tabled in the House of Commons on November 23, 1996. The report contained 440 recommendations.

Meanwhile, on March 22, 1996, Minister Irwin signed the Nisga'a Agreement in Principle, which provided that the precise legal mechanism for achieving certainty would be determined in the Final Agreement. This tossed the ball neatly into the court of the negotiators—just two months minus two days before I was assigned to the file.

The Final Agreement, according to the AIP,

> would constitute a full and final settlement, and will exhaustively set forth the Aboriginal title, rights and interests within Canada of the Nisga'a Nation and its people in respect of the Nisga'a Nation's rights recognized and affirmed by Section 35 of the *Constitution Act, 1982* in and to Nisga'a lands and other lands and resources in Canada, and the scope and geographic extent of all treaty rights of the Nisga'a Nation, including all jurisdictions, powers, rights and obligations of Nisga'a Government.

The issue was obviously vital to us, and though responsibility for the initiative ultimately rested with the Department, the federal negotiating team was very much part of the discussion. The conference calls with DIAND and the Department of Justice were numerous, intense, and sometimes frustrating, but we were finally coming to closure when a heavy spanner was abruptly thrown into the works. On December 11, 1997, the Supreme Court of Canada rendered its decision in the *Delgamuukw* case,[10] which sent us all back to the drawing board—Canada, British Columbia, and the Nisga'a alike. By February, though, it was becoming apparent that the *Delgamuukw* decision would not change the Nisga'a approach to treaty negotiations. The Nisga'a had been at this for years, after all. They knew what they wanted, and the Agreement in Principle reflected what their treaty would contain. I mourned the loss of time and effort, but at the same time I recognized that it had been unavoidable. If we had not examined the issue closely, it would have come back to haunt us.

On March 7, a Saturday, Premier Glen Clark addressed the annual convention of the provincial New Democratic Party. He was concerned about the growing divisiveness of land claims issues in the province, he said, as well as the possible ramifications of the *Delgamuukw* case.[11] For these reasons, he announced, he was sending Deputy Minister Jack Ebbels back to the negotiating table with instructions to conclude the Nisga'a treaty without further delay.[12] But he predicted a political firestorm as they carried the process forward.

"This will be a fight," he announced, "the likes of which I think we have never seen before in this province!"

How correct this statement would prove to be.

Clark also indicated for the first time publicly that the provincial government would be tabling alternative wording to achieve certainty in the Nisga'a treaty, avoiding the provocative phrase "cede, release, and surrender." Cabinet had approved several other proposals, he said, but he warned that the Province, Canada, and the Nisga'a were going to have to make some tough decisions, and all three would have to compromise. He capped his remarks with the announcement that there would be no province-wide referendum on the Final Agreement. There would, however, be a free vote in the legislature.[13]

Liberal Opposition Leader Gordon Campbell responded with a press release on March 11, 1998, stating that "British Columbians should have a right to openly assess and debate the provincial government's new negotiating mandate for the Nisga'a treaty talks." Referring to certainty, he wrote:

It is no exaggeration to say that the viability and success of the entire treaty process may well rest on how the government plans to tackle this thorny issue. We shouldn't have to wait until after the fact to find out how the government plans to proceed on our behalf on that issue or on the 70 other issues in the Nisga'a Agreement in Principle that were left completely open to negotiation.[14]

On the same day, the Province outlined its position on certainty. There was considerable discussion at the table over the issue in the ensuing weeks.

Canada was under significant pressure from British Columbia and the Nisga'a to table its own position, but the debate about certainty was still far from over in the federal system, and we had as yet no mandate from Cabinet to negotiate certainty. We could only discuss it, and that circumspectly.

In an attempt to resolve the issue, we went to Ottawa for a two-day session from March 30 to 31. We met with the federal caucus to update them on the negotiations and to outline our proposed approach to concluding the Final Agreement. We had a meeting with the DIAND internal caucus, and another with the central agencies: the Treasury Board, the Privy Council Office, the Department of Finance, and the Department of Justice. We also met with Deputy Minister Scott Serson, then with Minister Jane Stewart. Our meeting with the Minister was followed up by a conference call on April 7. The remainder of the month was marked by regular telephone conferences with Assistant Deputy Minister John Sinclair and others, including Scott Serson.

Meanwhile, in a pair of articles published in the Vancouver *Sun* in early April,[15] Liberal leader Gordon Campbell had suggested that one of the first steps in treaty making should be a mandate that was acceptable to the majority of British Columbians. This mandate, of course, could only come from a province-wide referendum. Certainty and equality, he insisted, could only be attained through extinguishment and the exclusion of "third order of government" arrangements. Not surprisingly, this did not go down well at the negotiating table, particularly among the Nisga'a. Joe Gosnell was quoted in the April 12 issue of the Vancouver *Province*: "It is not for the government to extinguish who we are as people, because they didn't place us on this land. We prefer to sit across the table and to discuss how to reconcile our rights as Nisga'a and your rights as Canadians."[16]

On April 18, Premier Clark announced his intention to launch a mailing campaign and a province-wide debate before his government would sign the Nisga'a Final Agreement.[17] He may have been acting under the influence of a Marktrend Poll that had recently found that 72 percent of British Columbians felt they had not been adequately consulted about the Nisga'a treaty and 68 percent wanted a referendum on land claims.

Gordon Campbell announced that the TNAC wanted two months to review each of the proposed eighteen chapters of the Final Agreement (in the end it ran to twenty-two chapters) before it was made public. He also stated that the Liberals expected a clause-by-clause debate in the legislature.[18]

The period from March to May 1998 was the most intense I had experienced since joining the Nisga'a table two years before. Work within the federal system was stepped up as the bureaucratic wheels ground toward a decision regarding certainty. The Cabinet document that would eventually give us a mandate to negotiate certainty was being drafted. Discussion and activity were at a fever pitch. Even so, both the Nisga'a and the Province seemed to assume that we were deliberately procrastinating, and they made no secret of their irritation.

I had several off-the-record discussions with negotiators for the Province and the Nisga'a to review the situation, sometimes separately, sometimes together. This had happened before during these negotiations. In my experience, an informal conversation—"a walk in the park to discuss the facts of life," as Assistant Deputy Minister John Sinclair called them—frequently helped provide the solutions that ultimately led to an agreement. But such talks, by their nature, require absolute trust and discretion. One must be assured that what is said during "a walk in the park" will never surface at the negotiation table or anywhere else. So, while I was assured that the other parties understood the dilemma we were in, that did not alter the impatience they felt at the table.

A partial timeline of the federal journey toward certainty would read as follows:

March 23, 1998: the issue of certainty is discussed by the Senior
  Policy Committee of DIAND
March 30–31: the federal team is in Ottawa to discuss the issue of
  certainty, among other items, with the Ottawa Federal Caucus,
  the DIAND Internal Caucus, the central agencies, the Deputy
  Minister, and finally the Minister
April 7: a conference call with Minister Stewart
April 8: a conference call with the Deputy Minister and senior
  Justice officials
April 20: the Senior Policy Committee reviews the draft
  memorandum to Cabinet
April 29: the Ottawa Federal Caucus reviews the draft
  memorandum to Cabinet
April 30: we brief TNAC

May 1: the Federal Steering Committee on Comprehensive Claims
reviews the draft memorandum to Cabinet
May 4: the Minister receives the final briefing and signs off the
document
May 12: the Cabinet Committee approves the mandate, and it
is eventually approved by full Cabinet

Throughout this period, there was also bilateral work with British
Columbia and with the TNAC Working Group. At the end of it, and for the
first time in the history of treaty negotiations in Canada, a federal negotiating team had a mandate to obtain certainty other than by "cede, release, and
surrender," thus ending one of the most extensive and lengthy policy reviews
that I have witnessed in the past nineteen years. It paid off, though. The government's position that certainty in the Nisga'a treaty provides the same
level of certainty as the surrender clauses commonly found in other treaties
has remained unchallenged, and appears to have the support of even the
treaty's most vocal critics.

Chapter Eight

....

NEGOTIATING CERTAINTY AT THE NISGA'A TABLE might have been a simpler task if the parties had had a clear and common definition of aboriginal rights. Unfortunately, there isn't one. Since George III issued his Royal Proclamation in 1763, consolidating British gains after the Seven Years' War and establishing governing structures in its new territories, the term "aboriginal rights" has undergone a process of evolution and some legal definition, but the nature and extent of aboriginal rights, and where they exist, are still very much open questions.

The following is not intended to be an exhaustive review of the case law; rather, it is a preliminary look at the legal theory upon which concepts of aboriginal rights are based.

The *St. Catharine's Milling*[1] case in the late nineteenth century established that provincial governments could not use Indian lands as a source of revenue until aboriginal title had been extinguished. A relevance of the case is explained by Carolyn Swayze in her biography of Thomas Berger:

In the Nishga [sic] case, the court looked, as do all Canadian inquiries into the nature of Indian title, to the *St. Catharines Milling Co.* case, which is familiar to every student of constitutional law. In 1883 the federal government, believing that it owned the lands and resources in a particular area with respect to which it had entered a treaty, granted a timber-cutting licence to the milling company. The Province of Ontario, however, claimed that the British North America Act gave it the land and negated any Indian interest there might have been on it. The then-final arbiter, the Judicial Committee of the Privy Council in England, held that after the treaty, the entire interest in the land and legislative jurisdiction over it fell to the province. In effect, this was a circuitous way of recognizing Indian title, for it recognized that the Crown's interest had existed concurrently with aboriginal title, which was something tangible and capable of extinguishment and which had originated with the Royal Proclamation.[2]

Nearly a century later, in 1973, *Calder et al v. the Attorney-General of British Columbia* established that aboriginal title existed at the time of European contact, regardless of whether Europeans recognized it. Although the court was split on the question of whether it continued to exist, and the claim was ultimately dismissed on a procedural technicality, the judgement did serve to negate the common assumption that First Nations in the sixteenth, seventeenth, and eighteenth centuries were not socially or politically advanced enough to have recognizable rights.

Key evidence during the *Calder* case was given by Wilson Duff, then associate professor of Anthropology at the University of British Columbia and author of *The Indian History of British Columbia*, long considered a classic of regional anthropology. Under examination by Thomas Berger, lawyer for the Nisga'a, Professor Duff spoke eloquently from a lifetime of experience and study. Berger first read from *The Indian History of British Columbia*, which had been marked as an exhibit in the courtroom:

At the time of contact the Indians of this area were among the world's most distinctive peoples. Fully one-third of the native population of Canada lived here. They were concentrated most heavily along the coastline and the main western rivers, and in these areas they developed their cultures to higher peaks, in many respects, than in any other part of the continent north of Mexico. Here, too, was the greatest linguistic diversity in the country, with two dozen languages spoken, belonging to seven of the eleven language families represented in Canada. The coastal tribes were, in some ways, different from all other American Indians. Their languages, true enough, were members of American families, and physically they were American Indians, though with decided traits of similarity to the peoples of North-eastern Asia. Their cultures, however, had a pronounced Asiatic tinge, evidence of basic kinship and long continued contact with the peoples around the North Pacific rim. Most of all, their cultures were distinguished by a local richness and originality, the product of vigorous and inventive people in a rich environment.

"Would that paragraph," asked Berger, "apply to the people who inhabited the area delineated on the map, Exhibit 2?" He indicated the Nass Valley.
"Yes," Professor Duff replied.
Berger continued, reading the next paragraph:

It is not correct to say that Indians did not own the land but only roamed over the face of it and used it. The patterns of ownership and utilization which they imposed upon the lands and waters were different from those recognized by our system of law, but were nonetheless clearly defined and mutually respected. Even if they didn't subdivide and cultivate the land, they did recognize ownership of plots used for village sites, fishing places, berry and root patches, and similar purposes. Even if they didn't subject the forest to wholesale logging, they did establish ownership of tracts used for hunting, trapping and food gathering. Even if they didn't sink mine shafts into the mountains, they did own peaks and valleys for mountain goat hunting and as sources of raw materials. Except for barren and inaccessible areas which are not utilized even today, every part of the province was formerly within the owned and recognized territory of one or other of the Indian Tribes.[3]

"Does that paragraph," Berger again asked, "apply to the people who inhabited the area delineated on the map, Exhibit 2?"
"Yes, it does," Duff replied, again.
"Does it apply"—Berger wanted to be certain—"to the Nisga'a tribe?"
"Yes, it does."
Berger then asked Duff to tell the court "the extent of the use to which the Nisga'a have put the lands and waters in the area delineated on Exhibit 2 and how intensive that use was."
The territories in general, the professor explained, were recognized by the people themselves and by neighbouring tribes as Nisga'a land. Certain areas would be used in common by the whole tribe, while others would be

allocated to family groups. Different parts of the territory would be exploited for different purposes at different times of the year, although the salmon streams were used fairly steadily, as different species spawned at different times.

The Nisga'a hunted and trapped in the lower parts of the valley, Duff continued, not just for their own immediate use but for commerce, for the Nisga'a were avid traders, first among other tribes and then among Europeans and Canadians. Some of the slopes farther up the valley were good areas for hunting mountain goats, others for trapping marmots. Lichen and moss were collected for dyes, minerals for tools. The water, too, was an abundantly exploited source of sea mammals and fish, shell fish and roe, and herring eggs, not to mention a means of transportation for trade and migration.

"To what extent," Berger asked Professor Duff, "would the use and exploitation of the resources of the Nisga'a territory have extended in terms of that territory? Would it have extended only through a limited part of the territory, or through a whole territory?"

"To a greater or lesser degree of intensity," the professor replied, "it would extend through a whole territory, except for the most barren and inaccessible parts, which were not used or wanted by anyone. But the ownership of an entire drainage basin marked out by the mountain peaks would be recognized as resting within one or other groups of Nisga'a Indians, and these boundaries, this ownership, would be respected by others."[4]

Contrast this pattern of ownership with the European and current North American practice, in which individual ownership is paramount, where parcels of land represent bundles of rights that can be divided among more than one person, and where the mineral estate can be separated from the surface estate while a mortgage and a lease can be granted for the same parcel. In the European concept of rights, it is necessary not only to define specific boundaries but also to develop a complex system of rights and a legal system to deal with them.

In the eighteenth century these two disparate and distinct concepts of land ownership collided in the Nass Valley.

Mr. Justice Emmett Hall, one of the seven justices who heard the *Calder* case, stated in his judgement that possession at common law was proof of ownership: "*prima facie*, therefore, the Nisghas [sic] are the owners of the lands that have been in their possession from time immemorial, and therefore, the burden of establishing that their rights have been extinguished rests squarely on the respondents [the province of British Columbia]."[5] He found from the evidence that the Nisga'a "in fact are and were from time immemorial a distinctive cultural entity with concepts of ownership indigenous to their culture and capable of articulations under common law . . . "

Justice Hall was clearly sensitive to the history of the issue, referring to the *St. Catharine's Milling* case and quoting extensively from Nisga'a elder and Chief David Mackay's presentation to a Royal Commission hearing in 1888. Speaking on behalf of the Nisga'a, Mackay said:

What we don't like about the Government is their saying this: "We will give you this much land." How can they give it when it is our own? We cannot understand it. They have never bought it from us or our forefathers. They have never fought and conquered our people and taken the land in that way, and yet they say now that they will give us so much land—our own land. These chiefs do not talk foolishly, they know the land is their own; our forefathers for generations and generations past had their land here all around us; chiefs have had their own hunting grounds, their salmon streams, and places where they got their berries; it has always been so. It is not only during the last four or five years that we have seen the land; we have always seen and owned it; it is no new thing, it has been ours for generations. If we had only seen it for twenty years and claimed it as our own, it would have been foolish, but it has been ours for thousands of years. If any strange person came here and saw the land for twenty years and claimed it, he would be foolish. We have always got our living from the land; we are not like white people who live in towns and have their own stores and other business, getting their living in that way, but we have always depended on the land for our food and clothes; we get our salmon, berries, and furs from the land.[6]

It was this concept of ownership as indigenous to aboriginal culture and capable of articulations under common law that was the basis on which aboriginal title law has developed in Canada following the *Calder* case. Its history in law, of course, went back much further than *Calder*, and it was not restricted to Canada. As early as 1822 Chief Justice John Marshall[7] of the United States had rendered a similar judgement, though with a different attitude toward the rights that Europeans had assumed in the Americas through power, war, and conquest. In *Worcester v. State of Georgia*, Marshall wrote:

America, separated from Europe by a wide ocean, was inhabited by a distinct people, divided into separate nations, independent of each other and of the rest of the world, having institutions of their own, and governing themselves by their own laws. It is difficult to comprehend the proposition, that the inhabitants of either quarter of the globe could have rightful original claims of dominion over the inhabitants of the other, or over the lands they occupied; or that the discovery of either by the other should give the discoverer rights in the country discovered, which annulled the pre-existing right of its ancient possessors.

After lying concealed for a series of ages, the enterprise of Europe, guided by nautical science, conducted some of her adventurous sons into this western world. They found it in possession of a people who had made small progress in agriculture or manufactures, and whose general employment was war, hunting and fishing.

Did these adventurers, by sailing along the coast, and occasionally landing on it, acquire for the several governments to whom they belonged, or by whom they were commissioned, a rightful property in the soil from the Atlantic to the Pacific; or rightful dominion over the numerous people who occupied it? Or has nature, or the great Creator of all things, conferred these rights over hunters and fishermen, on agriculturalists and manufacturers?

But power, war, conquest, give rights, which after possession, are conceded by the world; and which can never be controverted by those on whom they descend. We proceed, then, to the actual state of things, having glanced at their origin, because holding it in our recollection might shed some light on existing pretensions.

The great maritime powers of Europe discovered and visited different parts of this continent at nearly the same time. The object was too immense for any one of them to grasp the whole; and the claimants were too powerful to submit to the exclusive or unreasonable pretensions of any single potentate. To avoid bloody conflicts, which might terminate disastrously to all, it was necessary for the nations of Europe to establish some principle which all would acknowledge, and which should decide their respective rights as between themselves. This principle, suggested by the actual state of things, was "that discovery gave title to the government by whose subjects or by whose authority it was made, against all other European governments, which title might be consummated by possession" (8 Wheat. 573).

The principle, acknowledged by all Europeans, because it was the interest of all to acknowledge it, gave to the nation making the discovery, as its inevitable consequence, the sole right of acquiring the soil and of making settlements on it. It was an exclusive principle which shut out the right of competition among those who had agreed to it; not one which could annul the previous rights of those who had not agreed to it. It regulated the right given by discovery among the European discoverers; *but could not affect the rights of those already in possession, either as aboriginal occupants, or as occupants by virtue of a discovery made before the memory of man. It gave the exclusive right to purchase, but did not found that right on a denial of the right of the possessor to sell*[8]. (Emphasis added.)

Considering the manner in which the United States government and its citizens subsequently treated the original inhabitants of that nation—inflicting war and sometimes genocide upon them—it would seem that Justice Marshall's words were not taken very seriously, or at least not literally.

Another item of law that has sometimes not been taken very seriously is the Royal Proclamation of 1763, a document that has been referred to variously as the "Magna Carta of Indian Rights"[9] and "a historic expression of the common law rather than a source of legal rights."[10] It has been held by the courts to have "the force of a statute which has never been repealed,"[11] and it has been blithely ignored by successive federal, provincial, state, and territorial governments both above and below the forty-ninth parallel. It certainly failed to stifle the expansionist ambitions of the Thirteen Colonies—which, in any case, were soon beyond British control. At the same time, Native populations throughout Canada have regarded it very seriously, largely because, regardless of its political efficacy, it made two critical points: first, that all lands not purchased by the British Government from the Indians belonged to the Indians, and second, that further lands could be acquired from the Indians only by the government, and only after a public meeting of the Indians called for that purpose in the presence of an official. What a deal of trouble we might have spared ourselves had we only observed our own laws! Even so, it is interesting to note that the concept of aboriginal title existed in law as far back as the 1700s, and was in fact the underpinning for judgements ranging from *Worcester* to *Calder*. It was the basis of the Nisga'a petition to the Privy Council in 1913 and as recently as the *Delgamuukw* case, it was cited as a recognition of aboriginal title. But it was with the *Calder* case in 1973 that the principle of aboriginal rights was established in Canadian law for the first time.

The *Calder* case did not require the government to change its policy and begin to negotiate treaties.[12] It did, however, question title to Canadian lands and resources not then covered by treaties at a time when major projects were about to be undertaken. The Inuit and Cree of northern Quebec were beginning an action that threatened the James Bay hydro project. The Inuit of Baker Lake were commencing an action because of proposed mineral activity in the eastern Arctic. The Inuvialuit and the Dene-Métis were expressing concerns over the proposed Polar Gas Project and the Mackenzie Valley Pipeline. Economic development and activity were being threatened. The use and management of lands and resources were in a state of uncertainty. The issue had to be addressed.

On August 8, 1973, Jean Chrétien, then Minister of Indian Affairs, announced that the federal government intended to settle land claims, and issued a policy statement to that effect.[13] This reflected the government's, and particularly Prime Minister Pierre Trudeau's, altered thinking on the legitimacy of aboriginal title as a result of the *Calder* decision. Two new approaches would be taken, Chrétien announced. First, the federal government was prepared to accept land claims based on traditional use and occupancy. Second, any acceptance of such a claim would not be an admission of legal liability, but the federal government was willing to negotiate a settlement.

Although the Nisga'a had lost the *Calder* case on a procedural technicality, in reality they had scored a major victory. But their work would only now begin. For aboriginal rights was still a rather nebulous affair. Everyone agreed that they existed, but no one could agree on where and what they were. It was not until the *Baker Lake* case, seven years later, that the test for aboriginal title was established.

In 1980 a group of Inuit sought a declaration that the lands comprising the Baker Lake area of the Northwest Territories (now part of Nunavut) were "subject to the aboriginal right and title of the Inuit residing in or near that area to hunt and fish thereon." Relying on the *Calder* decision, the judge granted the declaration, but ruled that, in order to establish aboriginal title cognizable at common law, First Nations must prove:

1. that they and their ancestors were members of an organized society;
2. that the organized society occupied the specific territory over which they assert the aboriginal title;
3. that the occupation was to the exclusion of other organized societies;
4. that the occupation was an established fact at the time sovereignty was asserted by England.[14]

But there was still no clear interpretation or explanation of what aboriginal rights actually were. Even when the term was written into the Constitution Act, 1982, the Act did not define the nature, scope, or extent of aboriginal rights; it merely recognized and protected their existence. Section 25, for example, guarantees that the Charter of Rights and Freedoms "shall not be construed so as to abrogate or derogate from any aboriginal, treaty or other rights or freedoms that pertain to the aboriginal peoples of Canada," including "any rights or freedoms that have been recognized by the Royal Proclamation of October 7, 1763," and those "that may be acquired by the aboriginal peoples of Canada by way of land claims settlement." Section 35 recognizes and affirms the "existing aboriginal and treaty rights of the aboriginal peoples of Canada," defines those peoples as including "the Indian, Inuit, and Métis peoples," further defines treaty rights to include "rights that now exist by way of land claims agreements or may be so acquired," and provides that aboriginal and treaty rights are guaranteed equally to men and women.

It has been left to the courts to interpret the Act, and the courts have repeatedly urged negotiation over litigation. As Chief Justice Antonio Lamer said in *Delgamuukw*, "this litigation has been long and expensive, not only in economic but in human terms as well. By ordering a new trial, I do not necessarily encourage the parties to proceed to litigation and settle their disputes through the courts."[15] Joe Gosnell reiterated this sentiment at the initialling of the Final Agreement: "The Nisga'a treaty proves, beyond all doubt, that negotiations—not lawsuits, not roadblocks, not violence—are the most effective, most honourable way to resolve aboriginal issues in this country."[16]

Previous to 1982, aboriginal rights could be regulated by any level of government without recourse. The Constitution Act did finally provide that recourse, but it wasn't until 1990 that the courts began to define what rights might have existed in 1982 when section 35 came into force. In that year the Supreme Court of Canada ruled in *Sparrow vs. The Queen*, an aboriginal fishing rights case in British Columbia, that the rights protected by section 35 were those that had not been extinguished by statute or by consent of First Nations. The court further ruled that aboriginal and treaty rights could be regulated by competent government enactment—referred to as "justifiable infringement"—but that regulation of a right does not extinguish it. Governments also had to act in a manner that would uphold "the honour of the Crown"; there could be no appearance of sharp dealings. Legislative authority was linked to fiduciary duty.[17]

Neither *Sparrow* nor *Delgamuukw* provided the world with a clear definition of aboriginal rights. Indeed, given the diversity of aboriginal cultures in Canada—there are fifty-three distinct aboriginal languages spoken within our national borders, not including English and French—any such legal or philosophical clarity is a practical impossibility. The courts have indicated, however, that aboriginal rights are fact-specific, site-specific, and group-specific. In other words, in any case involving aboriginal rights, judgements will be made only in the context of that particular group and set of circumstances.

If it is through negotiations that aboriginal rights are defined, then the process is continual, and our efforts at the Nisga'a table represented only one step in the evolution of justice for Native peoples in Canada. But if specific rights cannot be applied to all of the nation's original inhabitants, broader, philosophical definitions are at least possible.

Broadly speaking, then, aboriginal rights are inherent, collective rights based on First Nations' pre-contact social order and their original occupation of the land. Most First Nations agree that aboriginal rights extend beyond the right to own and occupy land or maintain a traditional lifestyle. Ultimately, they embrace the concept of independence through self-determination. Most First Nations would also agree that the supreme source of aboriginal rights is the Creator. In this they are little different from the democracies of the Western world.

Human rights are based, first and last, on the simple fact of being human. Political rights are based on the human predilection for social order, and have their basis in human rights. To most intelligent people they are self-evident. Whether it is expressed in terms of "peace, order, and good government" or *"liberté, egalité, fraternité,"* the concept of rights held collectively and exercised individually is a common thread running through Western civilization. The tradition is equally strong, though somewhat older, in aboriginal societies.

To the First Nations of Canada, aboriginal rights are simply human and political rights, and they have been self-evident from time immemorial. Long before the upstart revolutionaries of the Thirteen Colonies declared, "We hold these truths to be self-evident, that all men are created equal, that they are endowed by their Creator with certain unalienable Rights"; long before the French Revolution resolved to set forth "the natural, unalienable, and sacred rights of man"; and centuries before the Parliament of Canada affirmed that we are a nation "founded upon the principles that recognize the supremacy of God and the rule of law," the people of the Nass River were living according to *Ayuukhl Nisga'a*, an ancient code of laws that will stand comparison to any modern constitution or declaration of statehood and nationality.

The tenets of *Ayuukhl Nisga'a*, though never written down, had survived and evolved in ceremony, tradition, and story for generations before that, embracing civil, criminal, and international law, a social code, a national history and mythology, political organizations, and religious institutions. Many pre-contact aboriginal societies in Canada ruled themselves according to similar unwritten constitutions and declarations, and were no doubt mightily vexed when well-meaning missionaries and less-well-meaning bureaucrats told them that they had no laws, no social order, and therefore no right to the land they lived on.

Many would say that it is the recognition of this historical wrong that is the moral basis of modern treaty making in Canada. Others might hold that redressing age-old grievances and resolving social inequities is simply practical politics. In any case, it is the right thing to do, and those who oppose treaty making on supposedly economic or social grounds haven't a moral or a practical leg to stand on.

A study done in the late 1990s by Price Waterhouse indicated that close to a billion dollars and fifteen hundred jobs had been lost in British Columbia's mining and forestry sectors as a result of disputes over land claims.[18] This figure did not take into account the hundreds of thousands of dollars that have been spent by industry and governments trying to deal with blockades and other forms of civil disobedience. Unresolved land claims have even become an issue on Wall Street in New York as various financial institutions analyse the province's economy. Not surprisingly, then, one of the stated objectives of treaty negotiations in British Columbia is to establish certainty over lands and resources and thus provide a more secure climate for investment and economic development.

On the other hand, a document entitled *Benefits and Costs of Treaty Settlements in British Columbia: A Financial and Economic Perspective* reported that British Columbia "can expect about $3 worth of total financial benefit for every dollar of provincial financial costs." The report, issued on January 17, 1996, by KPMG, another well-known firm of financial consultants, further reported that if the total costs to British Columbia were approximately $2 billion, at an average of $50 million a year over forty years it would represent about one quarter of 1 percent of the provincial annual budget.[19] This is a great deal of money, to be sure, but it pales in comparison to the costs of education, health care, and unemployment insurance. And it does not take into account the transfer of millions of dollars from the federal treasury.

There are compelling social as well as economic reasons for negotiating treaties. The Indian Act, as the main federal tool of governance over Indian affairs, has not always been administered even-handedly or with the best interests of human beings at heart. As a result, the social conditions of Native communities in British Columbia, like many in the rest of Canada, are, to greater and lesser degrees, substandard in comparison to those of other communities. First Nations have the lowest rates of literacy and education and the highest rates of infant mortality, unemployment, incarceration, and suicide of any single group in the province or in the country. The transfer of responsibility and control of aboriginal communities to aboriginal people is an essential step toward positive change. As Canada's laws and policies evolve in acceptance and understanding of the politics of the original inhabitants of the nation, the paternalism that has been a major part of what Duncan Campbell Scott called "the Indian problem"[20] will give way to mutual respect and cooperation, and the Canadian ideal of unity in diversity will evolve toward political reality.

It was in this spirit that DIAND Minister Ron Irwin and Minister Anne McLellan, then Federal Interlocutor for Métis and non-status Indians, announced a new policy to recognize the inherent right of self-government as an existing right within section 35 of the Constitution Act, 1982. The policy, first articulated publicly in a press release dated August 10, 1995, was based on the view that First Nations have a right to govern themselves in relation to matters "that are internal to Aboriginal communities; matters that are integral to Aboriginal cultures, identities, traditions, languages and institutions; and matters relating to their Aboriginal lands and their resources."[21] The policy was an explicit acknowledgement that the aboriginal peoples were the first inhabitants of Canada, and that they had developed governments, laws, and spiritual beliefs that allowed them to be fully functional societies centuries before the arrival of Europeans.[22]

The Ministers made it clear that "self-government will be exercised within the existing Canadian Constitution," and that "Federal, provincial, territorial and Aboriginal laws must work in harmony. Laws of overriding federal and provincial importance such as the Criminal Code will prevail." Moreover, "the Canadian Charter of Rights and Freedoms applies to all Canadians. The Charter will apply fully to Aboriginal governments as it does to other governments in Canada."[23] At the same time, "The current provisions of the Charter that respect the unique Aboriginal and treaty rights of Aboriginal peoples will continue to apply."[24]

The policy was seen as a vehicle to enhance the participation of aboriginal peoples in the Canadian federation, and it was critical to our deliberations at the Nisga'a table. As Joe Gosnell said repeatedly, "The Nisga'a are negotiating their way *into* Canada, not out of it." The concept of certainty was central to this process. Neither a world nation nor a First Nation can function effectively if its citizens are uncertain of where they can live, what they own, the limits of their territory, and to whose authority they are subject.

The approach to certainty used in the Nisga'a Final Agreement has been called the "Modified Aboriginal Rights Approach" in that it provides that whatever aboriginal rights and title the Nisga'a had at common law are modified to be the rights set out in the Final Agreement. Thus, rights are agreed to rather than extinguished, rendering obsolete the troublesome phrase "cede, release, and surrender." The Nisga'a have not surrendered their right to the land they have occupied since time immemorial; rather, that right has been modified to specify a particular area over which their rights of ownership continue to prevail.

Given the nature of the certainty provisions, it might be useful to look at how they weave together in the treaty to form the fabric of certainty. For those interested in object lessons—politicians take note—this will also demonstrate the importance in treaties of reviewing the entire document, for discussing or attacking one clause on its own is a meaningless exercise. It will also confirm that picking clauses from one treaty and replicating them in another—a fear frequently expressed among those who insist on viewing the Nisga'a treaty as a blueprint for all subsequent agreements in British Columbia—will be as fruitful an exercise as herding cats.

Paragraph 22 of Chapter 2, "General Provisions," asserts that the Final Agreement "constitutes the full and final settlement in respect of the aboriginal rights, including aboriginal title, in Canada of the Nisga'a Nation."

Paragraph 23 provides that the Final Agreement exhaustively sets out the "Nisga'a section 35 rights," a term defined in Chapter 1, "Definitions," as "the rights, anywhere in Canada, of the Nisga'a nation, that are recognized and affirmed by section 35 of the *Constitution Act, 1982.*" The parties agree that there are no exercisable rights beyond those set out in the treaty.

Paragraphs 24 and 25 provide that any aboriginal right the Nisga'a enjoyed prior to the Final Agreement is modified by the Final Agreement but continues as modified, including the attributes and geographic extent of those modified rights.

Paragraph 26 provides that if, despite the Final Agreement and the settlement legislation, the Nisga'a have an aboriginal right other than or different in attributes or geographic extent from Nisga'a section 35 rights, the Nisga'a release that right to Canada, but only to the extent of the difference. ("Settlement legislation" refers to the enactments of the British Columbia Legislature and the Parliament of Canada that give effect to the Agreement.)

In Paragraph 27, Canada, British Columbia, and all other persons are released from any liability for the infringement of any aboriginal rights of the Nisga'a prior to the effective date of the Final Agreement.

Paragraph 29 provides that, to the extent that provincial laws do not apply of their own force to the Nisga'a because of the constitutional division of powers, Canada would include a provision in its settlement legislation so that provincial law would apply to the Nisga'a in accordance with the Final Agreement. This paragraph is intended to operate with similar effect to section 88 of the Indian Act.

Four other paragraphs in the Final Agreement bear on the Modified Aboriginal Rights Approach to certainty:

§20: the parties will not challenge the validity of the Final Agreement

§21: a breach of the Final Agreement will not relieve the parties of their obligations

§57: there is to be no presumption in favour of any one party when interpreting the Final Agreement

§28: once Canada and British Columbia have consulted with or provided information to the Nisga'a in respect of any activity, including resource development or extraction, in accordance with their obligations under the Final Agreement, neither the Province nor Canada will have any additional obligations to consult with or provide information to the Nisga'a Nation in respect of that activity

The Nisga'a Nation represent and warrant that they enter into the Final Agreement on behalf of all persons who have any aboriginal rights based on their identity as Nisga'a. Further, the parties agree that the Final Agreement is binding on all parties to the Agreement and on all persons. The parties also agree that, by virtue of the modifications, there are no "lands reserved for the Indians" within the meaning of the Constitution Act, 1867, and no "reserves" as defined in the Indian Act.

The Preamble to the Final Agreement is also intended to assist in interpreting these certainty provisions, specifically the following clauses:

WHEREAS the Nisga'a Nation has sought a just and equitable settlement of the land question since the arrival of the British Crown, including the preparation of the Nisga'a Petition to His Majesty's Privy Council, dated 21 May, 1913, and the conduct of the litigation that led to the decision of the Supreme Court of Canada in *Calder v. the Attorney-General of British Columbia* in 1973, and this Agreement is intended to be the just and equitable settlement of the land question;

WHEREAS Canadian courts have stated that the reconciliation between the prior presence of aboriginal peoples and the assertion of sovereignty by the Crown is best achieved through negotiation and agreement, rather than through litigation or conflict;

WHEREAS the Parties intend that this Agreement will result in this reconciliation and establish a new relationship among them;

WHEREAS the Parties intend their relationship to be based on a new approach to mutual recognition and sharing, and to achieve this mutual recognition and sharing by agreeing on rights rather than by the extinguishment of rights; and

WHEREAS the Parties intend that this Agreement will provide certainty with respect to Nisga'a ownership and use of lands and resources, and the relationship of federal, provincial and Nisga'a laws, within the Nass Area . . .

We believe that these provisions provide the same level of certainty as do the clauses commonly found in previous treaties. We also believe that the courts will interpret these provisions in a manner consistent with the expressed intentions of the parties as set out in the Final Agreement. The courts have consistently said that these issues are best resolved at the negotiation table. I cannot imagine them now ruling that the only way certainty can be achieved is through a technique so fundamentally unacceptable to one of the parties that it makes negotiations virtually impossible on other issues.

True, the Final Agreement does contain approximately fifty provisions in which there is an obligation to negotiate. Critics say this is not certainty; they have mistaken certainty for finality. The treaty reflects a fundamental Canadian reality. Between Canada, the provinces, and the territories, for example, and between the provinces and territories and the municipal governments, negotiations are frequent and necessary to guide the evolving relationships. So, too, the Final Agreement recognizes a continuing relationship between the parties as a result of the treaty.

In some cases negotiations might never be required, or they might not be required until some future date. Final Agreements are not capable of predicting the future, but they can encourage certainty by identifying areas where further negotiation may be undertaken and making sure that systems are in place to reach decisions on issues that may arise. There is no binding obligation to reach an agreement with respect to these provisions, and any agreement that may result is not part of the treaty. The Custodial Arrangements Agreement with the Canadian Museum of Civilization, for example, or harmonization agreements for environmental assessment processes may arise from provisions in the Final Agreement, but they form no part of the Final Agreement itself.

In the final analysis, the issue that was most critical to third parties and to economic development—aboriginal rights, including aboriginal title and self-government—has been resolved.

Chapter Nine

....

IN THE MEANTIME, WORK CONTINUED at the main table. Matters were becoming more stressful, if that were possible. With certainty more or less out of the way, we were left with the difficult issues that had remained unresolved over the course of the negotiations. Canada and British Columbia did not help the mood much by revisiting previously agreed-to provisions at the behest of our respective bureaucracies.

In early May we were in Ottawa to brief Deputy Minister Scott Serson on our plans for bringing closure to the negotiations. We also met with Assistant Deputy Minister John Sinclair and others to review the outstanding federal issues.

On May 20, 1998, Frank Barton and James Robinson, the two dissident Nisga'a, announced that they had a court date in July for their ongoing challenge to the Nisga'a Tribal Council's authority to negotiate a treaty.[1] The action was worrisome, but there was nothing we could do but let justice and democracy take their course. No one involved in the negotiations imagined that Barton or Robinson spoke for the majority of the Nisga'a.

We were back in Terrace in the first half of June. On the 10th, Minister Stewart met with her provincial counterpart, Dale Lovick, to discuss Nisga'a issues and closing. That same evening, we had yet another meeting with the Kitimat-Stikine Regional Advisory Committee and reviewed in detail the six chapters that had been concluded: "Access," "Lands," "Fisheries," "Wildlife and Migratory Birds," "Administration of Justice," and "Cultural Artifacts and Heritage." We also discussed the outstanding issues and the federal and provincial governments' proposed approaches to them.

To Ottawa again on June 18 for meetings with DIAND, Heritage Canada, some members of the Federal Caucus, and representatives of the Prime Minister's Office.

On June 22 we brought Scott Serson up to date on the negotiations, and a bilateral Canada–British Columbia meeting was held to review where each government stood on the remaining issues.

We gave a further briefing to our Minister on the 23rd.

Negotiations can have an endless flow to them. This is the curse of the computer: no matter how often you read or rewrite a provision, you can always tinker with it. A word here, a phrase there, a comma or a semi-colon moved three words back or two phrases forward: the possibilities are endless, and they are all in the service of clarity. But there comes a point when you have to shift into closing mode and tackle the issues that have been constantly set aside. It's a "now or never" attitude. For the Nisga'a negotiations, it finally arrived in late June 1998.

The last round of negotiations began in Vancouver on June 24. All three parties agreed to stay at the table until the deal was done. From now on it would be seven days a week—no more weekend breaks.

It was at this time, to add to our joy, that other issues not directly related to the main table demanded our attention. Work had to begin on the timing and nature of the initialling ceremony. We needed third-party consultation on the final chapters. We needed a plan for the announcement, assuming there would be something to announce; nothing was certain until the final moment. We needed to plan for media briefings, for political briefings, and for the legal vetting, translating, proofreading, printing, and distribution of the final document.

Concurrently, I was involved in negotiations with two bands related to specific claims each had made against the federal government. Specific claims are brought in response to an alleged failure of Canada or the Province to meet the terms of an existing agreement. Unlike comprehensive land claims, which are based on aboriginal rights and title that have not been dealt with by treaty or other legal means, specific land claims are negotiated outside the treaty process. Though less important than an entire treaty, they are not minor matters by any means, and often they deal with issues that have been unresolved for decades. Specific claims might include:

◆ a claim that land was improperly pre-empted by settlers even though it had been reserved by the Crown;

◆ a claim that land was set aside as a reserve in an
Order-in-Council that Canada does not recognize or of which
Canada is unaware;

◆ a claim that the Crown promised to set aside land as a reserve
and has the obligation to carry through on the promise;

◆ a claim that land was an "Indian settlement" under colonial or
early provincial legislation, and therefore should have been set
aside as a reserve;

◆ a claim that the Crown failed to act adequately on behalf of a
band in advancing claims before the McKenna-McBride
Commission, and was thereby responsible for certain land not
being set aside as a reserve by the commission.

I had been hoping to get all the outstanding issues related to land out of
the way at the same time, but the federal government and the two bands
were as divided on the specific claims as they were on any topic being negotiated at the main table. As at the main table, flushed faces and muttered
asides were not uncommon. We usually managed to remain friendly, though,
and always avoided insult and blasphemy.

Thus, in the final days, the Chief Negotiators were juggling issues at the
main table with the remaining working groups as well as directing the ponderous task of legal drafting, planning the various and necessary ceremonies,
and continuing negotiations on the specific land claims. It was a frantic time.
I dare say it was doubly frantic for the federal team. Not only did we have to
give our full attention to the issues at hand; at the same time, we had to deal
with a much more petulant and overweight bureaucracy than did either the
Province or the Nisga'a. Tempers were frayed as often by an importunate
remark made in distant Ottawa as by an intemperate statement made across
the table. We started early in the morning and went until early the next
morning. Then, after a few hours' rest, a shower, and a change of clothes, we
were back at it. Meals were irregular and mostly unhealthy, fast foods served
with vinegar and ketchup (and a new twist offered by Brian Martin: Tabasco
sauce on french fries), often eaten at the negotiating table so we could keep
working. Every meeting room in the Federal Treaty Negotiation Office in
Vancouver was being used by one group or another involved in the Nisga'a
negotiations.

We moved to Terrace on July 8, 1998, on the principle that the Final

Agreement ought to be concluded as close to the Naṣs Valley as possible. We had wanted to do it in the Nass Valley but given the number of people involved and the equipment required to keep us in touch with one another and the outside world, it was utterly impracticable. I had a team of seventeen people in Terrace during the last week, as well as people in Vancouver and Ottawa with whom we were in daily, sometimes hourly, communication by phone, fax, and computer. The provincial and Nisga'a teams were of roughly the same numbers, all working at the same pace and living the same lifestyle. It was amazing how well we got along, all things considered. Treaty negotiations are as tough as any negotiations get, but despite the pressures, the exhaustion, and the perennial differences of opinion at the table, we remained civil to each other until the end; we could always share a joke or a meal together, no matter what seemed at stake in the negotiations.

We arrived in Terrace with an air of excitement and expectation, but with no illusions about the work that remained. An incredible number of hours had already been logged at the table since June 24. This is one of the critical times of any negotiation, when excitement and expectation battle against frustration and fatigue as the larger issues remain seemingly deadlocked. There is a temptation to panic at the amount of work that remains, to disavow all responsibility and simply stop, or climb the hotel walls (to the roof, on the outside), or run 150 kilometres to the sea and swim to Japan. The sleeplessness and inadequate nutrition add to the sum of your frustrations. It is critical, at this time, to pause, to take a breath, to sort out exactly what needs to be done, and to make a personal commitment to remain calm and allow the process to unfold. It is important to keep that perspective in front of your team, too; the last thing you need is seventeen people lining up for Valium at the all-night clinic.

During these last days we continued to brief Scott Serson, John Sinclair, John Watson from DIAND, and Doreen Mullins from the Federal Treaty Negotiation Office. We continued to deal with other federal departments, trying to break down the roadblocks we saw in front of us, many of which they had erected. At the same time I was involved in a small family negotiation, trying to bring my daughter Jennifer back from England in time for her to be present in British Columbia with me to experience the final days of the negotiations. She had been working in London since March.

As it happened, Jennifer arrived in Saskatoon on July 15, 1998. Perhaps her plane was touching down as, twenty-four hundred kilometres away, the negotiating teams were progressing triumphantly into the main room with Joe Gosnell holding the Agreement aloft like an acolyte carrying the Bible, or perhaps it was later as we were briefing the media, or later still while we were at supper with Premier Glen Clark. If the deal had been delayed by twenty-four hours, Jennifer might have been there for her father's proud moment. On the other hand, if the deal had been delayed by twenty-four hours, there might have been no deal at all.

At eight o'clock the next morning I was meeting with one of the bands that was hoping to close on its specific claim. It would happen eventually, but wasn't going to happen here. We were too far apart. Perhaps it was a portent of things to come. The euphoria of the day before was still with me—it clung to all of us like strong perfume—but little did we appreciate that the work was far from done!

We flew out of Terrace later that morning for a meeting with the Treaty Negotiation Advisory Committee in Vancouver. There we continued the planning that had begun in early July around obtaining final government approvals to allow for the initialling ceremony. We were also working on a strategy for briefing the press, the public, and the politicians.

On July 20, Jack Ebbels, Joe Gosnell, and I appeared on Bill Good's open line show on CKNW radio in Vancouver, fielding calls from opponents and supporters alike. The next day we were in Ottawa meeting with our federal caucus when the first major controversy broke out. Gordon Campbell, Leader of the Opposition in British Columbia, had tabled nineteen draft chapters of the Nisga'a Final Agreement in the legislature. Where he got them was anyone's guess. The negotiators had been reluctant to make the document public while the legal drafters were doing a final sweep for clerical and typographical errors and checking cross-references to ensure proper concordance between the twenty-two chapters of the Final Agreement and the thirteen appendices. We had been negotiating non-stop since late June, and hadn't had the luxury of time to do a full and careful check. Adding a paragraph here and deleting a paragraph there inevitably affects the numbering system and the cross-references, and we didn't want to hand the critics a non-issue over clerical and typographical errors. The parties never intended that there would be any changes of a material or substantial nature as a result of this final editing, but Gordon Campbell's action ensured that the controversy over the Nisga'a treaty would continue for many months to come.

Immediately, we were in a conference call with the Province and the

Nisga'a. We had to arrange a major press briefing in Vancouver as soon as possible. Luckily, I was able to get an early flight out of Ottawa the following day. We issued a press advisory late that night, and on July 22 we began our public education on the treaty. The press conference was carried live on CBC *Newsworld*. The numerous briefings and speaking engagements that would occupy a great portion of all the negotiators' time began now in earnest.

Internally, the federal team needed to review the treaty with the Ottawa Caucus, the Senior Policy Committee, and ultimately the Federal Steering Committee on Comprehensive Claims to obtain authority to initial the Final Agreement. When negotiators from all parties initial an agreement, they are expressing their intention to recommend the treaty to their respective authorities for ratification. For the Nisga'a, this authority meant not only the Tribal Council but also the entire community; for the Province, it meant the Legislative Assembly; for the federal negotiators, it meant the Parliament of Canada. It seemed a bit odd that we had to get authority from the federal government to present the treaty to the federal government, but that's the way governments seem to work; the *Calder* case, remember, was dismissed on the technicality that the Nisga'a had failed to get permission from the Crown to sue the Crown. In any case, we eventually got our approvals, and the initialling ceremony was scheduled for New Aiyansh on August 4, 1998.

On July 29, the Gitanyow issued a press release complaining about the effect of the Nisga'a treaty on their traditional territory.[2] No Memorandum of Understanding had yet been signed between the two nations—nor has been—and the Gitanyow were determined to proceed to the courts to resolve the issue of overlap with the Nisga'a. This was not the last we would hear from them, but I tried to put such matters out of my mind as the day of the initialling ceremony approached.

Jennifer arrived in good time, along with her sisters Corinne, Alison, and Kathryn, and my granddaughter, Hanna. I could not remember the last time the six of us had been together. The day before the ceremony I took them all to 'Ksan Village at the junction of the Bulkley and Skeena Rivers, where Gitksan and Wet'suwet'en artisans still practise the skills that have been passed down the generations for centuries. Examples of carving, painting, and jewellery in silver and gold are prominent at the 'Ksan Indian Village Museum, as well as at a gift shop to ensure that visitors do not to go away empty-handed. We drove past Delgamuukw's house, then along the north shore of the Skeena to the Tsimshian village of Kitwanga.

Tsimshian, which means "people inside the Skeena River," is a language as well as a First Nation. There are four main dialects: North Tsimshian is spoken along the lower Skeena and up the coast to Alaska; South Tsimshian is spoken in the coastal areas south of the Skeena; Gitksan is spoken on the upper Skeena; and Nisga'a, of course, is the language of the Nass Valley.

According to legend, Kitwanga was founded by members of the Raven clan and the Eagle clan after the flood. As Noah's Ark was set afloat on the far side of the globe, a group of the Raven clan found refuge from the rising waters on a nearby mountain. After the deluge receded, they descended and encountered a second group of survivors by the water's edge. Fortuitously— for Tsimshian custom frowns upon marriages within the same clan—these were members of the Eagle clan. Thus, the Eagle and the Raven united in community, and founded the village later known as Kitwanga.

More recently, but still far enough in the past to be called legend, Kitwanga was a centre of military and political conquest. Kitwanga Fort, four kilometres south of the village, is now a national historic site, but at the time of Nekt, a Gitksan warrior chief from the Queen Charlotte Islands, it was a base for raids against the peoples of the Nass River and the coast for food, slaves, and control of the lucrative trade routes. Kitwanga Fort is situated near the Grease Trail, where oolichan were transported for trade between the Skeena and the Nass Rivers. On Ta'awdzep, or Battle Hill, archaeologists have unearthed the remains of fortified houses. It is said that Nekt and his warriors hoisted enormous logs up the hill and onto the palisade walls, where they were secured with ropes of cedar bark; released at the critical moment, they pummelled down the hill and crushed their attackers. These feats and more are commemorated in the pts'aan of Kitwanga, now located in the village north of Battle Hill.

From Kitwanga we travelled west on the scenic Nisga'a highway to Gitwinksihlkw, known as Canyon City throughout much of the twentieth century. It was here, at its Tenth Annual Convention, that the Nisga'a Tribal Council had decided to proceed with the *Calder* case. We entered the village by the new bridge, which had been opened in 1995. Four totem poles, one at each corner, stand as sentries, both guarding the bridge and welcoming visitors to the village. The old bridge is a narrow footbridge, a windswept structure of wood and wire suspended above the river. It used to be the village's only link to the outside world, other than by boat. We walked partway across, imagining the previous generations hauling their groceries and supplies on their backs as they fought to keep their balance above the river. In winter it would have been especially harsh, with snow underfoot and the wind howling across the lava beds and whipping over the ice.

We had a picnic lunch with Doreen Mullins and her husband, Gary, and then we all left for New Aiyansh. This village, also known as Gitlaxt'aamiks, will be the home of the new Nisga'a government. The community centre, with its four majestic pts'aan guarding the entrance, was a beehive of activity as people prepared for the following day's celebrations. Outside, two satellite trucks were being set up to broadcast pictures around the world. Inside, a media centre was being erected in the basement. The floor was a writhing mass of cables and wires as telephones, computers, monitors, printers, lights, and the thousand other electronic devices the modern broadcaster cannot do without were put up and plugged in. Upstairs on the main floor, tables and chairs were being set up for a community feast that evening.

Our party of eight left them to it and journeyed on to Nass Camp, where we toured the property, inspecting the houses and the permanently installed trailers that are home to truckers, transient workers, and tourists. Nass Camp has the distinction of being the only community in the Nass Valley that is not Nisga'a. Though it is situated inside the Nisga'a core lands, it is private property, held in fee simple, which means it can be disposed of by sale or inheritance without encumbrance. The property is owned by Bill Young, a strong supporter of the treaty who appeared as a witness before both the House of Commons and the Senate Committees.

Nass Camp also has the only arena in the valley, and the only lounge. The former is optional, but a visit to the latter is a must. With its low ceilings and smoke-saturated furniture, it has an aura of frontier days and saloon justice, of easy women and dangerous men playing cards and smoking foul little cheroots. My own girls do not fit that mould, of course, but they are all quite tall. There were few other patrons in the lounge at the time, so I suppose they were quite noticeable as well, to the point that the bartender waylaid Alison on her way to the washroom and asked, "Are you guys part of some basketball team?" A Nisga'a chief in full regalia would have caused less comment, I am sure.

And that was precisely what we confronted the following day at the initialling ceremony. Or rather, it confronted us. It is difficult to describe the overpowering effect that several hundred faith-filled people in ceremonial garb can have on mere mortals such as myself. I have attended religious ceremonies and watched as a dozen vested priests made their way to the altar, preceded by a robed and mitred bishop, and I have felt the power of their collective faith wash over the congregation like a cleansing wave. I have felt the touch of the divine—or what seemed to me the divine—at moments of intensity and surrender: my marriage ceremony, the baptism of my children, my wife's funeral, the wedding of my daughter. As an Irish Catholic, I understand the power and the comfort of faith and tradition to a people who have been marginalized and shut out from the mainstream of society. What I did not understand until that moment was the purity of the joy such people feel when they have journeyed far and suffered long to achieve the goal the Nisga'a reached that day. After 111 years, they had finally negotiated their way into Canada. I felt no small pride in the part I had managed to play in that journey. I felt doubly blessed that my daughters and granddaughter were there to share it with me, along with members of our negotiating team.

At Nisga'a ceremonies the chiefs and the elders, like priests at Mass, vest themselves in exquisite traditional clothing. Red and black are the dominant colours, with splashes of startling white and yellow. Ankle-length robes are set off in intricate designs representing family crests and archetypal images from tribal cosmology. A wolf, an eagle, a raven, a killer whale spring from the folds of their vestments like live creatures in their natural habitat. Buttons abound, pearl white, outlining the designs of history and mythology that adorn the robes. White ermine pelts append to headpieces carved and inlaid with cedar bark and copper. The face of a bird or an animal appears above the human face of the wearer, abstracted and unreal, but somehow as real and natural as if the creature itself were there to join in the celebration. Rattles on leggings, and pants and boots of leather complete the attire. The chief will also carry a rattle, intricately carved in human or animal form.

Less exalted personages were no less regally attired, the women in calf-length black dresses with red tassels at the seams and hem, the men in black shirts with white buttons and trim. I felt quite underdressed in my suit and tie. But I also felt entirely welcome.

It was raining at first, but later the sky cleared and the day became perfect: a benevolent sun in an azure sky, the distant mountains standing like sentinels over the brash and poignant labours of humankind. The initialling ceremony was carried off with all the pomp and pageantry the Nisga'a could muster. The world was their witness, literally. The proceedings and celebrations were reported across the globe. Farmers in Saskatchewan read about it with people in Sweden and bureaucrats in Washington, Auckland, and Sydney. It was a day of speeches, awards, recognition, and celebration.

One speech, at least, is worth quoting in its entirety. The crowd fell silent as Joe Gosnell's voice filled the room:

> Back in 1887, our ancestors, pressing to settle the Nisga'a Land Question, climbed into their canoes and paddled down the British Columbia coast to Victoria's inner harbour, where, on the steps of the Parliament Buildings, they were sharply turned away by Premier Smithe.
>
> Like a handful of politicians today, Smithe refused to discuss the Nisga'a Land Question, wrongly convinced the assimilation of aboriginal people was inevitable. As a result, he plunged the province into 100 years of darkness for the Nisga'a and other First Nations.
>
> Today, that is changed forever, changed utterly. This ceremony is a triumph—for the Nisga'a people, the people of British Columbia, and the people of Canada. Today we make history as we correct the mistakes of the past and send a signal of hope around the world.
>
> Today, let us talk of reconciliation and a new understanding between cultures. Today we join Canada and British Columbia as free citizens—full and equal participants in the social, economic, and political life of this country. That has been our dream for more than a century. Today it becomes a reality.
>
> People sometimes wonder why we have struggled so long to sign a treaty. Why, we are asked, did our elders and elected officials dedicate their lives to a resolution of the Land Question? What is it about a treaty?
>
> To the Nisga'a people, a treaty is a sacred instrument. It represents an understanding between distinct cultures and shows respect for each other's way of life. It stands as a symbol of high idealism in a divided, fractious world. That is why we have fought so long and so hard.
>
> Has it been worth it? Yes, a resounding yes. But, believe me, it has been a long and hard-fought compromise. Some may have heard me say that a generation of Nisga'a men and women has grown old at the negotiating table. Sadly, it is very, very true.
>
> Words can only hint at our feelings. I am talking here about a

century of frustration, humiliation, and emotional devastation. We lived it every day. Devastated by smallpox, influenza, and other European diseases, our ancestors were torn from their homes, exiled to reserves, forbidden to speak the Nisga'a language and practise our own beliefs. In short, subjected to a system of cultural genocide for 130 years.

It still breaks my heart to see our young men and women sentenced to a life of seasonal, dead-end jobs. To see the despair and the disillusionment on the faces of my people.

Those are the reasons, ladies and gentlemen, I am still fighting to finalize the treaty. And will not stop until it is ratified and made into law. Look around you. Look at our faces. We are survivors. We intend to live here forever. And, under the treaty, we will flourish.

The treaty represents a monumental achievement for the Nisga'a people and for Canadian society as a whole. It shows the world that reasonable people can sit down and settle historical wrongs. It proves that a modern society can correct the mistakes of the past and ensures that minorities are treated fairly. As Canadians, we should all be very proud.

We have detractors, oh yes. Nay-sayers who say our interests should continue to be ignored. Those who say Canada and BC are "giving" us too much. And there are others, particularly within the aboriginal community, who say we settled for too little.

Our detractors do not understand, or, practising a willful ignorance, choose not to understand. Or worse, using carefully coded language, they are updating a venomous attitude familiar to First Nations of the world.

They are wrong. By playing politics with the aspirations of aboriginal people they are blighting the promise of the Nisga'a treaty, not only for the Nisga'a but for all Canadians.

No longer beggars in our own lands, we now go forward with dignity, equipped with the confidence that we can make important contributions—social, political, and economic—to Canadian society.

The Nisga'a treaty proves, beyond all doubt, that negotiations—not lawsuits, not roadblocks, not violence—are the most effective, most honourable way to resolve aboriginal issues in this country.

Today, as you are my witness, the Nisga'a canoe returns to the Nass River with a cargo of hope and reconciliation.[3]

It was a fine, proud moment, and a welcome pause after the months of effort and fatigue.

But it was only a pause, after all. We were brutally reminded of the fact later that day by news of a tragic airplane crash at Gingolx that took the lives of five people, including a nine-year-old boy, who had been returning from a medical emergency. The Vancouver *Sun* reported the incident:

KINCOLITH [Gingolx]—The deaths of all five people aboard a
float plane that crashed here Tuesday are a grim reminder that this
isolated Nass Valley town desperately needs improved medical
services and a road. The landmark Nisga'a treaty, initialled in nearby
New Aiyansh on the day of the accident, will provide both of those
necessities.[4]

It was a reminder, perhaps, that in some ways the work was just beginning.

In the 1880s, Nisga'a Chief Israel Sgat'iin had two government surveyors "escorted" off land near G̲itlaxt'aamiks in the Nass Valley. "These are our mountains and our river," he is reported to have said.

ROYAL BRITISH COLUMBIA MUSEUM/PN11430

First Nisga'a Land Committee, Cascade, BC (near Nass Harbour, 1883).
Top row: Jacob Russ, Alfred McKay, John Moore, James Percival, James Smythe, Henry Smart, William Gogag, Stephen Barton, William Lincoln, and Sam Munroe. *Bottom row:* Arthur Calder, Andrew Mercer, William Jefferies, Samuel Pollard, Amos Gosnell, Timothy Derrick, and Josiah Tait. ROYAL BRITISH COLUMBIA MUSEUM/PN23037

Victorian-style houses of the Nisga'a, at Gitlaxt'aamiks, 1927.
CANADIAN MUSEUM OF CIVILIZATION/69653

Totem poles at Gitlaxt'aamiks, nd. CANADIAN MUSEUM OF CIVILIZATION/70687B

Bridge to Gitwinksihlkw, Nass Valley. GARY FIEGEHEN/©NISGA'A NATION

Vetter Falls in Lava Bed Memorial Park. GARY FIEGEHEN/©NISGA'A NATION

Laxgalts'ap, on the Nass River. GARY FIEGEHEN/©NISGA'A NATION

A look at the structure of the main table negotiations. TOM MOLLOY

Rod Robinson, Ambassador of the Nisga'a Tribal Council, carries the sacred Talking Stick as he leads a procession of elders into an important general assembly in New Aiyansh, March 3, 1996. GREG JOYCE/CP PICTURE ARCHIVE

Fiscal Working Group at work. *Bottom left to right:* Liz Morin, Bill Stipdunk, John Cowell, Andrew Ali, Jay Kaufman, Tom Falconer, Jim Barkwell, and Jim Apostle. TOM MOLLOY

The Agreement in Principle was signed on March 22, 1996, in New Aiyansh. Federal Indian Affairs Minister Ron Irwin (*left*), Nisga'a Tribal Council President Joseph Gosnell (*centre*), and BC Aboriginal Affairs Minister John Cashore hold up the agreement after signing.

STEVE BOSCH/VANCOUVER *SUN*

BC Premier Glen Clark (*left*) and Tom Molloy at the dinner hosted by the Premier for the negotiation teams following the "handshake" agreement, July 15, 1998.

RICHARD INGLIS

Corinne Howe, Jennifer Molloy, President Emeritus of the Nisga'a Tribal Council, Frank Calder, Alison Molloy, Hanna Howe, and Kathryn Molloy in New Aiyansh at the initialling of the Final Agreement, August 4, 1998. TOM MOLLOY

Peter Baird and Grand Chief Phil Fontaine of the Assembly of First Nations, New Aiyansh, August 4, 1998. GARY FIEGEHEN/©NISGA'A NATION

The beginning of the Nisga'a procession to the initialling of the Final Agreement, New Aiyansh, August 4, 1998. GARY FIEGEHEN/©NISGA'A NATION

Ryan Lincoln of Kincolith Nisga'a Dancers, New Aiyansh, August 4, 1998.

NICK PROCAYLO/CP PICTURE ARCHIVE

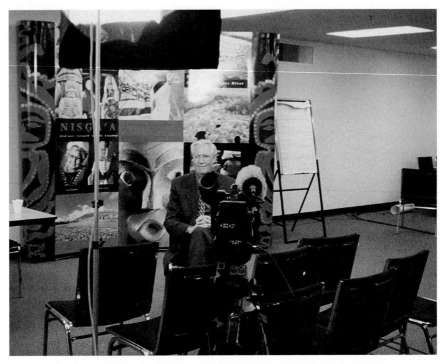

Tom Molloy on CBC Newsmagazine debating Rafe Mair, August 4, 1998.
JENNIFER MOLLOY

Part of the large crowd gathered at the Terrace Inn, Terrace, BC, awaiting
word on the progress of negotiation on July 15, 1999. TOM MOLLOY

Honourable Bob Nault, Chief Joseph Gosnell, Adele Gosnell, and Tom Molloy,
New Aiyansh, August 21, 1999. GARY FIEGEHEN/©NISGA'A NATION

Jack Ebbels, Deputy Minister of Aboriginal Affairs *(left)*, and Chief Joseph
Gosnell, with Nelson Leeson in background, New Aiyansh, August 4, 1998.
GARY FIEGEHEN/©NISGA'A NATION

The Nisga'a have often made reference to negotiating their way *into* Canada.

GARY FIEGEHEN/©NISGA'A NATION

Nisga'a and federal negotiators walk down Wellington Street, in Ottawa, led by Joseph Gosnell carrying the Final Agreement for formal signing by the Federal Government, May 4, 1999. *Far left to right:* Joseph Whiteside, Peter Baird, Joseph Gosnell, Jim Barkwell, and Tom Molloy. GARY FIEGEHEN/©NISGA'A NATION

Prime Minister Jean Chrétien salutes members of the Nisga'a Tribal Council in the House of Commons following his vote for final passage of the Nisga'a treaty bill, December 13, 1999.

TOM HANSON/CP PICTURE ARCHIVE

Formal signing by the Honourable Jane Stewart in the Hall of Honour, House of Commons, Ottawa, May 4, 1999. *Foreground, left to right:* Joseph Gosnell, Honourable Jane Stewart, and Tom Molloy. *Background, left to right:* Honourable Herb Dhaliwal, Honourable David Anderson, Edmond Wright, Jim Aldridge, Perry Azak, Harry Nyce, and Herb Morvan. GARY FIEGEHEN/©NISGA'A NATION

Tom Molloy *(left)*, John Watson, Regional Director for DIAND in BC *(centre, left)*, and Jean Chrétien during the Prime Minister's visit to the Nass Valley, August 21, 1999. DIANE MURPHY/OFFICE OF THE PRIME MINSTER

David Iftody, Parliamentary Secretary to the Minister, and Sue Barnes, Chair of the Standing Committee on Aboriginal Affairs, presenting Joe Gosnell with the flag that flew over the House of Commons on December 13, 1999—the day on which the Nisga'a Final Agreement passed in the House. Honourable Bob Nault *(left)*.
GARY FIEGEHEN/©NISGA'A NATION

The Governor General Her Excellency Adrienne Clarkson, Speaker of the Senate *(centre)* Gil Molgate, and Tom Molloy during the reception hosted by the Speaker following Royal Assent to the Nisga'a treaty bill, Ottawa, April 13, 2000.
ANDY SHOTT

Left to right: Andrew Beynon, Doug Wanamaker, Tom Molloy, Jim Barkwell, Brian Martin, and Doreen Mullins, poised with champagne in hand, receive official word at 12:01 AM on May 11, 2000, that all parties have found the documents in order and the Nisga'a treaty is in effect. TOM MOLLOY

The first sitting of the Wilp Si'Ayuuḵhl Nisga'a on May 11, 2000, in Gitwinksihlkw, BC. TOM MOLLOY

Chapter Ten

....

WHEN THE WORLD WAS IN TWILIGHT, Txeemsim stole fire from heaven and brought it to the people huddled in the frozen landscape below. He stocked the river with oolichan, then tossed a mountain into the channel to protect the fishing grounds from encroaching tribes. He flattened the valley between the four mountains to make space for houses and villages. He moulded the channels of the river to make spawning grounds for the salmon.

This was after the Flood, when Txeemsim descended from his home in the sky to do the bidding of K'amligihahlhaahl, the Supreme God and Chief of Heaven who lives at Magoonhl Lisims on the roof of the world. Txeemsim was a miracle worker, known for his kindness and his sense of humour, as well as his insatiable curiosity and his outrageous greed. He was a trickster who could appear in either human or animal form, and often set people and animals against themselves or one another just to see what would happen. He was a liar, a thief, an approachable but contradictory demi-god, much loved but rarely trusted, in constant battle against his own failings. This powerful inner conflict endeared him to the human hearts of those he had come to serve; his eventual victory has survived in the hearts of their descendants, down to the present generation. The Nisga'a feel that Txeemsim's struggle with his human failings makes him the finest of teachers; his eventual victory makes him the best that humankind can strive for.

Txeemsim roamed the shores of the Nass like a wandering preacher, teaching all who would listen. Anxious that his own hard-won experience should not be lost, he taught that every action is a moral action, that every human decision will affect others in one way or another, for good or ill. He taught that every creature, including woman and man, has a place in the world and a meaningful role to play in it. He taught, as he had learned through experience, that people need one another, that behaving selfishly and eschewing moral responsibility are both self-destructive and destructive of others, and will ultimately rend the very fabric of society. More practically, he taught people how to share the land with other creatures without disrupting the cycle of life. He taught the people how to build houses to survive the rains of summer and the snows of winter. He taught them to organize themselves into a coherent society, a political unity dependent not on race but on shared values and a common vision of life on Earth. Above all, he taught the sacred value of place. For it is the landscape that names you and defines you, the sacred earth that offers the means and the blessings of life itself.

Thus the messenger of K'amligihahlhaahl gave birth and shape to the tradition of oral history that survives to this day. Txeemsim is the very touchstone of Nisga'a identity. Indeed, according to Bert McKay, a revered elder and teacher, "Txeemsim and Nisga'a are one and the same."[1]

This is what it means to have lived in the Nass Valley since time immemorial. The Nisga'a do not remember the Flood as a literal, physical event any more than the peoples of Western Europe do. There is no document in Judaism or Christianity that bears witness to Noah's rainbow from first-hand observation. But when the Nisga'a invite the world to witness their history and their culture, it is understood that that culture has endured since Txeemsim and the Flood, handed down from generation to generation through the four clans of the Nisga'a nation: the Wolf, the Eagle, the Killer Whale, and the Raven. From time immemorial they have lived in villages along the Nass River, in wooden houses, governing themselves according to their ancient code. From time immemorial they have dwelt in the valley of the Nass, sharing their resources with one another as tradition and the law demand.

Sharing is an essential principle of Nisga'a society, a principle reflected not only in *Ayuukhl Nisga'a* and in the manner in which they have represented themselves to the courts and governments over the years, but in the very structure of their language. Like the Inuit to the north who have elevated the description of weather and hunting conditions to a fine art, and the Navajo far to the south who have evolved an elaborate vocabulary to describe the intricate interconnections and relationships among clans, the Nisga'a have developed words and phrases to describe sharing in ways that would likely never occur to a speaker of English or French.

The word *amnigwootkw*, for instance, describes a privilege granted to a son or sons by their father regarding the temporary use of the father's property; in the matrilineal society of the Nisga'a, *amnigwootkw* ceases on the death of the father. *Hagwin-yuu-wo'oskw* denotes a plot of land granted to a bride on her wedding day by her maternal uncle or grandfather on the understanding that her husband may have access to the land for the benefit of their children. The *yukw* is the feasting system that settles the estate of a chief and the passing on of the rights and privileges of chieftainship; the immediate sponsors of the feast include the maternal family of the deceased and, to a lesser degree, the extended family and clan, the spouses and children of the immediate family, and the in-laws. Overarching all is *saytk'ilhl wo'osihl Nisga'a*, the "sharing of a common bowl," the ruling canon of tribal ownership.[2]

When the Nisga'a Land Committee was first formed in 1890, they decided to claim a substantial portion of the Nass Valley on the basis of *saytk'ilhl wo'osihl Nisga'a*. Their petition to the British Privy Council in 1913, their clandestine activity throughout the period that the Indian Act made it illegal to pursue or contribute to aboriginal land claims, their claim before the provincial Supreme Court, and their subsequent appeal to the Supreme Court of Canada were all based on the cultural imperative of tribal ownership of lands and resources.

Perhaps if they had deviated from the course laid down by their grandmothers and forefathers, the issue might have been settled sooner. Among the detractors and nay-sayers Joe Gosnell spoke of at the initialling ceremony were several prominent politicians, including the leaders of at least one federal and two provincial political parties. Contemporary statements, repeatedly made and widely publicized, seem to suggest that if the Nisga'a had only abandoned the dangerous notions of communal ownership and self-government, all this fuss might have been avoided.

Gordon Campbell, leader of the Liberal Party in British Columbia, repeatedly attacked what he called "third order of government" arrangements—fearing, perhaps, that rational adults were not to be trusted to govern themselves, or that the Nisga'a were not rational adults. "What we are doing here," he wrote, in a call that would later be taken up by the federal Reform Party, "is virtually guaranteeing a future that consigns us all to live in the past. A future that enlarges and perpetuates a new reserve system under a different façade."[3]

Bill Vander Zalm, former Premier of British Columbia, lately trying to resurrect his political fortunes as leader of the BC Reform Party, clearly saw the malignant hand of communism directing Nisga'a affairs. Decrying "a system where no individual ownership exists and the tribal leadership is in full control," Vander Zalm proposed, simply, that the Nisga'a be "paid off." First Nations could only be "emancipated," he declared, if they were provided with "a means of individual ownership" that would "foster a sense of personal worth and value." To this end, he suggested that "every native man and woman and child" be given a parcel of land and "a one-time grant of $250,000," evidently to defray the costs of membership in a capitalist society. The size and location of the parcel of land were not revealed; it was enough, apparently, that it would be "the first land they will ever have owned."[4]

That this proposal constitutes both a moral and a practical contradiction of the stated desires of the Nisga'a themselves seems to have escaped Mr. Vander Zalm's notice—as have the provisions of the treaty itself, and the simple fact that every one of those provisions was negotiated and agreed upon by rational adults who paid each other the compliment of mutual respect. At the negotiating table, unlike politics, there is no place for paternalism—or, in the case of the Nisga'a, maternalism.

On the national stage, the federal leader of the Reform Party, too, was denouncing the Final Agreement as a document "based on socialist economics and collective ownership of land and resources." Characterizing the treaty as "a continuation of a failed approach to aboriginal development in Canada throughout the twentieth century," Preston Manning condemned "a system that denies aboriginal equality under the law, accountable and democratic government, and the basic right of free enterprise."[5]

It is tempting to say, as a *Globe and Mail* headline proclaimed, that the debate reveals a "conflict in ideology."[6] But to reduce the history and traditions of a distinct people to the narrow confines of ideology is, at best, a gross oversimplification. At worst, it reveals a near-transcendent ignorance of the development of human society in general, and of Nisga'a society in particular. Nisga'a culture and theology are no more communist, in the sense that Vander Zalm and Manning fear the term, than they are overtly capitalist. No one with any sense need dread the echo of Soviet jackboots marching down the Nass Valley. *Ayuuk̲hl Nisga'a* predates Marx by several millennia, and it was serving the people of the Nass Valley peacefully and well when the first Europeans sailed into Portland Inlet in the mid-eighteenth century. In any case, it is difficult to reconcile Mr. Manning's and Mr. Campbell's claim that the treaty will perpetuate poverty among the Nisga'a with their concurrent assertions that it grants rights and privileges under the Constitution not enjoyed by "ordinary" Canadians. It is doubly difficult to understand how granting the rights and responsibilities of citizenship and self-determination to a distinct people is somehow not in their own best interests.

Canada is not a melting pot, nor has it ever been one. What it is, according to the distinguished author John Ralston Saul, is a "permanently incomplete experiment built on a triangular foundation—aboriginal, francophone and anglophone."[7] Carrying the thought forward, Governor General Adrienne Clarkson in her installation speech before the Senate in October 1999 said:

> What we continue to create, today, began 450 years ago as a political project, when the French first met with the aboriginal people. It is an old experiment, complex and, in worldly terms, largely successful. Stumbling through darkness and racing through light, we have persisted in the creation of a Canadian civilization.[8]

To speak of "ordinary" Canadians is to do a disservice to the extraordinary Canadians who make up the bulk of the nation. Historically, socially, politically, and geographically, Canada is unique on Earth. We came into existence as a sovereign state not through conquest or revolution, not through bloodshed or decree, not even through evolution—social Darwinism could never have predicted a nation such as this—but through compromise and negotiation. This is the patrimony shared by every extraordinary Canadian, prominent among whom are those who have been here from time immemorial. Again according to John Ralston Saul, First Nations have "been a central factor in the shaping of Canada," and their increasingly noticeable presence in the social and political debates of the last quarter of the twentieth century should be seen as anything but an aberration:

> The gradual return of aboriginal influence, from the 1970s on, is often interpreted as a legal oddity or as a phenomenon of guilt or charity or as the annoying appearance of yet another interest group. Surely not. Surely it is the logic of history painfully kicking back into gear.[9]

Thomas Berger has called this phenomenon "the second discovery of America":

This is still the age of discovery, a discovery of the true meaning of the history of the New World and of the Native peoples' rightful place in that world. This is a discovery to be made in our own time, should we choose it—the second discovery of America.[10]

That First Nations should now be taking their rightful place as a distinct society among the distinct societies that make up Canada should surprise no one. The only surprise is that it has taken the rest of the nation 450 years to recognize that they are an essential part of who we are.

People like Sim'oogit Hleek have never been in any doubt. A man tall in stature, regal in bearing, and diplomatic in approach, he is the latest in a line of outstanding leaders to hold the position of President of the Nisga'a Tribal Council, which includes Frank Calder, James Gosnell, and Alvin McKay. He is also the last, as the council will cease to exist once the Final Agreement comes into effect. Better known to most Canadians as Joe Gosnell, Sim'oogit Hleek was first elected president of the Nisga'a Tribal Council in 1992, though he served as its executive chairman for many years before that, and as a council member before that. Concurrently, he has been active in the native Brotherhood of British Columbia, and for a time served as chairman of that body as well.

"Let me share some personal history," he said to the elected representatives of British Columbia in a speech to the Legislature on December 2, 1998:

When I began this process I was a young man. When I first became involved in our Tribal Council, I was twenty-five years old. Now I am sixty-three. Today, my hair is grey. The terms of six Prime Ministers chart the years I have grown old at the negotiating table: the right Honourable Pierre Trudeau, Joe Clark, John Turner, Brian Mulroney, Kim Campbell, and Jean Chrétien; and five British Columbia Premiers: Bill Bennett, William Vander Zalm, Rita Johnston, Mike Harcourt, and Glen Clark. I will spare you the list of Deputy Ministers, senior bureaucrats, and other officials we have met across the table during the past quarter century. Their names would paper the walls of this chamber. Twice, I'd bet.[11]

Born in New Aiyansh in the northwest corner of British Columbia, Joe Gosnell began his working life as a commercial fisherman. But it wasn't long before his natural eloquence and diplomatic skills were being put to a better use—though perhaps he would say they were simply being put to a different use. A hereditary chief of the Nisga'a nation as well as a fisherman, he was for a time Chief Councillor for the Gitlakdamix Band. He has also served on the board of the Northern Native Fishing Corporation, and on the Pacific Salmon Commission, which acted in an advisory capacity to the Canada-U.S. salmon treaty negotiations. He currently serves on the Pacific Regional Council, a senior advisory body to the federal Ministry of Fisheries and Oceans. An intensely private, quiet man, he would often prefer to be off on his own than socialize with the other negotiators during breaks. At the same time, he is a powerful and effective speaker, rational, persuasive, passionate without being bombastic—the type of statesman beleaguered nations dream of in times of upheaval and change. He describes the future in images from the past, cultural images that remind his people that what they once were, they can be again.

"Our canoe has landed," he said when the Agreement in Principle was signed. His words and thoughts—at the negotiating table or addressing an audience in Victoria or Ottawa or Europe—rarely stray far from the central, heroic image of those Nisga'a leaders who first journeyed from the Nass Valley in 1887. Clearly, his own work is a continuation of that journey, in homage not only to those who have gone before but to those who will come after.

Like Txeemsim before him, he is known for his kindness and his sense of humour, for his ability to hold an audience of five hundred as though he were speaking to each person individually, and for his willingness to speak to one person when five hundred might be waiting. That one person, after all, might change the world.

Although he has often characterized the Final Agreement as "the result of a long and hard-fought compromise,"[12] he also regards it as a triumph for the Nisga'a nation and for Canada—"a new and proud Canada,"[13] as he says. Canada is a constant theme in Joe Gosnell's political philosophy. Again and again he has emphasized that the Nisga'a have spent more than a century negotiating their way *into* Canada, not out of it. He sees the Final Agreement as equally a triumph for the larger nation, as he told a European audience in November 1998:

The Nisga'a Treaty is historic for many reasons. The *New York Times*, the *Asahi Shinbum* in Japan, the BBC World Service, and many other news organizations have noted its accomplishment. Treaty negotiations have been monitored by a variety of human rights watchdogs worldwide. It is noteworthy that it comes so closely on the eve of the fiftieth anniversary of the Universal Declaration of Human Rights.

I am also pleased to say that it rightly bolsters Canada's international reputation as a nation that respects human rights.

It was a proud day for Canada. It is worthy of international attention, because although Canada is a nation known for its peacekeeping activities, and for its role as a champion of human rights, it has rarely been able to come to the world with clean hands regarding aboriginal rights. I believe that has now changed.[14]

And as he told the Prime Minister in New Aiyansh the following year, "Together, we are sending an important message to an often fractious world. Negotiations, not confrontations, not violence, are the only way to resolve our differences."[15] The Final Agreement proves the value of sitting down as reasonable people to discuss the past without recrimination and settle historical wrongs. It proves that modern societies need not resort to confrontation or violence to correct the mistakes of the past.

Those who feel there are no mistakes to correct, those who feel the Nisga'a should be paid off and abandoned to the marketplace, those who fear the Final Agreement has created a kind of neo-feudal communistic autocracy in the northwest corner of British Columbia might benefit from taking a step or two along the same journey. Chief Gosnell is under no illusions as to the strength of the opposition to the treaty. Some critics, he says, feel that Canada and British Columbia are giving too much away. Others, "upholding the values of Smithe and Scott," are practising a kind of wilful ignorance, re-igniting the flames of fear and distrust that have blighted relations between aboriginals and non-aboriginals for generations and consigned the original inhabitants of the land to second- and third-class status in a society that should be theirs by birthright. Perhaps that is the critics' aim; if so, their tactics are desperate and ultimately doomed to failure. For the Nisga'a have not been negotiating emancipation. They have been negotiating membership, and in so doing they have contributed immeasurably to that "permanently incomplete experiment" that is Canada.

"The world is our witness," Joe Gosnell told the legislature. "Be strong. Be steadfast. Be true."[16]

For his strength and truth and loyalty, he has been awarded honorary doctorates from Royal Roads University in Victoria, the Open Learning University in Vancouver, Simon Fraser University in Burnaby, and the University of Northern British Columbia in Prince George; the Order of British Columbia from the province; a special award from the Canadian Labour Congress at their 1999 National Convention; and a Lifetime Achievement Award from the National Aboriginal Achievement Awards in March 2000. Truly, the world has been Joe Gosnell's witness as well.

But Dr. Gosnell, a typically extraordinary Canadian, would be the first to admit that his own achievements have been but a logical continuation of the efforts and sacrifices of those who have gone before. Prominent among these is the man who gave his name to the historic legal battle that finally brought the governments of Canada and British Columbia to the negotiating table.

Frank Calder, President Emeritus of the Nisga'a Tribal Council, began his public career in 1949 when he became the first aboriginal Canadian to be elected to the British Columbia Legislature. He served as an MLA for twenty-six years, from 1949 to 1956 and again from 1960 to 1979. In 1972 he became the first aboriginal to be named to the provincial cabinet. He was the Founding President of the Nisga'a Tribal Council in 1955, and served in that capacity for nineteen years. He is recognized as the driving force behind *Calder v. the Attorney-General of British Columbia*, which marks the beginning of the modern era of aboriginal policy.

As an octogenarian, Frank Calder remains a force to be reckoned with. He was an active and formidable presence throughout the negotiations that led to the Framework Agreement, the Agreement in Principle, and the Final Agreement. For his efforts on behalf of the Nisga'a, the province, and the nation, he, too, has been recognized by a broad spectrum of Canadian society. Among the many honours he has received are an Honorary Doctorate of Divinity from the Vancouver School of Theology and a Lifetime Achievement Award and citation from the province, which reads: "In honour of your outstanding contribution to the pursuit of Justice and a better tomorrow for all British Columbians, as demonstrated by your unwavering commitment to the achievement of the Nisga'a Final Agreement." He was named an Officer of the Order of Canada in 1987. His citation reads:

The first Indian to graduate from the Anglican Theological College of the University of British Columbia, he was also the first Native Indian to be elected to any Canadian parliament. He founded the Nisga'a Tribal Council, was instrumental in starting land settlement negotiations, and has been a strong advocate of aboriginal rights, setting an example for others that one route to redress is through the political system.

These do not sound like people who need to be emancipated, paid off, or lectured on the evils of socialism. Rather, they are people of grace, passion, and wisdom. Above all, they are people of patience.

They have needed it.

Chapter Eleven

....

On October 30, 1969, Jean Chrétien, then Minister of Indian Affairs and Northern Development, visited the Nass Valley to address the Twelfth Annual Convention of the Nisga'a Tribal Council and open the new community centre in Gingolx. The "Indian people have a right to a future as full citizens of their country," he declared:

> They have a right to be treated on the same basis as other citizens.
> They have the equally important right to remain what they are—
> Indian people with a proud heritage that promises a proud future.
> And they have the basic and fundamental right to be masters of their
> own future, to manage what is theirs, to be responsible for what is
> theirs, to profit from what is theirs.[1]

There can be little doubt that his listeners were heartened by these words. There can be little doubt, either, that more than a few of them were confused. Had not his boss, Pierre Trudeau, earlier that year in Vancouver declared that "We can't recognize aboriginal rights because no society can be built on historical 'might have beens'"?[2] Had not Chrétien himself in June 1969 introduced a White Paper that was intended to bring about the termination of Indians' distinctive status and relationship to the Crown?

Calder was before the courts even as Chrétien spoke.[3] It would be four more years before the Supreme Court ruling and another twenty-seven before the "right" he alluded to would be realized. But even when the Final Agreement was initialled in New Aiyansh on August 4, 1998, nothing was certain. It still had to be ratified at three levels—the Nisga'a, the Province, and Canada—before it could be proclaimed.

Indeed, as the drums beat and the dancers moved in a sea of red and black in the crowded community centre in New Aiyansh on that historic day in August 1998, no one fully appreciated that this was not only a celebration of the end of a long journey, but the beginning of one of the most raucous and provocative debates that had been heard in British Columbia for a very long time.

It started peacefully enough with the Nisga'a ratification process. Since 1975, a number of treaties have been concluded in Canada, none of which were put to referendum by federal, provincial, or territorial governments. As a matter of policy, however, the federal government requires that aboriginal groups ratify treaties through referenda. This is simply because it is their constitutionally protected, collectively held aboriginal rights that are directly affected and modified by treaties. A successful referendum by an aboriginal group is, therefore, another important element of certainty. It ensures that dissenting individuals cannot challenge the process at a later date. The parties to the Nisga'a negotiations agreed on the manner in which they would each ratify the Final Agreement early in the Agreement-in-Principle negotiations: the Nisga'a by referendum, the Province through a vote of the legislature, Canada through a vote in Parliament.

The procedures for the Nisga'a ratification process were detailed in Chapter 22 of the Final Agreement. The Ratification Committee was comprised of seven representatives from the Nisga'a and a representative each from Canada and British Columbia. The representative from Canada was Bill Wray, an experienced negotiator who had previously worked on Native land claims in Yukon and British Columbia. Later that year, he and I would work together with the Sechelt Indian Band in their AIP negotiations. He had my complete confidence as the federal representative on the Committee.

The Committee was responsible for compiling and publishing a list of Nisga'a voters, updating the list as necessary, approving the form and content of the ballot, and providing or creating an opportunity for members of the Nisga'a community to review the Final Agreement and draft constitution (the ratification process also included a vote to approve the Nisga'a Constitution, as required by Chapter 11 of the Final Agreement). To this end, they were responsible for several mail-outs, including copies of the Final Agreement and side agreements, appendices, treaty summaries, and the draft constitution. The Committee was also charged with naming the day or days of the referendum, authorizing and providing general directions for the voting, conducting the vote itself, counting the ballots, and verifying the process.

A first round of meetings took place in August 1998, following the initialling ceremony. The Nisga'a Tribal Council spent two days in each of the Nisga'a villages in the Nass Valley, and also with the three Nisga'a Urban Locals, located in Vancouver, Terrace, and Prince Rupert/Port Edward. At each meeting, representatives from the Council made presentations on the Final Agreement and the draft constitution, and people were given the opportunity to ask questions.

A special assembly of the Nisga'a Tribal Council was held in Laxgalts'ap on October 5 to 7, 1998. Once again, the provisions of the Final Agreement and draft constitution were reviewed. Two votes were then conducted, in accordance with the Final Agreement. When the votes were counted, a clear majority had approved the presenting of the Final Agreement and draft constitution to the Nisga'a nation for a referendum to be held on November 6 and 7, 1998.

Counting the vote was a harrowing experience, both for the vote-counters and for those of us who had to stand by and wait for the results. An enormous number of people had registered at the polls on the voting days, and the eligibility of each voter had to be verified while maintaining the secrecy of his or her vote. I hadn't been on the Committee myself, so I was not sure what was happening. At the best of times, I dislike not knowing what's going on. In this instance, with so much at stake, I found it nearly intolerable. If the Nisga'a themselves failed to ratify the treaty, all our work would have been for nothing.

Bill Wray phoned me in Vancouver at about 9:30 PM on Saturday, November 7. He couldn't talk, he said, which made me wonder why he had called. Then he said that the only thing he could say was that the results were inconclusive, although they did seem to be heading in the right direction. I did some calculations of my own based on what I thought he had said. I concluded that we were in trouble.

Saturday was a very long night.

On Sunday, I was told that the vote was going well, but a large number of ballots had yet to be verified and then counted. It was expected to take another couple of hours, at least. Doreen and Gary Mullins invited me for dinner. I brought a bottle of champagne in anticipation. We decided not to drink it until we had the official results.

We had a long wait.

Bill Wray called us from New Aiyansh to advise us that the count was proceeding, but so were the delays. In the end, we didn't get the final tally until Monday at 2:00 PM, when enough "yes" votes had been counted to declare a victory. A press release was issued:

> Based on the initial count of votes cast in the Nisga'a Referendum, a determination can be made that the Nisga'a Treaty has been accepted by members of the Nisga'a Nation.[4]

Of 2,384 eligible voters, 2,039 had cast ballots. Of those, 1,215 had voted "yes" and 422 had voted "no." There were ten spoiled ballots so far, and 382 ballots left to count. The Nisga'a nation had ratified the treaty.

At least, it was apparent to any reasonable person that they had ratified the treaty. But it was several more days before the final results were released, and in that time the critics managed to stir up a minor controversy. If there were 2,384 eligible voters, they pointed out, and 1,215 of them had voted in favour of the Agreement, then the majority was only 50.96%. The Final Agreement stipulated that the treaty could not be ratified with less than a majority of fifty percent plus one of all registered voters.

This stipulation added yet another measure of certainty to the results of the referendum and the validity of the Final Agreement. It also pointed up a distressing double standard in Canadian politics. The rules for the Nisga'a assumed not only that everyone who did not vote would have voted no, but that democracy should operate differently among First Nations than it does anywhere else on Earth. Any dispassionate observer—indeed, even a passionate one—with a sense of historical reality will conclude that the larger society demands a degree of unanimity among aboriginal communities that we do not expect from any other. In any national debate—the Free Trade Agreement, the Charlottetown Accord—dissent is not only accepted, but expected. In federal and provincial elections, the public will tolerate without question three, five, or more political parties; governments routinely get elected with less than 50 percent of the popular vote. Any dissent among First Nations, however, will call an entire agreement into question, and the winning side in any referendum cannot declare victory without a mandate that far exceeds any demanded in any other electoral process in Canada. It is a fine bit of sophistry, I have always thought, counting votes that have not been cast. But it seems to be necessary as long as critics in the larger society continue to vocalize their suspicion and distrust of aboriginal politics, and I cannot disagree with the higher standard as long as it serves the purpose of disarming such critics. The final tally indicated beyond doubt that a substantial majority of the Nisga'a, however one chose to count them, had cast their ballots in favour of the treaty.

That Monday after speaking with Bill Wray I phoned New Aiyansh and spoke, in quick succession, to Joe Gosnell, Edmund Wright, Nelson Leeson, and Edward Allen. They were understandably delighted, and described the air of excitement and celebration in the village. I could almost see it myself as they described the scene, with people driving through the village honking their horns and shouting, flying Canadian flags out their car windows. I wished I could have been there to celebrate with them.

For Joe Gosnell and the Nisga'a leadership, winning the referendum was no great surprise. They had assured us the treaty would pass, and it did. In retrospect, it was no great surprise for me, either. But the federal government and its servants always fret over whether an agreement will get ratified. It's almost like an election day, when the tiniest bit of information becomes fodder for discussion and dissection. I remember worrying inordinately over the Nunavut ratification vote, exhaustively discussing omens and items of negligible consequence or, alternatively, sitting silently and pondering the middle distance while demons wrestled in my gut. But there, too, the leadership assured us it would carry, and it did. They knew their people, and they knew what would be acceptable.

Again in retrospect, the Nisga'a victory should have been no surprise. Every year at the Annual Convention, the negotiators reported to the membership, reviewing the work that had been done and asking to have their mandate renewed. Representatives from the villages attended the negotiations when we met in their communities, as well as the elders and other interested Nisga'a when we met in Terrace or Prince Rupert. And each year the Nisga'a Tribal Council sought re-election on the basis of its accomplishments and service over the previous twelve months. Critics to the contrary, when it comes to deciding their collective future, many Native communities are among the most informed electorate on Earth. They are models of democratic process.

Eventually, the Ratification Committee issued its report, verifying that the process had met the criteria set down in the Final Agreement.[5]

Now it was the Province's turn.

On November 30, 1998, the legislature was recalled in Special Session to ratify the Nisga'a Final Agreement. Scott Serson, Doreen Mullins, Wendy John, the Assistant Regional Director General of DIAND for British Columbia, and I were invited to attend the opening. It was a day of pomp and pageantry—at which the Nisga'a excel—in a week of religious and cultural observation and celebration. The day before, a Sunday, members of the public had been invited to attend a Eucharistic service with the Nisga'a at St. Mary's Anglican Church in Oak Bay, followed by a seven-hour program of dancing and singing by the Nisga'a and other First Nations at the Da Vinci Centre in Victoria. The following morning, choirs and dancers representing both the Nisga'a and local schools performed on the steps of the legislature. Then in the afternoon, before the opening of the legislature, the Nisga'a made their way down Government Street by the inner harbour, a human river of flowing red and black in their button blankets, with an exquisitely carved canoe seemingly afloat in their midst. As they passed the Empress Hotel and moved on toward the legislature, it became apparent that the canoe was set on a bed of cedar branches on a trailer. It was carrying Nisga'a elders in a triumphal re-enactment of the journey of 1887. In the previous century they had arrived alone and were turned away in humiliation. Now they were led by drummers and dancers in elaborate wooden head-dresses, and instead of being banished they were welcomed.

The procession stopped at the entrance to the legislature grounds for a necessary formality. According to Pacific Coast tradition, the Songees nation greeted the Nisga'a at the border of their own traditional lands, and welcomed them. Only after this protocol had been duly observed would the Nisga'a move onto the grounds of the provincial parliament.

The vast iron doors of the building remained shut. Before them stood Premier Glen Clark, who welcomed them in the name of the Province and his government. Joe Gosnell replied, "We ask all aboriginal people, all British Columbians, and all Canadians to walk with us on the final part of our journey."[6] RCMP officers, the scarlet of their traditional uniforms rivalling the red of the Nisga'a traditional dress, swung open the giant doors. A sea of red and black swarmed up the stairs and into the building from which they had been barred 111 years before.

In the upper rotunda, the company paused. They stood in silence on the mosaic floor, beneath the soaring, light-filled dome with its gilded mould-ings, and uttered the names of the Nisga'a who had gone before. Then they moved onto the floor of the legislature, which they soon filled, overflowing into the gallery. Looking distinctly underdressed in the midst of all that brilliant colour, the Premier introduced the legislation, Bill 51. During his speech he introduced the Nisga'a to the legislature, as well as the provincial negotiators and myself. The official business done, the Nisga'a drummers began performing in the upper rotunda. The sounds reverberated throughout the building, drowning out the human voices of those who had come to celebrate as well as those who had come to dispute.

"We are not naïve," Joe Gosnell would later say to that same assembly. "We know that some people do not want this treaty."[7] But for those few hours, at least, their voices were not heard.

On Tuesday, Nisga'a dancers and singers performed at Market Square in Victoria, and the following day they performed at the Eaton Centre. On Thursday, December 3, the Nisga'a officially ended their visit to the provincial capital with another Eucharistic service, this time at the Church of St. John the Divine on Quadra Street. The Nisga'a encounter with Christianity has been less volatile than that of some other First Nations in Canada. Whether this is a function of the Nisga'a or of Christianity is difficult to say, but it is interesting to note that the church has been a vocal ally in the struggle for aboriginal rights in northern British Columbia.

The evening of the ceremony at the legislature, Gloria Macarenko of the local CBC television station moderated a debate featuring Premier Glen Clark, Leader of the Opposition Gordon Campbell, Bill Vander Zalm of the Reform Party, and Gordon Wilson of the Progressive Democratic Alliance. No new issues emerged, and the debate cast more heat than light on the old ones. Later, on the Knowledge TV Network, Joanne Piros hosted an interactive discussion with Joe Gosnell, Jack Ebbels, and me, with a studio audience and telephone lines open to the wider audience across the province. Again, no new issues emerged, but I would like to think we spoke somewhat more rationally than the politicians did.

A few days later Gordon Campbell attacked the treaty, calling once again for a provincial referendum.[8] A by-election in Parksville-Qualicum resulted in a crushing defeat for the NDP and Reform candidates. The Liberals interpreted their victory as an endorsement of their policy regarding the Nisga'a treaty. As the legislature adjourned in mid-December for Christmas, the field was arrayed for battle.

Supporters and detractors lined up on both sides of the issue. All the tools of social debate were brought into play: letters to the editor, phone-in shows on the radio, public television, public forums, and private debates. And of course the politicians were everywhere, reiterating well-rehearsed positions or offering pithy, off-the-cuff sound-bites to eager journalists for the evening news.

Supporters of the treaty included the federal and provincial negotiators and their respective ministers, the Nisga'a, environmentalists such as David Suzuki, former politicians Mike Harcourt, Iona Campagnolo, and Judd Buchanan, labour leader Ken Georgetti, and a host of business leaders, including Milton Wong, David MacLean, Brian Smith, Wendy McDonald, Chuck Conneghan, and Win Stothard, to name the most prominent. The opposition, a more predictable alliance, included the provincial Liberal and Reform Parties, the federal Reform caucus in British Columbia, and individual opinion-makers such as broadcaster Rafe Mair, occasional newspaper columnist Gordon Gibson of the Fraser Institute, and Mel Smith, a former advisor to the Social Credit government.

Reform MP Mike Scott, whose vast Skeena riding includes the Nass Valley, was one of the most vocal critics of the Final Agreement both federally and provincially. His commitment to serving his constituents was later illustrated in a November 1999 Canadian Press story, reproduced here in its entirety:

OTTAWA (CP)—The controversial Nisga'a land-claim treaty set off fireworks as a Commons committee began reviewing it Wednesday.

An all-party committee heard Indian Affairs Minister Robert Nault repeat high praise for the deal to give about 5,000 B.C. Nisga'a self-government, land and cash.

But sparks flew when NDP MP Svend Robinson said it's appalling that Reform MP Mike Scott, who represents the Nisga'a, hasn't met their leaders in five years.

"That's bull," Scott said before chair and Liberal MP Sue Barnes admonished him.

"Mr. Scott, you're out of order," she said.

"So is he," Scott yelled.

Scott's later effort to clarify the issue confirmed he hadn't met Nisga'a representatives since 1993.[9]

While Bill 51 was still before the BC Legislature, the Province launched a massive advertising campaign that included a web site, a toll-free information line, newspaper, television, and radio advertisements, and a summary of the treaty mailed to every household in British Columbia. The cost of the campaign, estimated at over $7 million, became almost as controversial as the treaty itself.

Meanwhile, at their own expense, thirty-three prominent British Columbians took out a full-page advertisement in a number of daily newspapers across the province. The copy read, in part:

[We] strongly encourage Members of the Legislative Assembly of British Columbia and the House of Commons of Canada to ratify the Nisga'a Final Agreement when it comes before the respective Houses. We do so because we firmly believe that such action will put in place a cornerstone of justice for all people in the building of our beloved country, Canada.

Articles and editorials for and against the treaty appeared in Canada's national newspapers and magazines. Lawsuits were launched by provincial Liberal leader Gordon Campbell, by a group calling itself the Fisheries Survival Coalition, and by Lloyd Brinston, a resident of the Nass valley. Concurrently, the claims of the Gitanyow and of the two dissident Nisga'a, Barton and Robinson, were before the courts. While each of the lawsuits attacked a specific aspect of the treaty, all sought to scuttle it entirely.

In a peculiar, perhaps a unique, response to one of its own paid advertisers, the newspapers of David Black's print empire published a series of seven rebuttals of the various advertisements that had been taken out by the provincial government. "The government," they declared, "is misleading you about the Nisga'a Treaty." They then itemized what they considered to be untruthful in the Province's ads. From my perspective, all their charges had been met and all their questions answered before they even went to press. Of course, to know that, they would have had to read the Agreement itself and follow something of the exhaustive process of negotiation and public consultation of which it was the result.

But David Black (no relation to Conrad), the publisher of some sixty daily and weekly newspapers in British Columbia, was not content simply to contradict his own paid advertisers. He also issued a directive to his editors to the effect that "all commentary and editorials in his papers must attack the treaty."[10]

"The opinions to be expressed in our papers," he declared in a CBC radio interview, "are going to be against the treaty. This treaty is wrong. It is going to destroy the province as we know it."[11] Mr. Black further revealed that he had hired Mel Smith, a self-styled constitutional expert and vocal opponent of the Nisga'a Final Agreement, to write a series of eight articles delineating his opposition.

The provincial government announced that it was going to file a formal complaint with the Press Council. Black countered with a complaint against the Province to be filed with the Advertising Standards Council about alleged inaccuracies in the government's advertising about the treaty.

The Nisga'a responded with a media advisory. "We are disappointed that an influential newspaper owner in British Columbia is trying to censor certain views about the Nisga'a Treaty," it said:

We are engaged in a serious programme of public information presentations to all people who care to listen, and think carefully about this historic Treaty.

But, given the history of the struggle for aboriginal rights in this province, we are not surprised by the crude and capricious censorship of a big newspaper magnate like Mr. Black. Such is the nature of some others' so-called "information campaigns."[12]

The advisory further pointed out that, in addition to the Nisga'a Tribal Council's community information work, Chief Gosnell had written a piece for the editorial page of the Vancouver *Sun*; he had served on a panel of the Northwest College in Terrace; he had spoken at a public meeting in Prince Rupert; he had spoken to members of the Vancouver diplomatic corps, which included the consuls and vice-consuls of many foreign countries; he had spoken to a forum at the University of Victoria; he had participated in a panel discussion at the Pacific Business and Law Institute; and he would shortly be speaking at the annual convention of the Union of British Columbia Municipalities.

It was odd, to say the least, that while the academic, economic, labour, and diplomatic communities were busily informing themselves about the Final Agreement, the print media were busily telling them that they were misinformed. What is the role of responsible journalism in Canada? If issues requiring public debate depend on a free exchange of opinions and ideas in the media, then the actions of David Black were directly contrary to the interests of democracy. This is to say nothing of the moral fibre of those editors who tossed their journalistic integrity out the window and folded beneath Mr. Black's directive.

Minister Jane Stewart rightly characterized Black's directive as "an insult to the people of British Columbia who by and large understand that we have legal obligations here, and they want those obligations reconciled in a peaceful fashion. Not with bloodshed, not with barricades, not with difficult rhetoric, but around a negotiating table!" The Minister, who has subsequently suffered from unrelated controversies, showed her mettle when she said, further, "Quite frankly [David Black and Mel Smith] offer nothing as an alternative. If what they see as being appropriate is continued chaos, continued frustration, continued uncertainty, I won't have it!"[13]

In the midst of the verbal affray, it was regrettable that Premier Clark chose to indulge his apparently inexhaustible facility for playing into the hands of his enemies. Ensuing events in the former Premier's career have amply demonstrated this ability, and he has paid a high price in terms of political ostracism and disgrace. There may be no moral culpability in many of his words and actions, but there are unquestionably political ramifications, and he really should not have said that the Nisga'a treaty was a template for other negotiations. It was certainly not a term one heard on the lips of any federal representatives. Nonetheless, he said it, and in saying it managed to enrage First Nations and third parties alike.

There are a myriad of reasons why the specific provisions of the Nisga'a Final Agreement cannot and should not be "templated." Chief among them are the sheer size of the negotiating parties, the differing locations of the various First Nations in the geographically diverse landscapes of British Columbia and Canada, their proximity to established municipalities, the complexity of urban as opposed to largely rural land claims, and the fundamental diversity of aboriginal societies across Canada. As a negotiator, I must understand and accept the distinct interests of the communities I deal with and their divergent approaches to the goal we all seek, which is nothing less than equality and justice—equality not only before the law but in society at large, and justice not only according to our present lights but according to the history and traditions of the culture in question. Every culture on

Earth has traditions it holds inviolable. I could no more tolerate the closing of my church by government decree than Joe Gosnell could tolerate the abolishment of traditional Nisga'a feasting ceremonies or a Cree from Saskatchewan could tolerate the sudden illegality of sweetgrass in time-honoured rituals. Like the Irish, the English, the Ukrainians, and the French, individual First Nations are just that: individual, with unique histories, cultures, geographies, languages, customs, and political structures.

The treaty process, if it is to be successful, depends not on imposed solutions but on complex and *appropriate* negotiations. As Joe Gosnell has said:

Opponents, who refer to the "Nisga'a template" and not the "Nisga'a treaty," insist the Nisga'a agreement will be applied like a cookie cutter in all of the other negotiations under way in the province. This suggestion would be too absurd to be taken seriously if it were not repeated so frequently.

The Nisga'a Tribal Council had neither the desire nor the mandate to negotiate for anyone other than the Nisga'a nation.[14]

Premier Clark made another unfortunate error when he said that Canada had agreed to forgive the negotiating loan made to the Nisga'a. The statement was both inaccurate and troublesome, as it played further into the hands of those who claimed the nation and the Province had already given away too much. For many years, Canada has had a policy of advancing funds to First Nations to allow them to hire the necessary resources to conduct complex and long-lasting negotiations, but the same policy has always recognized that a loan is a loan and must be repaid. From my own experience and the experience of my colleagues through many federal negotiations, I know that loan forgiveness is always an issue, often right down to the moment of closing. To date, however, the federal government has stood firm in requiring loan repayments as part of final agreements. The Nisga'a could not be an exception. The loan was not forgiven. The final document contains a loan repayment schedule.

Despite the erroneous observations of the Premier and the ongoing attempts by others to help him shoot himself in the foot, Bill 51 passed second reading in the British Columbia Legislature on January 13, 1999, the day after MLAs returned from the Christmas recess. "We are now one step closer to the ratification by BC of this landmark treaty," Clark stated, "but we still have a way to go before our task as legislators is complete."[15]

With second reading, Bill 51 moved into the committee stage. A news release from the Office of the Premier read, in part:

> "We expect that committee stage debate will be very similar to procedures used during budget estimates debates, with detailed examination of all aspects of the legislation and the final agreement," said Aboriginal Affairs Minister Dale Lovick. "This is a complex piece of legislation, and the government will have the necessary resources on hand to provide thorough and complete answers to any questions MLAs may have on all sections of the bill."[16]

On January 29, Gordon Wilson, former leader of the Progressive Democratic Alliance and the British Columbia Liberal Party, announced that he was joining the NDP, swelling government ranks to a five-seat majority. Premier Clark made him Minister of Aboriginal Affairs, replacing Dale Lovick. On April 7, Minister Wilson, who had always been in favour of the treaty, indicated that he wanted the debate concluded by April 22 to coincide with the 42nd Annual Convention of the Nisga'a nation. The announcement effectively put a limit on what had seemed, at times, a never-ending process.

Indeed, after some 120 hours of debate, the government had apparently had enough of providing thorough and complete answers to the filibustering Liberals. By that time, the legislature had debated Bill 51 longer than any other piece of legislation in the province's history. To howls of protest from the Opposition, the government moved to cut off debate. Gordon Campbell characterized the move as "an unprecedented abuse of democracy," and the new Aboriginal Affairs Minister Gordon Wilson as "a toady for Glen Clark's dictatorial assault on democracy."[17]

Closure was invoked on April 21, 1999. The vote would occur the next day at 5:45 PM. As Premier Clark had previously announced, it would be a free vote.

I watched the last hour of debate on television. The Liberals, in a final show of protest, walked out of the legislature. The bells rang at precisely 5:45. The Liberals returned to vote. At approximately 6:00 PM the Speaker of the House rose and announced: "It is an Act, the Nisga'a Treaty Act."

The vote had gone as expected: all the New Democrats supported it, all the Liberals opposed it. Jack Weisgerber, who as Aboriginal Affairs Minister in Bill Vander Zalm's Social Credit Government had signed the Framework Agreement that brought the Province to the negotiating table in the first place, also voted against it.

On April 26, the legislation was given Royal Assent by Chief Justice Allan MacEachern, acting on behalf of the Lieutenant-Governor, who was out of the province.

On April 27, the Final Agreement was signed by representatives of the Nisga'a nation and the Province of British Columbia in the Terrace arena, where the Nisga'a were assembled for their Annual Convention. It was the usual colourful ceremony, with dancers and drummers in traditional costume, and the occasional elaborate and imposing head-dress visible above the heads of the throng. As we proceeded into the arena—the Nisga'a leadership, Premier Clark, Minister Wilson, the provincial negotiators, myself, and Peter Baird, who headed up the Public Information and Consultation Unit for the federal negotiating team—the procession would stop from time to time and ceremonially bow to the four directions. Because we were meeting in Terrace, traditional territory of the Tsimshian, they were present to welcome us before the ceremony.

The Province and the Nisga'a executed six copies of the Final Agreement. During the actual signing, Mercy Thomas began to read a statement of protest. Ms Thomas, a Nisga'a matriarch, had been extremely critical of the Final Agreement, particularly the provisions on certainty. "No matter how you look at it, it still means extinguishment," she had told a national audience during a broadcast of "Cross Country Checkup" on CBC Radio.[18] The press immediately focused on her, but she was drowned out by the drummers. There were no other signs of protest or dissent.

Following the signing, Nisga'a Ambassador Rod Robinson formally presented Chief Gosnell with a copy of the document, instructing him, on behalf of the elders, to travel immediately to Ottawa to seek the signature of the representative of the federal government.

The bound document consisted of the Final Agreement and appendices in English and French. Each of the six signed copies was contained in a three-post expansion binder. Marcus Bartley, Boris Tyzuk, Peter Baird, and I, representing the three parties to the negotiations, crazy-glued the expansion posts so they could not thereafter be tampered with. I had not known that this was one of the functions of the Chief Federal Negotiator.

I could not help but be overwhelmed by the sheer size of the document.

In addition to the Final Agreement and appendices, there was the Implementation Plan, the Fiscal Finance Agreement, the Tax Agreement, the Harvest Agreement, and the Own Source Revenue Agreement. Taken together, the English version ran to 854 pages. The French version effectively doubled that. In contrast, the Agreement in Principle, including appendices, had totalled only 175 pages. When I considered that literally every phrase, word, and punctuation mark in those 854 pages were the result of the con-sidered positions and opinions of many people on three negotiating teams, I was amazed that it had been accomplished so quickly. In the end, the com-plete package, English and French, exceeded 1,700 pages.

The ball was now in Canada's court.

Chapter Twelve

....

IN DECEMBER 1998 I travelled with my daughter Jennifer to Victoria, where I was to appear on the CBC radio program "Cross Country Checkup," hosted by Rex Murphy. The other guests included Joe Gosnell, Mercy Thomas, and Gordon Gibson of the Fraser Institute. We arrived in Victoria the night before, and Jennifer was in the studio audience the next day as the program was broadcast across Canada. Everyone on the panel but Gibson agreed that a referendum on the Final Agreement was neither advisable nor necessary. The program held no surprises, aside from an outburst from a member of the studio audience. The Victoria *Times Colonist* reported the incident:

> Although Gibson deplored the "down and dirty poor-ass politics" that have made the treaty a partisan issue, he observed that 60 per cent of British Columbians are in favour of a referendum. And referendums, said Gibson, such as the vote on the Charlottetown accord, have become a defining Canadian tradition.
>
> But audience member Mark Tyrell launched a personal tirade against Gibson, telling him he had "a hell of a nerve" to voice those opinions.
>
> "The majority is not always right. Minority rights are not protected by a bigoted majority."[1]

That evening Jennifer and I caught a late flight to Winnipeg, where we spent the night. We caught an early flight to Ottawa the following morning, where I attended an awards ceremony with other Nisga'a team representatives. We had received the Head of the Public Service Award for Excellence in Service Delivery. Presented by Jocelyn Bourgue, Clerk of the Privy Council and Secretary to the Cabinet, the citation accompanying the award said, in part:

> Critical to the success of this remarkable achievement was a team of dedicated people working in Vancouver and Ottawa. With dogged determination, perseverance, inexhaustible energy and an unwavering commitment to concluding a final agreement, the team overcame many obstacles.
>
> The tripartite negotiations required innovative work across many departments, an elaborate public consultation mechanism, and teamwork that thrived over many arduous years. The negotiations themselves were intricate, complex and often intense. Yet, in the end, they resulted in a covenant that corrected an historic wrong and addressed uncertainty in the Nass River Valley that had tempered investment for years.
>
> All Canadians can take great pride in this product, which holds exceptional value for all of us.

Jennifer and I caught a flight back to Saskatoon early the next morning. In the space of three days we had crossed more than half the continent twice. It was nothing unusual for me, but at the end of it Jennifer said, "Dad, I can't keep up with you. I don't know how you do this day after day."

Neither do I, to tell the truth, but it seems that when the energy is needed, it's there. More remarkable, to me, is the result of all that travel and energy: the Final Agreement. I am still overcome, sometimes, by that mixture of disbelief, triumph, and joy that accompanied me into the hotel room in Terrace when I announced, "We have a deal!" Perhaps it is time now to take a look at what that "deal" contains.

The Preamble to the Final Agreement recognizes and affirms the historical rights of the Nisga'a nation as an aboriginal people who have lived in the Nass area since time immemorial. It sets out the objectives of the parties in entering into the Agreement, notably "the reconciliation between the prior presence of aboriginal peoples and the assertion of sovereignty by the Crown." It states, further, that the parties intend the Agreement to be "the just and equitable settlement of the land question" that the Nisga'a have sought "since the arrival of the British Crown," and that the parties "intend their relationship to be based on a new approach to mutual recognition and sharing, and to achieve this mutual recognition and sharing by agreeing to rights, rather than by the extinguishment of rights." The Preamble states, finally, that Canada, British Columbia, and the Nisga'a nation "intend that this Agreement will provide certainty with respect to Nisga'a ownership and use of lands and resources, and the relationship of federal, provincial and Nisga'a laws within the Nass Area."

"Now therefore the parties agree as follows," the Preamble concludes, and there follow twenty-two chapters and thirteen appendices, comprising hundreds of pages of clauses and provisions—each phrase, word, and punctuation mark of which was debated, reflected on, and agreed to by all parties at the negotiating table

The General Provisions chapter takes its logical place in the document, following immediately upon the Preamble and an exhaustive list of definitions that sets out the precise meaning of terms and phrases as they apply in the Agreement. The General Provisions chapter is of particular importance because it sets out the treaty's approach to certainty. The Final Agreement, it states, provides a full and final settlement of Nisga'a aboriginal rights and title, which are modified and continue as set out therein. The treaty exhaustively sets out the Nisga'a section 35 rights under the Constitution Act, 1982, which, as we have seen, recognizes and affirms the "existing aboriginal and treaty rights of the aboriginal peoples of Canada," defines those peoples as including "the Indian, Inuit, and Métis peoples," further defines treaty rights to include "rights that now exist by way of land claims agreements or may be so acquired," and provides that aboriginal and treaty rights are guaranteed equally to men and women. Under the Final Agreement, the Nisga'a agree to indemnify Canada and British Columbia against any claims for aboriginal rights not identified in the treaty, and further agree to release any aboriginal rights, including aboriginal title, that are not delineated in the treaty or that are different in attributes or geographical extent from the Nisga'a section 35 rights set out in the treaty.

The General Provisions chapter affirms that the Nisga'a continue to be an aboriginal people under the Constitution Act, 1982, enjoying the same rights and benefits as other Canadians. It also states that the Charter of Rights and Freedoms applies equally to the Nisga'a government and its institutions as it does to other local governments and institutions across Canada, and that, critics to the contrary, federal and provincial laws continue to apply to

Nisga'a citizens and others who reside, temporarily or permanently, on Nisga'a lands. Of equal importance to those who want to see an end to the brutal hegemony of the Indian Act is the provision specifying that lands owned by the Nisga'a will no longer be reserve lands under the Act. The chapter also contains key clauses that allow the parties to proceed with the treaty despite the absence of certain overlap agreements; the provisions ensure that the rights of other aboriginal groups are protected, and that Nisga'a rights do not affect the aboriginal rights of other First Nations. The chapter provides, finally, that the treaty is amendable with the consent of the three parties.

The Lands chapter—the longest in the Agreement—identifies Nisga'a lands as comprising some 2,000 square kilometres, consisting of 1,930 square kilometres of former British Columbia Crown land and a further 62 square kilometres of former Indian reserves—in total, approximately 8 percent of the traditional territory the Nisga'a originally claimed. Further, all Nisga'a lands will be held in fee simple estate ("fee" = unencumbered ownership; "simple" = unlimited as to category of heir) and will not be considered as federal lands reserved for Indians; it is basically the same type of land interest that every private landowner in British Columbia enjoys. Nisga'a lands do not include existing fee simple lands within Nisga'a lands—no one is going to be forced off his or her property as a result of the Agreement—nor do they include the Nisga'a highway or lands currently subject to agricultural leases and woodlot licences. Existing legal interests on Nisga'a lands will continue or be re-issued as tenures by the Nisga'a government. The Nisga'a will be able to issue new tenures in the future.

The Nisga'a will own all subsurface resources, such as minerals and fossil fuels, on Nisga'a lands. The Agreement further provides for Nisga'a government ownership of certain fee simple lands that lie outside the main area of tribal ownership, including eighteen former Indian reserves and some 12.5 square kilometres of adjacent property. The Nisga'a will own all subsurface resources on these lands as well. However, in a remaining fifteen small parcels of fee simple land identified in the Final Agreement as Nisga'a lands —approximately 2.5 square kilometres in total—subsurface resources will continue to be owned by British Columbia, which will retain its jurisdiction as it does over other privately held land in the province.

Important cultural sites on Nisga'a land will be designated and protected as heritage sites, and some key geographic features will be re-designated with

Nisga'a names. The Province will retain its authority and responsibility with regard to the Nisga'a Memorial Lava Bed Park and the Gingietl Creek Ecological Reserve. Nisga'a culture and history will continue to be promoted as the chief features of the park. Appropriately, Nisga'a citizens preserve the right to use the lands and resources within both the park and the ecological reserve for traditional purposes. The Nisga'a will receive, on application, a commercial recreation tenure that will operate under provincial laws; the intent of this provision is to allow the Nisga'a to provide, for example, professional guides for hiking parties and ecological tours on Crown lands.

The Lands chapter also addresses the critical issue of water. The Agreement provides that existing water licences will remain in place, while British Columbia will establish a Nisga'a water reservation of 300,000 cubic decametres per year from the Nass River and other streams wholly or partially within Nisga'a lands for domestic, industrial, and agricultural purposes. This provision assures that the Nisga'a will have access to sufficient water for their present and future needs without depriving others who may be relying on the Nass River for similar purposes. A further provision enables the Nisga'a to investigate the suitability of streams flowing through Nisga'a lands for purposes of generating hydroelectric power.

The Land Title chapter affirms that Nisga'a lands will be owned by the Nisga'a. Any fee simple parcels existing within Nisga'a lands on the day the treaty comes into effect will remain subject to the Land Title Act and the provincial land title system. Individual parcels within Nisga'a lands will initially be registered under a Nisga'a land title system, and may subsequently be registered under the provincial land title system.

The Forest Resources chapter addresses five key issues: ownership, regulation, harvesting, processing, and forest resources outside Nisga'a lands. Not surprisingly, the Nisga'a will own all forest resources on Nisga'a land. The annual allowable cut is specified in the Agreement, which also provides for a five-year transition period to allow existing licensees to adjust their operations. Such licensees will be required to meet certain obligations, including silviculture, through the transition period and beyond. Following the transition period, the Nisga'a will manage all forestry operations on Nisga'a lands, but their forest management standards must meet or exceed existing provincial standards, including the Forest Practices Code. Further, provincial laws pertaining to the manufacture of timber harvested on Crown lands will apply equally to timber harvested on Nisga'a lands. To protect existing interests and to allow for an equitable period of transition and adjustment, the Nisga'a agree not to establish a primary timber processing facility for ten years following the effective date of the Agreement. Subject to ministerial approval under the provincial Forest Act, the Nisga'a, like any other entrepreneur or group of entrepreneurs, may acquire forest tenures outside Nisga'a lands, with an aggregate allowable cut of up to 150,000 cubic metres.

The Access chapter and the Roads and Rights of Way chapter address issues of key importance to local business interests and area residents. These issues were material to all three parties throughout the negotiations, and the Final Agreement reflects the concerns both of the negotiators and of the third parties who frequently met with us throughout the process.

The Agreement provides, first, for reasonable public access to public Nisga'a lands for non-commercial pursuits such as hunting and fishing, though the Nisga'a government may regulate such access in the interests of public safety, for the protection of environmental, cultural, or historical areas, or for habitat protection. Owners of privately held land within Nisga'a lands will, of course, retain free access to their properties. The federal and provincial governments will also retain access to Nisga'a lands for the delivery or management of government services, and for emergency response purposes. Similarly, representatives of the Nisga'a government may, in accordance with the laws of general application, have temporary access to adjacent Crown lands for similar purposes. ("Laws of general application" are defined in the Agreement as including "federal and provincial laws that apply generally in British Columbia," but not "federal laws in respect of Indians or lands reserved for the Indians.")

Under the Final Agreement, British Columbia retains ownership and control of the Nisga'a highway, an unpaved provincial highway that runs through the Nass Valley from Laxgalts'ap to a point north of Nass Camp. The Province also enjoys exclusive and perpetual right of way on all secondary provincial roads on Nisga'a lands, and may acquire portions of Nisga'a land to create additional rights of way for roads or public utilities. Nisga'a roads will be regulated and maintained by the Nisga'a government.

The Fisheries chapter, one of the longest in the Agreement, is set out under ten subheadings plus Schedules A to G. The chapter addresses such issues as salmon, perennially critical to the Nisga'a economy, enhancements, non-salmon species and aquatic plants, fisheries management, the Lisims Fisheries Conservation Trust, participation in the general commercial fishery, international arrangements, and processing facilities, among others, while the schedules specify formulae, percentages, allocations, and funding arrangements for the topics addressed under the subheadings. Replete with cross-references and technical data, the Fisheries chapter reflects the complexity of the negotiations perhaps better than any other.

Briefly, the Fisheries chapter provides that Nisga'a citizens will have the right to harvest fish and aquatic plants subject to the requirements of conservation and legislation enacted to protect public health and safety. Again, critics to the contrary, by no means will they enjoy the profligate rights to do what they want, when they want, and for any reason they want without reference to the laws and constrictions that apply to other Canadians. In the absence of a Nisga'a police force, the RCMP will continue to serve on Nisga'a lands as they have in the past.

Under the treaty and a separate Harvest Agreement, the Nisga'a will receive an annual salmon allocation that will, on average, comprise approximately 26 percent of the Canadian Nass River total allowable catch. The Harvest Agreement, which will be entered into by the three parties on the effective date of the treaty, will allow for the harvesting of sockeye and pink salmon; this harvesting will be included in the 26 percent mentioned above. The Nisga'a will be able to sell their salmon, but not unrestrictedly; they will be subject to the same monitoring, enforcement, and laws of general application that apply to any other fisheries concern; such laws and regulations will be enforced, as they always have been, by the Department of Fisheries and Oceans and the RCMP. Similarly, if in any year there is no directed Canadian commercial or recreational fishery for any given species of Nass salmon, no Nisga'a commercial fishery will be permitted for that species, either.

The Nisga'a will have the right to harvest steelhead as well as non-salmon species and aquatic plants, but for domestic purposes only. The Agreement also provides for a shellfish allocation and for the further negotiation of allocations for other species such as halibut and crab. This latter provision was one of the issues that critics of the Agreement raised in an attempt to show that certainty had not been achieved. What they showed, in fact, was the shallowness of their perceptions. Nothing is absolute. Certainty depends on the goodwill of the parties as well as the provisions of the Agreement.

The Nisga'a may conduct enhancement activities for Nass salmon, but only with the approval of the Minister. Enhancement activities include such initiatives as hatcheries, stream reclamation, and environmental operations that result in the return to Canadian waters of those salmon species included in the proposal to the Minister. The Joint Fisheries Management Committee (JFMC), an advisory body established by the parties to facilitate the cooperative planning and conduct of Nisga'a fisheries and enhancement activities, may offer recommendations in respect of any initiatives proposed by the Nisga'a. The Nisga'a may harvest any surplus Nass salmon resulting from their approved enhancement initiatives in proportion to their contribution to the total cost of the initiative. Unlike the sockeye and pink salmon covered under the Harvest Agreement, this surplus will be in addition to the Nisga'a fish allocations cited previously.

On the critical issue of fisheries management, the Minister of Fisheries and Oceans and the Province of British Columbia will retain responsibility for the conservation and management of the fisheries and fish habitat, according to their respective jurisdictions. The Nisga'a government may pass laws to manage the Nisga'a harvest, but those laws must be consistent with the Nisga'a Annual Fishing Plan, must be recommended by the JFMC, and must be approved by the Minister. The Annual Fishing Plan, prepared by the Nisga'a for all species of salmon and other fish, will be reviewed by the JFMC and, if satisfactory, approved by the Minister of Fisheries and Oceans. The treaty also provides for Nisga'a participation in any future regional or watershed-based fisheries management proposals.

Lisims is the Nisga'a name for the Nass River. Appropriately, a Lisims Fisheries Conservation Trust will be established to promote the conservation and protection of Nass area fish species, to facilitate the sustainable management of the fisheries for the benefit of all Canadians, and to promote and support Nisga'a participation in the stewardship of this crucial resource. Under the Agreement, the federal government will contribute $10 million toward this initiative, the Nisga'a $3 million. Canada and British Columbia will provide a further $11.5 million to enable and increase Nisga'a participation in the commercial fishery. As with the forestry sector, the Nisga'a have agreed not to establish a large-scale fish-processing facility for some years—eight, in this instance—following the effective date of the treaty.

Another chapter of the Final Agreement deals with Wildlife and Migratory Birds. Appropriate to their culture and traditions, the Nisga'a will receive a wildlife hunting allocation for domestic purposes. This allocation includes specific figures for moose, grizzly, and mountain goats. Other animals and allocations may be designated and established in the future. Such allocations are based on percentages of the total allowable hunt for each species. In this manner, the Agreement reflects the sensitivity of the negotiators and their respective governments toward the reality of fluctuating wildlife populations, the needs of wildlife management, and the interests of other hunters. The activity of hunting itself, whether for recreation or subsistence purposes, remains subject to conservation requirements and applicable provincial and federal legislation enacted in the interests of public health and safety. Further, the right of the Nisga'a to hunt does not preclude other authorized uses of Crown land, nor does it prevent the Crown from authorizing such uses or dispositions.

The Nisga'a may harvest migratory birds for domestic purposes, and they may trade or barter wildlife, wildlife parts, and migratory birds among themselves or with other aboriginal peoples—but again, subject to conservation concerns and laws enacted to protect public health and safety. The Agreement provides for a wildlife committee to be established to promote the cooperative management of the resource in the Nass area and advise the Minister on management and hunting matters. The committee will have equal representation from the Nisga'a and British Columbia, and one federal representative. The Nisga'a will develop an annual management plan for their hunt to be reviewed by the committee and approved by the Minister.

Nisga'a citizens who hunt outside the management area will be subject to all applicable provincial laws, including those that deal with licensing. Trapping, too, will be regulated in accordance with British Columbia laws, while guiding activities will continue to be subject to the laws of general application. The Nisga'a may receive a guide outfitter's certificate if a certificate that currently covers all or part of Nisga'a lands ceases to apply. The Nisga'a will also receive an angling guide licence for certain watercourses outside Nisga'a lands. The Minister of the Environment, Lands, and Parks continues to be responsible for all wildlife.

The Environmental Assessment and Protection chapter provides that the Nisga'a government will have the power to pass laws in that area on Nisga'a lands, but the standards defined in those laws must meet or exceed federal and provincial standards. The Nisga'a may also undertake environmental assessments of proposed projects on their own lands, but these assessments must include public participation, and the results must be made available to the public, except where information is kept confidential by law. If a proposed project on Nisga'a lands will have effects outside those lands, Canada and British Columbia will participate in any environmental assessments. Federal and provincial environmental assessment processes continue to apply on Nisga'a lands. To avoid duplication, the Agreement provides for the harmonization of Nisga'a environmental assessment procedures with those of Canada and British Columbia.

The chapter on Nisga'a government is unique among treaties in Canada, in that the Nisga'a Final Agreement represents the first time that land claims and self-government have been addressed together. The provisions set out in the Nisga'a Government chapter not only allow the Nisga'a to take their rightful place in the Canadian political system and the larger society, but it allows them also to take control of those matters that are internal to their communities and distinctive to their culture.

The Nisga'a will be governed by the Nisga'a Lisims Government (their central government) and four village governments. A constitution will set out the terms of governance and recognize the rights and freedoms of Nisga'a citizens. The constitution will be devised and negotiated among the Nisga'a, and must be ratified by at least 70 percent of the voters who were registered to vote to ratify the Final Agreement.

Under the Agreement, the Nisga'a government will be required to consult with non-Nisga'a residents of Nisga'a lands about decisions that significantly and directly affect them. Likewise, residents who are not Nisga'a will be able to participate in the deliberations of elected bodies that directly and significantly affect them. The means of participation can vary according to circumstance. In one instance, the opportunity to make representations to the Nisga'a government may be sufficient to protect a third party's interests. In another, adequate participation may mean being able to vote for or seek election to Nisga'a public institutions. Non-Nisga'a residents will have the same means of appeal as Nisga'a citizens. Some local laws, such as traffic codes and transportation regulations, will apply to all residents of Nisga'a lands, but in the majority of cases Nisga'a laws will only pertain to Nisga'a citizens.

Nisga'a jurisdiction is limited by the Agreement, and is concurrent with federal and provincial laws. The Nisga'a government will have the power to make the laws required to carry out its responsibilities and exercise its authority as set out in the Agreement. Its principal authority rests in its responsibility to pass laws governing Nisga'a citizenship, language, and culture, Nisga'a property in Nisga'a lands, and the Nisga'a government itself.

Areas of concurrent jurisdiction with Canada and British Columbia include buildings and public works, traffic and transportation, health and social services, adoption, and education. Federal and provincial laws continue to apply to Nisga'a citizens and Nisga'a lands, as they apply to any property owners in Canada. The relationship between federal and provincial laws and Nisga'a laws is clearly delineated in the Final Agreement, with stipulations as to which law will prevail in case of conflict or inconsistency.

The transition provisions in the Final Agreement stipulate that the first elections for the Nisga'a government must be held no later than six months after the effective date of the treaty. Although the Nisga'a Tribal Council and the Band Councils formally cease to exist once the treaty is proclaimed, members of both bodies will continue to manage Nisga'a affairs until the new governments are formed.

The administration of justice on Nisga'a lands is the subject of a separate chapter in the Final Agreement. Briefly, the Nisga'a government may provide policing, corrections, and court services on Nisga'a lands. If it decides to provide its own police service, it may do so with the approval of the Lieutenant-Governor in Council; it does not require an Act of the provincial legislature or of Parliament. Any proposed Nisga'a police service will be both independent and accountable. Peace officers will be required to meet provincial standards in qualification and training, and, as such, they will have the authority to enforce Nisga'a, provincial, and federal laws, including the *Criminal Code of Canada*, on Nisga'a lands. Again, in the absence of a Nisga'a police force, the RCMP will continue to serve in their traditional capacity.

A Nisga'a court may be established with the approval, once again, of the Lieutenant-Governor in Council. The court will have the authority to adjudicate prosecutions and civil disputes arising under Nisga'a laws, and to review the administrative decisions of Nisga'a public institutions. Judges of the court will be appointed by the Nisga'a government according to a method of selection approved by the Lieutenant-Governor in Council; they will meet the expectations and comply with generally recognized principles of judicial fairness, independence, and impartiality. In any proceedings that may result in imprisonment under Nisga'a law, the accused may elect to be tried in the Provincial Court of British Columbia. Decisions by the Nisga'a court may be appealed to the Supreme Court of British Columbia on the same basis as decisions handed down in the provincial court.

If they choose, the Nisga'a may also enter into agreements with Canada or British Columbia for the provision of community correctional services. Such facilities will function in accordance with generally accepted standards and be consistent with the needs and priorities of the Nisga'a government.

The Indian Act Transition chapter, though brief, is essential to facilitate the transition from the Act to provincial or Nisga'a jurisdiction. So pervasive was—and in many cases still is—the Act in the life of every "status" Indian in Canada that provisions have to be made to ensure that such things as wills and the administration of estates remain valid after the effective date of the treaty. Governance arrangements, too, will have to be reviewed to assure their validity under provincial or federal law.

Three chapters of the Final Agreement deal with fiscal and financial matters: Capital Transfer and Negotiation Loan Repayment, Fiscal Relations, and Taxation. As has been widely reported in the media—generally accurately, though often selectively—enormous sums of money will be changing hands as a result of the Final Agreement. This is to be expected in an enterprise of this size and complexity. But the actual expenditures of the federal and provincial governments pale in comparison to the projected benefits to the economy of northwest British Columbia, not to mention the rest of the province and the nation as a whole. The cash settlement of $190 million to be paid to the Nisga'a through capital transfers over a period of fifteen years seems almost trivial compared to the estimated $1.25 billion it would take to "pay off" the Nisga'a according to Bill Vander Zalm's formula for emancipating the Natives. Even the loans made to the Nisga'a to support their participation in treaty negotiations will be fully repaid over a period of fifteen years.

The Nisga'a government will be responsible for ensuring the delivery of programs and services at levels reasonably comparable to those generally available in northwest British Columbia. Every five years the parties will be required to negotiate a Fiscal Financing Agreement. Under this agreement, funding will be provided to enable the Nisga'a government to deliver essential programs and services, including health, education, and social services, local government services, and capital asset maintenance and replacement. The Fiscal Financing Agreement will take into account the Nisga'a government's ability to raise its own revenues according to an Own Source Revenue Agreement that, in turn, will be phased in over a period of twelve years. After the initial term, the Own Source Revenue Agreement may be renegotiated every two years at the request of any of the parties.

The Final Agreement affirms that the funding of the Nisga'a government is a shared responsibility, but it is the intention of all parties that Nisga'a reliance on capital transfers will be substantially reduced over time. The establishment of the principle of own source revenue in the Final Agreement is an important indication that a new relationship is being created with the Nisga'a—and, by this precedent, possibly with other First Nations negotiating self-government in federal, provincial, and territorial jurisdictions.

Taxation is ever a troublesome issue. But the ineluctable reality any government must face is that, in order to deliver services, it must have the ability to tax its citizens. The Nisga'a government is no different. Under the Final Agreement, therefore, the Nisga'a government assumes the power to tax Nisga'a citizens on Nisga'a lands. It does not have the power directly to tax non-Nisga'a citizens, though the parties may negotiate tax delegation agreements with a view to coordinating their respective systems of taxation on Nisga'a lands. The traditional tax exemption for Nisga'a citizens under the Indian Act will be eliminated after a transitional period of eight years for transaction taxes and twelve years for other taxes; the former includes such items as the sales tax, the latter such things as income tax. Pursuant to a taxation agreement, the Nisga'a central government and the four village governments will be treated in the same way as municipalities for tax purposes. Nisga'a citizens will thus pay taxes to the federal and provincial government and to the Nisga'a government.

Under the Cultural Artifacts and Heritage chapter, the Royal British Columbia Museum and the Canadian Museum of Civilization agree to return a portion of their collections of Nisga'a artifacts to the Nisga'a. The Nisga'a have agreed, in turn, that some collections will be retained by the museums for the purposes of public exhibition and education. With respect to heritage sites on Nisga'a lands, the Nisga'a government and the Province will coordinate their activities to manage the sites and preserve them.

The Local and Regional Government Relationships chapter is, with only six provisions, one of the briefest in the Final Agreement. Simply, it provides that Nisga'a lands will continue to be part of Electoral Area "A" in the Regional District of Kitimat-Stikine, and that the Nisga'a and the Regional District may enter into servicing agreements or otherwise coordinate their activities with respect to common areas of responsibility. Like all Canadian citizens, eligible Nisga'a will continue to vote in federal, provincial, and regional district elections.

The Dispute Resolution chapter is somewhat longer, with further details delineated in an appendix. No matter how careful the parties were in drafting each provision in the Final Agreement, no matter how thorough, it is virtually inevitable that disagreements will arise with respect to the interpretation, application, or implementation of the treaty. In such instances, it is expected that the parties will first attempt to come to a resolution through consultation and cooperation. Failing that, they may have recourse to mediation or some other form of dispute resolution. Failing even that, the parties may resort to arbitration or, in the last resort, the Supreme Court of British Columbia and any appropriate appeals.

The chapter on Eligibility and Enrolment, though historically logical, unfortunately raises the spectre of race-based government. While it is true that, to be eligible to receive benefits from the Nisga'a treaty, a person must meet enrolment criteria that are largely based on Nisga'a ancestry, to condemn the process as racist is to ignore fundamental aspects of the development of human societies. Any community of persons exists first as a physical entity. If it governs itself according to laws and customs that have evolved over time, it becomes a political entity. If race is a dominant factor in the community, it is a function of history, not intention. The Nisga'a negotiated the Final Agreement not as a separate race but as a political community. They had lived in a particular place, according to particular customs, laws, and social structures, since time immemorial—and had to prove as much to every level of government and court in Canada before they were even allowed to sit at the negotiating table. That the Nisga'a nation is predominantly made up of Nisga'a should surprise no one, but their common racial origin is incidental to their social and political aspirations.

The task of determining eligibility has largely been carried out, for it was necessary to identify Nisga'a voters during the ratification process. Under the Agreement, the Nisga'a were required to strike an eight-member Enrolment Committee that would create a register of names during an initial enrolment period. Thereafter, the Nisga'a government would maintain the register. The decisions of the committee and the Nisga'a government with respect to eligibility and enrolment are final and binding, subject to an appeal process.

The provisions of the Ratification chapter, again, have been largely fulfilled. The Final Agreement states explicitly that it has no force or effect unless ratified by the Nisga'a, British Columbia, and Canada. For the Nisga'a, those citizens who were enrolled by the Enrolment Committee and who met the voting criteria were eligible to vote on the Agreement by secret ballot. A Ratification Committee, with representation from all parties, oversaw the conduct of the vote. To be approved, the Agreement had to be ratified by a simple majority of all eligible voters.

This has been accomplished.

For British Columbia, the Agreement had to be ratified in the Legislative Assembly by the enactment of legislation giving effect to the treaty.

This, too, has been accomplished.

Then it was Canada's turn.

But before we get to that, there is one more chapter to discuss: the Implementation chapter. It contains only five provisions, to the effect that the Final Agreement will be implemented according to an Implementation Plan that is separate from the Agreement itself and is not constitutionally protected under section 35. The plan sets out the steps to be taken to make the treaty work "on the ground." The Implementation Plan will be in effect for a period of ten years, commencing on the date the treaty comes into effect.

In summary, the Nisga'a Final Agreement includes a number of breakthrough elements in treaty negotiations in Canada:

◆ Certainty has been achieved without the use of the objectionable phrase, "cede, release, and surrender."

◆ Past uncertainties relating to the extent and scope of the fishing rights of a First Nation in British Columbia have been conclusively eliminated. The Nisga'a fisheries arrangements are the first of their kind. The fisheries management provisions and the Lisims Fisheries Conservation Trust confirm the role of the Nisga'a in the stewardship of the Nass River fisheries.

◆ For the Nisga'a, Indian reserves will cease to exist. The Final Agreement demonstrated that lands can be brought into the provincial land registration system without affecting the integrity of the system.

◆ The governance provisions of the Final Agreement demonstrate that it is possible to reach agreement on a number of matters raised by the federal inherent right policy. The Nisga'a government, for example, will operate within the framework of the Canadian Constitution. The Final Agreement clearly defines

the scope of Nisga'a authorities and their relationship to federal
and provincial jurisdictions. It also addresses the rights of those
people residing within Nisga'a lands who are not Nisga'a citizens.

◆ The treaty provides a fair opportunity for the Nisga'a to manage
their own affairs in a fashion similar to other local governments,
and subject to overarching laws such as the Canadian Charter of
Rights and Freedoms and the *Criminal Code of Canada.*

◆ For the first time in a Canadian treaty, a substantial portion of a
First Nation's artifacts held in museums (the Canadian Museum
of Civilization and The Royal Museum of British Columbia) will
be permanently returned.

◆ For the first time in British Columbia, a First Nation has agreed
to end its tax-exempt status.

◆ An own source revenue agreement has been negotiated, providing
for a phased-in contribution of Nisga'a revenues.

In all these areas, and many more, each of the parties was required to
make major concessions and compromises. None of those compromises can
be viewed in isolation from the rest of the Agreement. The taxation provisions are integral to other provisions such as self-government, lands
acquired by the treaty, and fish. Land Title is basic to Forest Resources, Forest
Resources to Access, Access to Roads and Rights of Way, and so on. Each
chapter is an essential corollary of the others. The Agreement cannot be
picked apart. You cannot say, "I like the tax chapter, keep it. But I don't like
self-government," or "I don't like some parts in the fish chapter, take them
out. But keep the environmental provisions." Treaties are about the resolution of differences through negotiated compromise.

Remove one thread and the whole garment may unravel.

Chapter Thirteen

....

As with any drawn-out, complex process, the negotiation and subsequent ratification of the Nisga'a Final Agreement has attracted its share of critics. I would be inclined to say it has attracted more than its share. Many have been reasonable people with sincere concerns about their country and the aboriginal peoples who share it with them. Others have been ideologically driven— equally sincere, and no doubt reasonable according to their own lights, but unable to see beyond the self-constructed walls of their ideology. Still others have been utterly frivolous in their condemnation of a document they have obviously not read, or at least have not understood, or perhaps have not wanted to understand. Trying to reason with such people is like trying to teach pigs to sing. It is frustrating and ultimately futile, and it annoys the pigs.

Nonetheless, it is important to answer at least some of the criticisms, if not the critics, for a number of unfounded allegations have been made that, if allowed to go unchallenged, could poison future negotiations. A treaty is a catalyst for that which will unfold. It is a law, but it is also a guide. Through the process of negotiating the Nisga'a treaty, we have learned valuable lessons, understood concerns, and found solutions. The process was effective, the result successful. A good catalyst was developed at the Nisga'a table. It is by no means a template for other treaties, but it would be foolish to ignore the lessons we have learned, or refuse to apply them wisely and consistently in future negotiations.

As a Chief Federal Negotiator, I have answers and explanations for everything I did at the Nisga'a table, as do the negotiators for the Province and the Nisga'a. However, those answers and explanations are often bound up in legal and constitutional issues that make them rather difficult to elucidate in a ten-second sound-bite on television. It is much easier to create a negative image by mouthing slogans—"This must be settled by referendum!" "This is taxation without representation!" "This creates a third order of government!"— which conveniently relieve one of the necessity of critical thought. Without impugning anyone's motives, therefore, and without trying to teach pigs to sing, let me now touch on a few of the major issues raised by the treaty that have not already been addressed.

It has been said that Nisga'a law will displace federal and provincial law on Nisga'a lands—that the Final Agreement, in fact, creates a "third order" of government. It does no such thing. Canada's law-making authorities are set out in section 91 of the Constitution Act, 1867 (the British North America Act), and those of the provinces are delineated in section 92. Together, these represent the bulk of the powers enjoyed by the two constitutionally established levels of government. Superficially, it would seem that for one government to make laws about items on another's list is beyond the power of each. Thus, they are exclusive powers. But they are not shut up in watertight compartments; there can be leakage between the two lists. Canada may pass a law on a matter that falls within its jurisdiction, but which may have an incidental impact on a matter on the provincial list. Thus, there are some circumstances where federal and provincial legislation may cover the same matter. If the laws conflict or are inconsistent with one another, the courts must determine which law prevails, according to constitutional rules and legal jurisprudence that has evolved over the years. The court first attempts to see if the laws are valid; it next considers whether it is possible to have both laws continue to apply; finally, it must rule on whether one law prevails over the other. The outcome of any legal action is never predictable; it takes time and can result in uncertainty.

The Final Agreement avoids this uncertainty by providing detailed rules to determine which law prevails in the event of a conflict or inconsistency between Nisga'a law and federal or provincial law. The Nisga'a cannot displace the law-making authority of Canada or British Columbia. Canada and British Columbia continue to make laws, while the Nisga'a have concurrent jurisdiction in defined areas, usually areas in which the federal or provincial governments are unlikely to pass laws in any event.

For example, the Nisga'a may make laws in respect of Nisga'a citizenship, but conferring Nisga'a citizenship on a person does not counter or deny that person's rights of entry into Canada, Canadian citizenship, the right to be registered as an Indian under the Indian Act, or any rights or benefits under the Act. Nor does it impose any obligation on Canada or British Columbia to provide rights or benefits. Similarly, the Nisga'a may make laws to preserve, promote, and develop Nisga'a culture and language; they may pass laws with respect to Nisga'a cultural symbols and practices and the teaching of the Nisga'a language. But that does not include the power to make laws in respect of intellectual property, the official languages of Canada, or activities outside Nisga'a lands.

The Nisga'a may make laws establishing and operating a land titles system for Nisga'a lands, for the designation of Nisga'a lands as Nisga'a private or Nisga'a village lands, and laws with respect to expropriations for public purposes and public works. They cannot, however, carry out expropriations in certain categories of lands specified in the Final Agreement. These include lands for which replacement tenures were provided by the Final Agreement, lands or interests expropriated by Canada under the Final Agreement, and rights of way acquired by British Columbia or a public utility.

The Nisga'a have the authority to make laws with respect to health services, but these laws would prevail only to the extent that they govern the organization and structure of the delivery of health services on Nisga'a lands; otherwise, federal and provincial laws prevail. In the same manner, the Nisga'a can make laws in respect of the authorization or licensing of aboriginal healers on Nisga'a lands, but that does not include the authority to regulate products or substances that are regulated by the federal or provincial governments. Such laws must also consider issues of competence, ethics, and quality of practice that are reasonably required to protect the public.

Not to belabour the point, the Nisga'a can make laws regarding child and family services on Nisga'a lands, provided those laws include standards that are comparable to provincial standards. However, in the event of an emergency in which a child on Nisga'a lands is at risk, the Province may act to protect that child. Laws of general application regarding the reporting of child abuse continue to apply on Nisga'a lands.

As should be obvious from these few examples, the Nisga'a, unlike our constitutionally established federal and provincial governments, do not receive under the treaty any one area of exclusive law-making authority. Indeed, there are many areas in which the Nisga'a have no law-making authority whatever. Unless it is specifically provided for in the Final Agreement, it does not exist.

It has been said that the Final Agreement changes or amends the Constitution of Canada. The Final Agreement itself explicitly states that this is not so. In fact, section 35 of the Constitution Act, 1982, explicitly contemplates the negotiation of new treaties. As Patrick Macklem, Associate Professor of Law at the University of Toronto, wrote in *The Globe and Mail*:

> Your recent editorial asserting that the Nisga'a treaty amends the Constitution of Canada is spectacularly wrong. The Constitution does not require a constitutional amendment in order to negotiate, ratify or implement the Nisga'a Treaty . . . A constitutional amendment is only necessary when a government wants to do something that the Constitution prohibits. The Constitution authorizes governments to negotiate treaties that establish constitutionally protected rights.[1]

And as Peter Hogg, Dean of Osgoode Hall Law School, wrote to the Deputy Attorney General of British Columbia:

> It is true that once the Nisga'a treaty has come into effect it will be constitutionally protected by s.35 of the *Constitution Act, 1982* which recognizes and affirms "aboriginal and treaty rights." But this occurs automatically by virtue of s.35. Section 35 is not amended when a treaty is entered into. Nor does the treaty become part of the Constitution of Canada.[2]

Despite such authoritative opinions, the issue is even now before the courts in an action launched by Gordon Campbell, Leader of the Opposition in the British Columbia Legislature. It is fair to say, however, that it has always been the position of the Canadian government that the provisions of the Nisga'a Final Agreement do not constitute a change to the Constitution; rather, they fall within the scope of section 35. A number of legal experts in addition to Professors Macklem and Hogg have spoken out on the matter and agree with Canada's position, notably Doug Saunders from the University of British Columbia, Brad Morse from the University of Ottawa, Patrick Monahan, Bruce Ryder, and Kent McNeil of Osgoode Law School, and Joel Bakan, Professor of Constitutional Law at UBC. Professor Bakan referred to the Constitution as "a living tree":

One of the great virtues of our constitutional system is its capacity to accommodate change in the wider society without formal constitutional amendment. That is why the Constitution is often called a living tree. This Nisga'a agreement will be one more branch on that living tree.[3]

It has been said that the Final Agreement does not address the rights of those who are not Nisga'a citizens, specifically with respect to Nisga'a elections, in which they do not have the right to vote. This accusation ignores the fact that the rights of all residents on Nisga'a lands are protected by the Charter of Rights and Freedoms. Moreover, the Final Agreement requires that the views and concerns of non-Nisga'a living on Nisga'a lands be given full and fair consideration in any matter that might significantly and directly affect them. They also have access to administrative appeal processes, and ultimately judicial review by the courts.

In the final analysis, though, it must be stated that the Nisga'a Final Agreement is for the Nisga'a. It defines Nisga'a rights and responsibilities as they enter into full partnership in the Canadian confederation. In the vast majority of cases, the law-making authority of the Nisga'a government will apply only to Nisga'a citizens living on Nisga'a land.

As to the cry of "taxation without representation," one can only wonder how a rallying cry from a revolution south of the border has gained such favour in Canada 224 years later. In any case, it is inaccurate in terms of the provisions of the Final Agreement. The Nisga'a have no right to tax persons who are not Nisga'a.

The spectre of race-based government was discussed in the previous chapter. It remains only to say that Canada's policy of self-government is an attempt to recognize and honour the fact that aboriginal peoples were organized in self-governing communities long before the arrival of Europeans. On a purely practical level, the Nisga'a have lived under the provisions of the Indian Act for generations; since, under the Final Agreement, the Act no longer applies, it was necessary that another form of government be created. The Final Agreement successfully establishes a form of self-government within the constitutional structure of Canada. To quote Patrick Macklem again:

Nor does the treaty's significance lie in what you incorrectly and irresponsibly describe as a racially based form of self-government. Aboriginal self-government is not based on race; it is based on domestic and international legal recognition that aboriginal nations were self-governing societies prior to European contact and that their law-making authority has not been extinguished by the emergence of Canada as a Nation-State.[4]

Another allegation related to self-government is that it will result in "gated communities." More likely, the opposite will occur. Indian reserves in Canada are basically federal enclaves located within a province. Most bands remain governed by the Indian Act, and their ability to deal with their lands and assets is severely limited by the Act. Provincial laws apply only to the extent defined in section 88 of the Act. The Final Agreement, on the other hand, brings Nisga'a lands into provincial jurisdiction, where provincial laws apply. Nisga'a title is similar to the title held by other private land holders, who also make their own decisions about their lands and assets. In short, the Final Agreement gives the Nisga'a far more in common with their immediate neighbours and other British Columbians than the Indian Act ever could. Add to this that the Nisga'a will soon enough be able to whine along with the rest of us about the exorbitant rates of tax imposed by the provincial and federal governments. Shared circumstances—especially shared grievances—generally lead to more openness among people.

There have been calls for a referendum, strident, insistent—and somewhat belated. Successive federal governments for more than twenty years have supported a policy of resolving the outstanding land claims of aboriginal peoples through negotiation. These governments, and every provincial government that came to power in the same period, were given mandates by the electorate to carry out their policy initiatives. The basic terms of the Final Agreement had been in the public domain for at least two and a half years before the ratification process began. Both federal and provincial elections were held in the period between the Agreement in Principle and the Final Agreement. Citizens of Canada and British Columbia have made their voices heard through their duly elected legislative and parliamentary representatives. No referendum was called for when Canada entered the treaty process in the 1970s. Referenda were not required for other social initiatives such as Medicare and the Old Age Pension, both of which cost far more than the

Nisga'a treaty ever will. In fact, Canada has held only three referenda in the nation's history: one on prohibition in 1898, one on conscription in 1942, and one on the Charlottetown Accord in 1992—and there is some scholarly argument as to whether these were real referenda or merely plebiscites. As I said to Ann Petrie on a CBC television broadcast, "Governments in Canada have negotiated thirteen modern day treaties in the last twenty-three years without a referendum, so why should the rule suddenly change in British Columbia?"[5] To quote Peter Hogg again:

> In my opinion, it would be undesirable to hold a referendum every time a treaty is entered into with aboriginal people. These treaties are intended to provide clarity and certainty to aboriginal rights that have been held by aboriginal people since before European settlement. The treaties are long, complicated documents reflecting years of negotiation and much compromise on both sides. It would be very difficult to communicate all the issues in a balanced way in a province-wide referendum campaign.[6]

Dean Hogg's observations raise the further question of who would vote in such a referendum. Would it be just the people of British Columbia, or would it be Canada-wide? And what would people vote on, the document as a whole, or would it be chapter by chapter, clause by clause? As with any negotiated agreement, some provisions will enjoy more public support than will others. Would the majority vote in favour of a treaty because it brings an end to tax-exempt status for First Nations citizens, or would the majority vote against a treaty because it grants a measure of self-government to those same citizens? It is the same treaty, after all, the same record of negotiation and compromise. If the Final Agreement were rejected in a referendum, what then? Are we back at square one, or do we return to the table and try to renegotiate a more acceptable arrangement to the public without knowing what chapters, provisions, or clauses the public objected to in the first place? The mind boggles at the bureaucratic morass such a situation would precipitate. In any case, as a point of political and moral principle, minority rights should not be decided by polling the majority.

It has been argued, of course, that the Nisga'a got a referendum, so why not the rest of us? It is simply because aboriginal rights are held by the collectivity of people. To modify or define those rights requires the consent of the collective. The best evidence that that consent has been obtained would be to have everyone sign the treaty. Bureaucrats might rub their hands in anticipation of the paperwork this would produce, but in the practical world it is not a reasonable option. The best alternative is the democratic one: a vote, with a high enough majority required for approval that, if the Agreement were challenged, the courts would find that it had been approved by a sufficiently high percentage of registered voters that the result fairly represented the will of the majority.

To my mind, though, the most cogent argument against a province- or nation-wide referendum is that the Nisga'a Final Agreement did not provide for one. The document set out how each of the parties would ratify the Agreement. To later call for a referendum would be a significant and unilateral change to the Agreement itself. It would be an act of bad faith.

Of course, bad faith is no stranger to politics. But it never ceases to amaze me that any indiscretion or evidence of human frailty on the part of a First Nations leader causes people in the wider society to question the advisability of aboriginal self-government in general and the competence of band councils in particular. Yet we don't apply the same standards to municipal, provincial, or federal governments. In 1999 the Minister of Education for Alberta disbanded a school board because it was dysfunctional. In British Columbia, three recent premiers have been forced to resign because of perceived scandals in their administrations. In Saskatchewan a whole gang of MLAs, including several cabinet ministers, have been convicted of fraud. A senator in Ottawa was recently convicted of influence peddling.

The record is no better in the private sector. I have had the unfortunate experience of sitting on the board of a non-profit organization whose senior executive officer was convicted of theft to the tune of hundreds of thousands of dollars—this despite a board that included business leaders, lawyers, and other professionals, despite financial statements regularly reviewed by audit committees and the board. As a lawyer I have had clients, both large and small, who have been the victims of internal fraud. It happens. This is not to excuse the occasional and much-publicized indiscretions of First Nations leaders and band governments. All organizations must be vigilant against attacks on their integrity, whatever the source. But sweeping generalizations based on isolated incidents should not be the basis on which to judge a society or its concepts of governance.

On the other side of the coin, we seem to expect a degree of unanimity among First Nations that we demand from no other group of citizens. Any dissent among First Nations in Canada has the immediate effect of calling whole approaches to issues into question. Yet, in the general population, we can debate the Free Trade Agreement, the Charlottetown Accord, or any other issue, and dissent is accepted. Indeed, it is expected. In federal or provincial elections we will tolerate without question three, four, even five or more political parties. Governments routinely get elected with far less than 50 percent of the popular vote. Treaties such as the Nisga'a Final Agreement and the Nunavut Land Claim Agreement set the bar for acceptance far higher than any mandate any other government in Canada is expected to achieve. Why must a different standard be applied against First Nations governments? I can't help thinking of Charlotte Whitton's famous remark: "Whatever women do they must do twice as well as men to be thought half as good. Luckily, this is not difficult."[7]

For those concerned about accountability and democratic processes, the Nisga'a Final Agreement has built-in safeguards comparable to any governmental or organizational constitution in Canada. Subject to restrictions of age and residency, all Nisga'a citizens are eligible to vote and hold office. Under the Agreement, the Nisga'a government must be democratically and financially accountable to its citizens. It must hold elections at least every five years. It must establish financial administration systems and conflict-of-interest rules comparable to standards generally acceptable for governments in Canada. And it must adhere to the General Provision that explicitly states that the Charter of Rights and Freedoms applies to the Nisga'a government and all Nisga'a citizens.

Overlaps are often considered obstacles to the successful resolution of land claims. As we have seen, an overlap is a geographical area used or occupied by two or more aboriginal groups. Animals, birds, and fish migrate. Similarly, plants and trees generally do not limit their existence to politically defined geographical areas. Neither did early hunting and gathering societies. Owing to the diverse geography of British Columbia, the differing cultural backgrounds of its earliest human inhabitants, and the availability of certain species of fish and wildlife, First Nations territories tended to vary in size and location. Often more than one aboriginal group used the same areas, either simultaneously or at different times throughout the year. Given the large number of First Nations in British Columbia and the importance of salmon to the Native economy, overlapping territories are extremely common. When the British Columbia Treaty Commission was launched and First Nations began to identify their traditional territories, the resultant claims eventually added up to 125 percent of the province. Anyone cognizant of even some of the information in this paragraph could easily see why. Nonetheless, detractors of the process immediately and vociferously jumped to the conclusion that there would never be enough land to satisfy all the demands. This, I am convinced, was a deliberate failure to recognize both the nature of the claims and the history of treaty making in Canada. At the end of the day, the difference between claimed territories and settlement lands is enormous. Nisga'a lands, for example, comprise only 8 percent of the area originally claimed.

Over time, the Nisga'a have entered into overlap agreements with the Tsimshian and the Tahltan. No agreements have yet been reached with the Gitanyow and the Gitksan, and in fact the Gitanyow have launched a legal challenge to the treaty. This is worrisome, to a degree, but there is nothing in the Final Agreement that would preclude other First Nations from negotiating harvesting or management rights in the Nass area. As the General Provisions chapter states, "Nothing in this Agreement affects, recognizes or provides any rights under Section 35 of the *Constitution Act, 1982* for any aboriginal people other than the Nisga'a Nation." In fact, in fish and wildlife management, there is no exclusive right or benefit accruing to the Nisga'a. Similarly, the water provisions are not exclusive. The access provisions in the Final Agreement stipulate that the Nisga'a will allow reasonable access to others for temporary non-commercial and recreational uses. Public rights of access on navigable waters within Nisga'a lands are not affected by the treaty. In short, there is every reason to believe that other rights that might be found to exist can be accommodated, the Final Agreement notwithstanding. Those who argue to the contrary are ignoring the express provisions of the Final Agreement.

The financial component of the treaty is obviously of critical importance not only to the functioning of its provisions "on the ground," so to speak, but in the public perception. The goal of the parties in negotiation and in the working groups and committees was to break the cycle of dependency between First Nations and governments, and, in the longer term, through economic growth and own source revenues to reduce Nisga'a reliance on fiscal transfers.

Some who have reviewed the Final Agreement say the sum of money to be transferred is too large. Others say it is insufficient. Some recommend more land and less cash, others more cash and less land. Despite the explicit provisions in the Final Agreement, its total cost to governments remains a matter of some debate. This is partly due to the wilful ignorance of those who oppose treaties on principle and the misinformation being spread by the more radical among them, but it is also partly due to a 1999 study by R. M. Richardson and Associates, *A Comparative Analysis of the Nisga'a Treaty*,[8] which suggests that the total costs could exceed $1.3 billion. As we shall see, this comparative analysis demands a somewhat more careful analysis.

As specified in the treaty, the Nisga'a will receive a capital transfer payment of $190 million, to be paid over fifteen years. A fund to enhance Nisga'a participation in the commercial fishing industry through the purchase of vessels and licences accounts for a further $11.5 million. Transition, training, and other costs associated with such things as the construction of a government building, community capital costs, forestry transition, land management, communications, fish studies, the preparation of laws and the replication of cultural artifacts amount to $40.4 million, to be paid out over five years. Added to this is British Columbia's estimate of payments to the Nisga'a for trees harvested during the five-year forest transition period, which comes to another $4.4 million. Thus, the total one-time payments to the Nisga'a amount to some $246.3 million—a sum that falls somewhat short of $1.3 billion.

But there are other, related costs to Canada and British Columbia. The latter, for example, has agreed to pave the Nisga'a highway, at a cost of $41 million. Other items on the provincial ledger include land values of $106 million and costs to forestry revenue of $36 million. On the federal side of the ledger, Canada's contribution to the Lisims Fisheries Conservation Trust to support fish science amounts to $10 million (the Nisga'a will also contribute $3 million to the Trust). Surveys of land parcels cost the federal government $3.1 million. The purchase of third-party interests are estimated at $30 million. In addition, Canada will pay $3 million to British Columbia in adjustment assistance.

Adding all these figures, the one-time costs to government amount to some $475.4 million—still considerably short of the 1.3 billion projected by Richardson and Associates. But even this is deceptive, for not all of that money goes to the Nisga'a. The costs of surveys, third-party interests, the transition fund, and the Nisga'a highway will in large part be paid to others.

The ascribed costs of the lands is not really money out of the government's pocket. And the money for the Trust will benefit more than the Nisga'a.

So these are the one-time costs of the Final Agreement. There are, in addition, ongoing costs of $32.1 million annually during the five years of the Fiscal Financing Agreement. This represents the costs of Nisga'a government services such as education, social programs, health, land and resource management, and housing, to name a few. The amount represents an approximate 10 percent increase in monies presently provided to the Nisga'a, recognizing that they will have increased costs related to the management and administration of these programs. On the other hand, the overall cost of government should diminish with the transition of management and administration.

It is also important to keep in mind that, eight years after the effective date of the treaty, the Nisga'a will be paying sales and other transaction taxes, and after twelve years they will be paying income tax. In time, as well, the Own Source Revenue Agreement will offset these transfers. Tax payments and own source revenues should reduce government transfers by approximately 25 percent in fifteen years. Other residents of the region will also enjoy spin-off benefits as a result of greater economic activity. This, too, will result in further revenues for government. And, while difficult to quantify, one might reasonably expect the cost of social programs, health services, and similar costs to go down as economic and social changes improve the lifestyle of the Nisga'a.

So how do firms like R. M. Richardson and Associates escalate the value of the Final Agreement so dramatically? Simply by overstating the costs, misinterpreting the Agreement, and falling prey to methodological errors. For example, the Richardson report's valuation of the forests is based on "liquidation value"—as if all the trees will be cut down at once. In British Columbia—indeed, everywhere in Canada—entire forests are not liquidated. They are cut sustainably. In the real world, the basis of the report's estimate would be unlawful, environmentally disastrous, and economically foolish. The error: $162 million. The report also assumes that the Crown's ability to develop lands in the Nass Wildlife Area is severely limited by the Final Agreement. But the Nisga'a do not get a veto. The error: $208 million. With respect to the fishery, the report is based first on a value ascribed by the Nisga'a to their cumulative losses from 1878 to 1992. It also wrongly assumes that the Nisga'a catch will disappear into some kind of vacuum, or a "gated homeland," and it fails to recognize that the Final Agreement brings the Nisga'a into the regional economy. The error: $100 million. These are only three examples, but they account for errors in the Richardson report amounting to $470 million. As other errors are uncovered, the amount of the discrepancy grows.

Critics have also said that the Final Agreement gives the Nisga'a government jurisdiction over matrimonial property law and the division of property on the break-up of marriage. This is simply not so. The Indian Act is silent on the division of matrimonial property. The case of *Derrickson v. Derrickson*[9] held that provincial laws regarding the division of real property in the event of marriage breakdown do not apply on Indian reserves. As the Nisga'a Indian Reserves will cease to be reserves on the effective date of the treaty, the provincial Family Relations Act will apply. The law-making authority of the Nisga'a government is exhaustively set out in the Final Agreement; it does not include law-making authority over matrimonial property.

Other critics raise concerns that the Nisga'a have been given the authority to make laws respecting labour relations. Again, this is not the case. While other bands in British Columbia and Saskatchewan have asserted aboriginal rights over labour relations, the Final Agreement provides that both federal and provincial labour laws continue to apply. There is no law-making authority related to this field of jurisdiction in the treaty. The Nisga'a may make representations to regulatory bodies, but such representations must be made in accordance with the rules of that regulatory body and will not affect the regulatory body's ability to control its processes.

At the end of the day, the Nisga'a Final Agreement remains what it was meant to be: a document of compromise and negotiation, certainly, but also a just and reasonable settlement of age-old grievances, and the beginning of a new era in Canadian and aboriginal history.

Chapter Fourteen

....

WHILE THE DEBATE WAS BUBBLING, and occasionally boiling over, in Canada, the significance of the Nisga'a treaty was not lost on the rest of the world. The day after the initialling ceremony at New Aiyansh, *The New York Times* featured a front-page story on the "landmark treaty" that was "seen as a model for dozens of other Indian Bands." The article compared the Nisga'a to the First Nations of the United States, and pointed out that initiatives to grant indigenous peoples greater autonomy or self-government have tended to lead to greater economic prosperity for them. The story also focused on some of the opposition to the Final Agreement.[1] Other major U.S. papers covered the initialling ceremony, including the *Baltimore Sun*, the Albany *Times-Union*, the Seattle *Post-Intelligence*, and the *Los Angeles Times*. Many noted that the United States Consul-General, Jay Bruns, had attended.

In Sweden, both newspapers and television carried some coverage of the initialling ceremony, while in the United Kingdom, two British dailies ran stories plus pictures. BBC World Television featured stories throughout the day.

Later that week, *The Economist* magazine made mention of the treaty in the "Politics This Week" feature, and on page thirty-four it carried a thoughtful story discussing aboriginal issues in general and the Nisga'a treaty in particular. The story also touched on opposition to the treaty, but closed with the comment, "maybe they [British Columbians] just want to end the long dispute and move on."[2] In the same period, I was interviewed by a reporter for the *Manchester Guardian*, which was doing a feature article.

Christian Jaekl, Ottawa correspondent for *Neue Zurcher Zertung*, a Zurich newspaper, told me that there was great interest in the Nisga'a Final Agreement not only in Switzerland, but in Germany and Austria as well. The

Asahi Shinbum, Japan's pre-eminent newspaper, carried a story on the treaty, as did media in South America, Australia, and New Zealand, where governments are facing similar issues.

On November 2, 1998, the federal negotiating team met with the Right Honourable Douglas Graham, Minister of Justice for New Zealand, to review the Final Agreement and answer questions on the Canadian approach to treaty making. Minister Graham was accompanied by five officials from the New Zealand government, including Ross Philipson, Director of the Office of Treaty Settlements. We were surprised at the extent of the Minister's knowledge of Canadian jurisdictions. Handling most of the discussion himself, he made frequent and specific references to Canadian legal decisions and how they applied. Following the meeting, he confided that Canada was somewhat ahead of New Zealand in its approach to aboriginal land claims. Citing our policy of self-government, he said that Canada appeared to be more proactive, whereas New Zealand tended to be reactive to particular situations.

On the same day, David MacLean, Chair of CN, and Brian Smith, Chair of BC Hydro, both advocates for the treaty, hosted a luncheon of business leaders in Vancouver. The keynote speaker was Gilbert Grosvenor, Chair of the National Geographic Society in Washington, DC. Mr. Grosvenor stressed the importance of building new relationships with and between peoples of different nationalities and cultures, including aboriginal peoples. He heard Canadian leaders talk about the importance of the Nisga'a treaty, and expressed an interest in featuring the Nisga'a in an upcoming issue of the Society's magazine.

On November 4 the federal negotiators met with François Garde of the French Secretariat of State *À L'Outre-Mer.* The French had expressed interest in the Final Agreement, as they had a number of colonies, particularly in the South Pacific, where aboriginal issues were gaining importance.

Also in November, Joe Gosnell undertook a ten-day speaking tour of Europe and the United Kingdom. In the course of the tour, he spoke to academics, government officials, business leaders, and the media in Bonn, Vienna, The Hague, London, and Cambridge. The previous year he had addressed world leaders at the Asia Pacific Economic Conference in Vancouver. The following year he attended an international conference on federalism in Mont Tremblant, Quebec. That conference, no doubt to the annoyance of the secessionist government in Quebec, was attended by a number of world federalist leaders, including Prime Minister Jean Chrétien, United States President Bill Clinton, and Mexican President Ernesto Zedillo. Chief Gosnell participated in a number of round-table discussions involving federalism and the role of aboriginal peoples in the federalist state.

In addition to the media attention, and no doubt partly because of it, DIAND was inundated with requests for information on the treaty from academics, journalists, and government officials in countries around the world.

In March 1999, while in New York to brief a number of foreign journalists on the creation of Nunavut and the Nunavut Final Agreement, I met with three members of the editorial board of the *Wall Street Journal.* During our interview, the discussion came round to the Nisga'a Final Agreement. I confess I was surprised, first by their awareness of the treaty, and then by the depth of their knowledge of many of the issues, particularly the issue of collective rather than individual rights. The Nisga'a Final Agreement also came up during a briefing session with four Japanese papers that included several German, Australian, and American journalists as well. I also discussed it briefly during an interview on BBC television's *World Business News.* I could not help but wish, during my stay in New York, that some of our Canadian politicians had been as well informed on the issues as many of the foreign journalists I met.

Ratification was now in Canada's court. For reasons that continue to escape me, both the Nisga'a and Premier Clark, as well as various editorial writers[3] were expressing uncertainty about Canada's commitment to ratify the treaty—this after twenty-two years at the negotiating table, and after the negotiation and ratification of thirteen modern treaties since the 1970s. Some even questioned the Prime Minister's commitment to the process, overlooking the fact that it was Jean Chrétien, as Indian Affairs Minister, who was responsible for bringing Canada to the negotiating table, and that it was his policy that had started modern-day treaty making. There was never any doubt in my mind that Canada would ratify the treaty. And indeed, Minister Jane Stewart had little trouble steering the Final Agreement through Cabinet, or in getting Cabinet's authorization to sign it. At the same time, Cabinet authorized the drafting of the settlement legislation that would allow the document to move to Parliament.

From November 4 to 6, 1998, Minister Stewart visited Terrace, Prince George, and Kelowna, where she met with representatives from local governments, the business sector, the resource industry, concerned citizens, students, and others to discuss the Final Agreement. She appeared on open-line shows and was widely interviewed by the local media. That same month her Parliamentary Secretary, David Iftody, MP for Provencher, made the first of several trips to British Columbia in connection with the Final Agreement. Later in the month, shortly before the provincial legislature was recalled to ratify the Nisga'a Final Agreement, Minister Stewart was again in British Columbia. Her visit this time included a breakfast meeting with elected officials and business leaders in Vancouver and Victoria, an appearance on *The Bill Good Show*, and meetings with the Laurier Institute and the Treaty Negotiation Advisory Committee.

On March 3, 1999, the negotiating team briefed the Liberal Parliamentary Research Group and members of the Parliamentary Staff. A separate briefing was held with representatives of the policy staff of the Honourable Ralph Goodale, Minister of Natural Resources. Later that evening Minister Stewart hosted a dinner for several MPs and senators to discuss strategy and building support for the Final Agreement. As Chief Federal Negotiator, I attended most of these functions, though not for my conversational skills. I often felt like a frequent-access subsystem on a computer disc, recalling the same data over and over in an infinite loop of variable sequence and order.

On March 22, a month before Glen Clark's government finally invoked closure on Bill 51 in British Columbia, *The Globe and Mail* reported that Canada was debating the wisdom of moving forward with its settlement legislation.[4] The possibility that Canada might move on the treaty before it had been ratified by the province brought a predictable response from Reform MP Mike Scott. "It is an insult to British Columbians," he declared in the *Terrace Standard*, "to have Ottawa planning on debating the Nisga'a Treaty in the House of Commons before it has been democratically ratified in British Columbia."[5]

The Reform Party had threatened to slow down business in the House of Commons if the Bill was introduced before it had been passed in the British Columbia Legislature. Reform House Leader Randy White vowed that there would be no peace in Parliament if the government tried to move ahead on the issue. Meanwhile, the summer recess was approaching, and time was running out on the parliamentary calendar.

On April 16, 1999, Minister Stewart signed the Sechelt Agreement in Principle on behalf of the federal government. I had been appointed Chief Federal Negotiator with the Sechelt Indian Band in September 1998, and regarded the minister's signature as a continuing demonstration of Canada's commitment to the treaty process.

On April 23, the day after Bill 51 was passed in the British Columbia Legislature, David Iftody reaffirmed Canada's commitment. Both the Prime Minister and the Minister, he indicated, had made it clear that Canada would be living up to its commitments. But on April 29, I was asked to phone Joe Gosnell. I had to advise him of the government's decision to introduce the Nisga'a ratification legislation in the fall owing to a lack of parliamentary time for a full debate before the summer recess. But Minister Stewart was anxious to have the Final Agreement signed regardless.

On May 4, 1999, the Nisga'a leadership, John Watson, Jim Barkwell, Peter Baird, Joseph Whiteside, and Don Durell, Manager of Administration for DIAND in Vancouver, and I assembled in the lobby of the Chateau Laurier Hotel in Ottawa. At the appointed hour, we marched up the street to the Parliament Buildings; Chief Gosnell carried the enormous bound document under his arm. I walked beside him. As we ascended Parliament Hill, he spoke about what a historic day it was for his people, a day he had often doubted would ever arrive. A treaty signed by all parties! Pointing to the red volume, he remarked on how much blood, sweat, tears, and compromise had gone into it. I was moved by his words, and proud that I had played some part in this day.

The signing ceremony took place in the Hall of Honour in the main corridor of the Parliament Buildings. A large representation from the British Columbia Liberal caucus were on hand, including the Honourable Herb Dhaliwal, the Honourable Hedy Fry, Sophia Leung, and Ted McWhinney. Parliamentary Secretary David Iftody was present, as well as Nancy Karatak-Lindell, Member of Parliament for Nunavut, and several other MPs. The Honourable David Anderson, then Minister of Fisheries and Oceans and the political Minister responsible for British Columbia, spoke words of welcome and introduction. Minister Stewart and Chief Gosnell also spoke.

Following the ceremony, David Iftody hosted a luncheon in the parliamentary restaurant, during which a host of people dropped by to offer congratulations. Prominent among these were the Honourable Anne McLellan, Minister of Justice, and Phil Fontaine, Chief of the Assembly of First Nations. Several MPs and representatives of British Columbia municipalities also dropped by.

After lunch, we attended Question Period in the House of Commons and watched as members of the Reform Party launched their first major assault against the treaty on the national stage. Much of what I heard that afternoon was spoken—shouted, rather—in obvious, if not deliberate, ignorance. I wondered how they could not know they were making fools of themselves. The treaty was replete with provisions and clauses that anyone with a modicum of intelligence could make an issue of. Instead, Her Majesty's Loyal Opposition was engaged in mouthing slogans at the nation's expense.

Later in the summer, on August 3, Bob Nault, MP for Kenora–Rainy River, was appointed the new Minister of DIAND, which meant another round of briefings to bring him up to speed, as he would be charged with the responsibility of steering the Nisga'a legislation through Parliament. Two days later the new Minister was being urged to introduce the Bill by MP Claude Bachand, Indian Affairs critic for the Bloc Québecois. M. Bachand had recently visited the Nass Valley and was greatly impressed at how the Nisga'a had prepared themselves to set up their own government.

On August 21, 1999, Jean Chrétien became the first prime minister in Canadian history to visit the Nass Valley. He was accompanied by his wife, Aline, their daughter France Desmarais, and her three children, Jacqueline, Phillipe, and Max, as well as Ministers David Anderson and Bob Nault. The Nisga'a could not have asked for a more meaningful expression of the federal government's commitment to the treaty.

"I want to tell every one of you," he said, "that the commitment of our government to the Final Agreement is unwavering."

"You don't have to say anything," Joe Gosnell replied, beaming. "Just your presence here indicates your support."

Later, during a media scrum, the Prime Minister reminded reporters that his party enjoyed a substantial majority in the House of Commons, and the Liberals were not the only ones supporting the bill. To me, he said, "You negotiated the treaty, now I am here to start implementing it!"

Ironically, this was the day Glen Clark resigned as Premier of British Columbia. I was saddened that he would not be there now that the Nisga'a Agreement was truly moving onto the national stage. For British Columbia, the negotiation and ratification of the treaty had been a major political event. For Canada, it was business as usual. Not that it wasn't exciting or a truly historic event, but the nation had been negotiating and ratifying treaties since the 1970s. This was one more event in the day-to-day business of the national government.

"Business as usual," for us, meant long hours travelling throughout British Columbia. Members of the federal negotiating team participated on panels, gave radio and television interviews, appeared on open-line shows, gave background briefings, constantly met with newspaper reporters, and frequently had to rebut their columns and editorials in Letters to the Editor. We spoke to the academic community, business leaders, and other citizens. When Norman Spector complained in *The Globe and Mail* about the lack of federal presence in the debate, stating that "even Federal Negotiator Tom Molloy refuses to be booked for one speech per week,"[6] Doreen Mullins responded in a Letter to the Editor:

This is an outrageous statement in light of the extraordinary lengths to which Mr. Molloy has gone to proactively represent the federal position at a multitude of speaking events all across this province. Mr. Molloy has been and continues to be available to explain the substance of the agreement wherever and whenever there is an opportunity. He has been involved in no fewer than 13 engagements in a 4 1/2-week span.[7]

The allegation, both erroneous and bizarre, was similar to previous rumours about the negotiating process, in which terms like "secrecy" and "back-room deals" figured prominently. We had to learn to ignore them, however false and sometimes painful they were.

The pace continued for some months, and was matched in Ottawa by the ongoing work to prepare for the introduction of the legislation. Government House Leader Don Boudria personally reviewed the draft legislation and Final Agreement. In September he announced that, in the new session of Parliament, the government would bring forward several major bills; he singled out the Nisga'a legislation as a priority. As House Leader, he would be responsible for the timing and strategy of introducing the legislation, the timing of the debate, and further strategy to take the bill through Parliament and the Parliamentary Standing Committee.

While Boudria was preparing for the return of Parliament, Minister Nault's office was responsible for overseeing the preparation of materials to support the passage of the legislation. The responsibility for passing the bill and the conduct of the debate in the House of Commons were now on his shoulders.

A tremendous amount of work goes on behind the scenes before the introduction of any piece of legislation. In this case, briefing documents in both official languages were prepared for all members of Parliament and senators, providing each with substantial information about the Final Agreement, the legislation, and the key issues raised by the Agreement. More exhaustive briefing materials were prepared for members of the Standing Committee on Aboriginal Affairs. As the treaty would be referred to the Standing Committee for hearings, a list of potential witnesses had also to be prepared.

Between speaking engagements and briefing sessions in British Columbia, members of the federal team and DIAND established an office in Ottawa to assist in briefing members of Parliament, the senate, and the media, and to prepare speeches and other materials that would be required from time to time. The Nisga'a did likewise.

In the midst of this activity, the issue of a referendum on the Nisga'a Final Agreement once again raised its head. In September the BC Fisheries Survival Coalition had written to 137 British Columbia municipalities, asking them to include a referendum question on their November 20, 1999, municipal ballots: "Do you support the Nisga'a Final Agreement as it stands today?" The request received short shrift. John Ranta, President of the Union of BC Municipalities, said simply, "There's nothing we can do about Nisga'a."[8]

During the week of October 4, the Nisga'a leadership were in Ottawa to begin lobbying for the passage of the legislation—Bill C-9, as it would be called. They met with MPs and officials from all political parties. Joe Gosnell, Greg Gauld, and I participated in a Library of Parliament seminar series for parliamentarians and staff, focusing on self-government generally and the Nisga'a self-government provisions specifically.

On October 12, 1999, the Thirty-Sixth Session of Parliament opened, its pomp and pageantry rivalling those of the Nisga'a. Speaking in the ornate Red Chamber of the Senate, recently sworn in Governor General Adrienne Clarkson promised that the government would introduce legislation to implement the Nisga'a Final Agreement.

Fostering good government and strong accountability in First Nations communities will increase investor confidence, support economic partnerships and improve living conditions. Land claim agreements, in particular, are essential to create certainty for Aboriginal people and their surrounding communities—providing the climate needed for partnerships, investments, and economic opportunities. Early in the new session of Parliament, the Government will introduce legislation to implement the historic agreement with the Nisga'a.

On the floor of the Senate Chamber, in full regalia, sat Chief Gosnell and Frank Calder.

On October 19 the government tabled a ways and means motion related to the proposed legislation. Once this motion was passed, the legislation could be introduced. The government gave every indication that it expected the Bill to pass quickly. The Reform Party, contrarily, indicated that it would use every means at its disposal to delay it.

On Thursday, October 22, Minister Nault introduced Bill C-9: An Act to give effect to the Nisga'a Final Agreement. Harry Nyce was present, representing the Nisga'a, and later spoke at a press conference with the Minister. Minister Dale Lovick and other officials from British Columbia were present in the gallery. When the bill was introduced, the Nisga'a negotiators received a standing ovation from all members in the House, except Reform. Later, Minister Nault made it clear that he intended aggressively to push through the bill, and threatened to cut off debate if the Reform Party became "nonsensical."

We will debate the facts, we will debate the Agreement, we will debate aboriginal rights if that's what people would like to do in this country. But we will not hold up people's lives and their future aspirations for political reasons, which I think this is all about![9]

He would not be proved wrong. On October 26, concerned about the misinformation being spread about the treaty by the Official Opposition, the Minister issued a document entitled "The Facts About the Nisga'a Treaty— Building Partnerships Through Negotiations." It began:

Over the summer, the Reform Party has published a document entitled "Top 10 Concerns with the Nisga'a Agreement." That document contains a number of allegations about the Nisga'a Treaty that are incorrect. In "The Facts About the Nisga'a Treaty" the Federal Government dispels the myths propagated by the Reform Party. It is only fair that Canadian citizens know the real facts. The document answers these 10 top myths which were continually being referred to in speeches and articles by the Reform members. It was a constant frustration for us to show them to be factually wrong only to have them continue to rely on their misstatements.[10]

On October 29, 1999, the Government House Leader gave notice of a motion to move time allocation to complete second reading of the Bill. Meanwhile, the Standing Committee on Aboriginal Affairs and Northern Development had met, and elected Sue Barnes, MP for London West, as chair. The opposition members of the Committee wanted it to be able to travel; this requires the unanimous consent of the Committee, and the government members objected. At the same time, dealing with other business, the Finance Committee wanted to travel to allow Finance Minister Paul Martin to appear before it to deliver his annual fiscal and economic update. The Reform members objected. A deal was cut: if the Finance Committee can travel, so can the Aboriginal Affairs Committee.

On November 1, the Liberals used their majority to invoke closure on preliminary debate on the treaty. The measure was approved 120 to 66, provoking Reform House Leader Randy White to declare, "This tells the people of British Columbia to go to hell!" The Reform Party took every opportunity thereafter to speak on the Nisga'a treaty, including during a debate on a bill pertaining to the international space station.[11]

On November 3, 1999, Minister Bob Nault, John Watson from the British Columbia office of DIAND, and I were the first witnesses the Committee heard. The hearing lasted three hours. Almost immediately, a controversy arose over the number and nature of the proposed witnesses. Opponents of the treaty complained that the list had been skewed in favour of its backers. In fact, the witnesses included people on all sides of the debate, but the controversy dogged its footsteps wherever it went, making Sue Barnes's job an exceptionally difficult one. Outside Ottawa, the committee held hearings in Smithers, Terrace, Prince George, Vancouver, and Victoria. No issues or arguments emerged that had not been heard before. But the myths and misinformation continued to be given credence in certain quarters, leading Nelson Leeson, who appeared on behalf of the Nisga'a Tribal Council, to say that there seemed to be two Nisga'a treaties: the real one, and the one everyone was debating.

In a press release dated November 16, 1999, Reform MPs, led by Preston Manning, demanded that the federal government hold a province-wide referendum.[12]

In Vancouver on November 18, former Premier Bill Vander Zalm led a demonstration outside the hotel where the Committee was meeting. He had not been allowed to appear, he claimed. It was after that that he wrote his piece in *The Globe and Mail* urging that the Nisga'a be "paid off."[13] I responded several days later, on November 22. "It is sad," I wrote, "that Mr. Vander Zalm, who as premier, initiated so much in bringing British Columbia to the negotiating table in 1990, could not take pride in the realization of this accomplishment."[14] He was soundly defeated in a provincial by-election the following month.

On November 23, during Question Period, the Prime Minister said:

Mr. Speaker, we have an obligation which was given to the people of Canada at the time that the British came to Canada. They decided that treaties would be signed with the First Nations who were here. This was an obligation that was given to us and it is our obligation to live up to the commitments that were made by the Government of England 200 years ago.

The Reform motion for a province-wide referendum was defeated 191 to 55 that same day.

On November 25 the Committee met in Ottawa and undertook a clause-by-clause study of the Bill. To everyone's surprise, there were only six amendments proposed, and none of them carried. The Bill was presented to Parliament without amendment.

On December 2, the Bill was debated throughout the day. Reform MPs attacked the Final Agreement on several fronts, including its treatment of the overlap issue, the constitutional protection given to aboriginal self-government, the fishery provisions, and the consultation and ratification process. While continuing to demand a province-wide referendum, they also raised a procedural point in an attempt to delay the debate. The Government House Leader indicated that he planned to resume the report stage of the debate on Monday, December 6. On Friday, December 10, the government tabled a notice of time allocation concerning the completion of the report stage and third reading of Bill C-9. At that point, the legislation had been before either the House or the Committee for 61.4 hours.

The Reform Party filed 348 amendments to the Bill, but Commons officials found that only 225 of them were in order. Overnight, another 300 or more appeared. In the end, the total number accepted reached 471. For a bill with only twenty-seven sections, seven of which were consequential amendments to other statutes, it seemed excessive. *The Globe and Mail* later reported, on January 30, 2000, that Reform House Leader Randy White had spent months coming up with the plan to fight the treaty, trying to block its passage at every step of the process and ultimately requiring Parliament to vote one by one on all 471 amendments, a process that required forty-two consecutive hours.

To give some sense of the depth of Reform's understanding of the treaty, the first amendment proposed "that Bill C-9 be amended by deleting the title" ("An Act to give effect to the Nisga'a Final Agreement"). Another proposed "that Bill C-9 be amended by replacing the title with the following, 'An Act to implement the Nisga'a Final Agreement.'" Yet another proposed "that Bill C-9 be amended by replacing the title with the following, 'An Act to give effect to the agreement between Her Majesty in Right of Canada, Her Majesty in Right of British Columbia and the Nisga'a Nation.'" Other amendments dealt with the placement of punctuation marks.

Deep stuff.

To conduct the vote, the Speaker of the House first read the amendment in English, then in French. Those in favour responded "Yea," those opposed said "Nay." The Speaker then declared the motion defeated, as it invariably was. But Reform always challenged the ruling, as was their right, and requested a recorded vote. Those in favour then rose, one by one, the clerk calling out each person's name twice. Those opposed then rose, one by one. The motion was once again declared to have been defeated. This occurred 471 times, a mindless exercise aimed not at improving the Bill but at obstructing its passage. Whole sections of the treaty might have been financed with what the Opposition squandered in terms of keeping Parliament open during that exhausting and pointless marathon.

Finally, on December 13, 1999, the bill received third and final reading as the last of the amendments failed. I spent the day in the government lobby, except for Question Period and the vote on the final amendment just before

12:00 noon. Don Boudria assured us that the bill could only be derailed now by an adjournment motion by a cabinet minister. Barring that extremely unlikely possibility, the vote would occur at 6:15 PM.

The Minister led off the debate at noon, followed by Mike Scott of Reform, Laura Davies of the NDP, Claude Bachand of the Bloc Québecois, and Gerald Keddy of the Progressive Conservatives; all but Scott supported the treaty. The rest of the day was taken up, largely and not surprisingly, by the Reform Party with motions, points of order, and other last-minute attempts to demonstrate their determination, if not their intelligence. One by one the government members who had been slated to speak were removed from the roster. In the end, only David Anderson got to speak, and that was to close the debate with seven or eight minutes to spare.

The bells rang promptly at 6:15. Just before 6:30, with the Prime Minister in the House, the Party whips approached the Speaker and the voting began. The Commons applauded the Committee members as each one rose, as well as the Minister, David Iftody, Jane Stewart, and the Prime Minister.

The Bill carried 217 to 48.

Following the vote, the House rose and applauded the Nisga'a and federal negotiating teams where we stood in the gallery. It was an emotional moment. The applause lasted for some time, and then they spontaneously broke into "O Canada." Reform refrained from applauding, then the Bloc refrained from singing. Reform stood for the national anthem, but they did not sing. A silly display of petulance, I later thought. But at the moment nothing could spoil the mood.

As we left the gallery there were handshakes and hugs. Everyone wanted to show their support. Especially meaningful for the Nisga'a was the presence of Phil Fontaine, Chief of the Assembly of First Nations, who had strongly criticized Reform's stance on the treaty, and the Dogrib negotiators from the Northwest Territories who happened to be in Ottawa for meetings with the federal government. After the vote Minister Nault, David Iftody, and Sue Barnes hosted a reception at which the Nisga'a were presented with the flag that had flown over the Parliament Buildings that day. It was a fitting gesture.

Joe Gosnell summed it up: "Let me repeat the score here today with respect to the motions that were voted upon by the House of Commons. Nisga'a: 471; Reform Party: zero."[15]

On December 14 the bill, under the sponsorship of Senator Jack Austin, went to the Senate for first reading beginning a long senate process.

Over the next few months, work continued among the three parties. Details and procedures needed to be in place to make the treaty come into existence, assuming it passed this final hurdle in the legislative process. A number of Orders-in-Council needed to be drafted and approved. The individuals to be appointed to the Joint Fisheries Management Committee, Wildlife Committee, Lisims Trust, Enrolment Appeal Board, Implementation Committee, and Tripartite Finance Committee had to be identified and approved. The Province and the Nisga'a had their own lists. The work never seemed to end. Joe Gosnell had over two thousand documents to execute, and they had to be prepared first. The Nisga'a needed to draft more than twenty pieces of legislation to be passed by their government on the effective date. They were consulting their own communities and governments as well as Canada and British Columbia. Tripartite and bilateral meetings continued to the very end as all the documents required to give effect to the countless provisions of the treaty were prepared, approved, executed, and delivered to the appropriate party.

On Thursday, January 20, 2000, Peter Baird and I met with Her Excellency the Governor General and members of her staff at Government House to review the treaty. I found her sensitive to the key issues, and supportive of the treaty process. Later, I spoke on the telephone with His Excellency John Ralston Saul.

On Tuesday, February 8, 2000, the Senate reconvened after the Christmas break. Senator Dan Hays, Deputy House Leader, tabled the Nisga'a Final Agreement, the Appendices, and the Tax Agreement. The Senate Committee on Aboriginal Peoples was reconstituted, and Senator Jack Austin of Vancouver was appointed chair. The responsibility of guiding the Bill through the whole Senate process thus fell to him, and he had to call on reserves of political skill to accomplish it. Our team met with him several times over the next few weeks to discuss issues as they arose in the Committee deliberations and debate. Several other Senators from both sides of the Upper House also requested briefings.

On February 16, Minister Nault, Andrew Beynon, and I testified before the Senate Standing Committee. We were the first witnesses to appear. The beginning of the Minister's presentation was interrupted by a fire alarm. It turned out to be false, but I hoped it did not augur things to come. In the end, we spent over three hours testifying. The minister agreed to appear again at the conclusion of the hearings, but hoped it would be with less fanfare. The Nisga'a appeared the following day.

The committee generally sat on Tuesday mornings and Wednesday evenings. The list of witnesses included many of the same people as had appeared before the House of Commons Committee. There was some talk of the committee travelling outside Ottawa, but it came to nothing.

The week of March 6 was a parliamentary recess, and no hearings were held. Owing to a lack of legislation to consider, the Senate decided that it would not meet the following week, either. Everyone but the Senators, it seemed, were becoming frustrated at the slowness of the process. The hearings, when they occurred at all, were conducted in a much more civilized manner than those of the House of Commons Committee, but they produced no new information. Things proceeded slowly, but smoothly.

The media, which had been largely ignoring the process, suddenly came to attention when a gang of new witnesses materialized. A group calling itself CANFREE—Canadians for Reconciliation, Equality, and Equity—had enlisted the support of former Supreme Court of Canada Judge Willard Estey, who questioned the constitutionality of the Nisga'a Final Agreement and recommended that the Senate refer the matter to the Supreme Court of Canada. The founders and directors of CANFREE remained largely unknown, as did their reasons for coming forward, unannounced and unanticipated, toward the end of the hearings.

John Weston, who also appeared on behalf of Mel Smith, represented the group. He accompanied Willard Estey during his presentation, and assisted Nisga'a dissident Mercy Thomas when she testified on behalf of herself and Frank Barton. CANFREE, it was revealed, were also assisting Thomas and Barton in their new legal challenge to the Treaty—a last-minute attempt to get an injunction to stop its passing—which failed in both the lower court of British Columbia and the Appeal Court.

During the course of the Senate hearings, attention focused mainly on five issues:

◆ how the Nisga'a Final Agreement operated within the Canadian legal context
◆ the matter of Nisga'a citizenship
◆ minority rights
◆ the fishery
◆ overlaps

Each of these issues was addressed by Minister Nault when he and I appeared again before the committee on March 24. The Minister stated, in part,

ON THE CONSTITUTION:

I would respectfully draw the attention of Honourable Senators to the many ways that the Nisga'a Final Agreement has been negotiated within the constitutional framework of Canada. The General Provisions chapter, paragraph 8 on page 17 of the English text, expressly states that the Nisga'a Final Agreement does not alter the Constitution.

This reflects our intentions that the Final Agreement should be interpreted in a manner consistent with the Constitution. The General Provisions chapter, paragraph 13, on page 18 also expressly confirms that federal and provincial laws apply to the Nisga'a, and to Nisga'a lands. Moreover, the Preamble of the Nisga'a Final Agreement Act states that the Constitution is the supreme law of Canada. It also restates that the Nisga'a Final Agreement does not alter the Constitution. This language in the Preamble can be used by the courts when interpreting the Nisga'a Final Agreement Act. Finally, consistent with the Nisga'a Final Agreement, the Nisga'a themselves have adopted an internal constitution which expressly states that their constitution is subject to the Constitution of Canada.

ON CITIZENSHIP:

Webster defines citizen as "an inhabitant of a city or town, especially one that is entitled to its privileges or franchises." The Nisga'a will no longer have Indian Act bands under the Final Agreement. Therefore, the concept of Nisga'a band membership will no longer apply. Having said that, the Nisga'a right to determine Nisga'a citizenship would be similar to the authority of the many Indian Act bands who currently control their membership. The defined term "Nisga'a citizen" will be used instead to identify those who have the rights set out in the Final Agreement.

ON MINORITY RIGHTS:

Senators, the treaty provides a practical arrangement to provide real protections for the minority population. Most Nisga'a laws will deal

212

with issues that only affect Nisga'a citizens (such as decisions on how to spend money obtained under the treaty). Consequently, the Treaty will ensure that those Nisga'a citizens have control over their government on these matters. At the same time, this is balanced with provisions to protect the political rights of non-Nisga'a on matters that affect them.

Not only are there rights of political participation for non-Nisga'a, but there is also an obligation on the Nisga'a to consult in respect of the activities of Nisga'a Public Institutions. Senators, this is a very substantial protection because the Treaty defines consultation as including a guarantee of a reasonable amount of time to present views on a proposal, and an obligation on the Nisga'a to provide a full and fair consideration of any views. This is the kind of protection that those people asked for and that is appropriate and fair.

ON FISH:

Some try to say that the Nisga'a Treaty creates exclusive fishery rights because only the Nisga'a have the rights to fish set out in the Treaty. Senators, it should hardly be surprising that the Nisga'a Treaty deals with Nisga'a rights—the rights of other Canadians are already found in the ordinary law. The Treaty was negotiated taking into account those rights of other Canadians, such as existing property rights, the protections of the Charter, the rights of other Aboriginal groups, and the fishing rights of other Canadians, including those non-Nisga'a commercial and recreational fisheries.

The Treaty does not deny or take away fishing rights from non-Nisga'a fishers. The Nisga'a will not have any property right to fish. The public right of navigation on the Nass River will continue.

AND ON OVERLAP:

We recognize that, sometimes, groups may find it difficult to reach agreement and to address such situations in a way that resolves them. As you know, over a number of years, attempts have been made to facilitate a resolution of the overlap issue between the Nisga'a and the Gitanyow. The federal government has arranged meetings between the parties and supported mediation.

Unfortunately, resolution has not yet been possible, but we remain optimistic that it is still achievable.

Let me be clear that the Federal Government is prepared to move forward in the absence of an overlap agreement if, and only if, the following criteria apply:

◆ the group that is ready to settle has negotiated with it neighbours in good faith

◆ measures taken to resolve the impasse have proven to be unsuccessful and

◆ the Treaty contains an explicit statement that it will not affect any aboriginal or Treaty rights of any other aboriginal group

The federal policy on overlaps recognizes that, in the face of unresolveable impasses on overlap issues, the only solution may be to negotiate a treaty with each group in turn, while respecting the rights of other affected aboriginal groups.[16]

On Tuesday, March 28, after hearing some thirty witnesses over a total of twenty-five hours of hearings, the committee concluded its review and reported back to the Senate, without amendment to the Act but with a single observation related to overlap. Senator Jack Austin, in moving the third reading of Bill C-9 to give effect to the Nisga'a Final Agreement on March 29, thoroughly reviewed the issues, and concluded:

My final comment in opening the third reading debate is to remind honourable senators that the Nisga'a Final Agreement is the product of many years of negotiations—negotiations that are complex because they had to meet the requirements of the Government of Canada, the Province of British Columbia, the Nisga'a themselves and, wherever possible, the other stakeholders in the province of British Columbia. It has taken many years to reach the conclusion that is before us now. We are the last legislative step in this process. As such, we have a particular responsibility for care. We have a particular responsibility, in my submission, to the Nisga'a people to treat their agreement with the Government of Canada and the Province of British Columbia with the utmost seriousness, with support, and with our endorsement.[17]

214

The final debate concluded, Senate Speaker Gil Molgat called for the vote at 3:00 P.M. on April 13, 2000. Three amendments were proposed; all failed. At 3:53 P.M. the legislation passed the Senate by a vote of 52-15, with 13 abstentions. In a rare occurrence, the Governor General personally attended the Senate Chamber to give Royal Assent to the legislation. The task is typically delegated to a justice of the Supreme Court. She later told me how delighted and honoured she had been to perform the task personally.

By telephone, the Nisga'a reported to us on the celebrations that were beginning in each of their communities. We could hear the church bells ringing in the background. In Kincolith, we were told, the chiefs had assembled the people and they were marching down the street waving Canadian flags—full citizens at last.

Chief Joe Gosnell, jubilant and triumphant, stood on the steps of the Senate Chamber, surrounded by his fellow Nisga'a and supporters from both houses of Parliament. He spoke with typical eloquence:

The Royal Assent of our Treaty signifies the end of the colonial era for the Nisga'a people. It is a great and historic day for all Canadians, and this achievement is a beacon of hope for colonized people in our own country and throughout the world. Today, the Nisga'a people become full-fledged Canadians as we step out from under the Indian Act—forever. Finally, after a struggle of more than 130 years, the government of this country clearly recognizes that the Nisga'a were a self-governing people since well before European contact. We remain self-governing today, and we are proud to say that this inherent right is now clearly recognized and protected in the Constitution of Canada.[18]

The Nisga'a Final Agreement took effect on May 11, 2000.

Appendix I: Dramatis Personae

....

THE THREE SENIOR PEOPLE IN BRITISH COLUMBIA involved in the Nisga'a treaty were John Watson, Doreen Mullins, and Lorne Bownsey. One could not ask for a better triumvirate to work with. The three worked well together, and I with them. Each of them brought complementary skills to their tasks. A great deal of credit must go to them for their contributions to getting the critical support of the Department and others.

In Ottawa they were complemented by the skills of Deputy Minister Scott Serson and later Shirley Serafini, Associate Deputy Ministers that included Shirley Serafini, followed by Gary Wouters and then Dennis Wallace, Assistant Deputy Minister John Sinclair and then Bill Austin, Director General Greg Gauld, Christine Cram, and Caroline Davis.

In Justice, Bill Elliot, then Claire Beckton, Ann McAllister, and Daniel Ricard and other Justice lawyers worked with their opposite numbers in Vancouver, which included, among others, Denis de Keruzec, Andrew Beynon, Maureen Parkes, Peggy Stone, and DIAND fish lawyers Hugh MacAulay and Cheryl Webb. Our legal guru on certainty was Fred Morris. Scott Cowan from Justice, our "dirt lawyer," was invaluable on the land issues. Joe Friday (not a policeman) was our expert on dispute resolution techniques, and Sarah Kelleher was our lawyer on specific claims. Legislative drafting lawyers included Doug Stoltz for the English legislative draft and Claude Bisaillon for the French draft.

Al Gould from the Department of Fisheries and Oceans worked tirelessly on all our fish issues with his other departmental representatives and lawyers.

On implementation, the experience of Barrie Robb, now DIAND Regional Director General for Alberta, and Liz Morin, who had both worked with me in the Nunavut implementation negotiation proved invaluable, together with Henry Drysteck, Ian Redmond and others, including Pat Yakura and Chris Lee, who will oversee the implementation of the treaty from the federal perspective.

Jay Kaufman, a former Deputy Minister of Finance in Ontario, Jim Apostle, and Bill Stipdunk, working with our fiscal arrangements and cost-sharing group, facilitated the fiscal and other financial issues and negotiations, particularly on the departure of Florence Roberge in December 1997.

Sylvain Dubois from Ottawa headed our large French translation team.

Our Public Information and Consultation Unit was headed by Peter Baird, a.k.a. "Wag the Dog," who could always be counted on to pull together press conferences and briefings on short notice, and chair them as well. His contacts are legendary; his ideas and organizational skills resulted in many a successful event. Joseph Whiteside's political experience was constantly being put to the test with the Regional Advisory Committees, sectorial groups, and the Treaty

Negotiation Advisory Committee. Lucie Zaharoff came on our team to assist with drafting Cabinet documents and the innumerable briefing notes and dockets required from day to day. She would later help Peter, Joseph, and Lyse Cantin turn out an endless number of speaking notes and speeches, as required by everyone.

The legislative team consisted of Pat Barlow from the Legislative Branch of DIAND, and Erin Gorman and Kevin Langlands from the Minister's Office, plus many others from the Department and the Minister's Office.

Don Durrell, Manager of Finance and Administration, and his crew effectively kept the machinery of government oiled, the "machinery of government" being phones, faxes, photocopiers, computers, and all the rest of the long list of physical facilities and requirements—including record-keeping and payment of accounts—necessary to keep our large team functioning.

Bill Zaharoff, who had worked with me on a number of tables prior to my joining the Nisga'a team, helped to facilitate some program issues on assuming the role of Director of Funding Services in the Regional Office.

And the long, long list of members of the chorus included other people over time from Indian and Northern Affairs in Vancouver and at Headquarters, Canadian Heritage, Canadian Museum of Civilization, Environment, Canadian Environmental Assessment Agency, Fisheries and Oceans, Finance, Foreign Affairs, Health Canada, Human Resources, Industry and Science, Justice, National Defence, Natural Resources, the Prime Minister's Office, the Privy Council Office, Public Works and Government Services, Transport, and Treasury Board, whose representatives would appear at the table as required.

One cannot overlook the important role of the ministers and members of their staffs, whose commitment made the entire process possible. Ron Irwin, Jane Stewart, and Bob Nault brought different skills and talents to solving the many difficult issues that culminated in the Nisga'a treaty. Minister Irwin steered the Agreement in Principle through Cabinet, obtained the mandate for us to conclude the negotiations, and began the process for a new approach to certainty. Minister Stewart concluded the certainty process in Cabinet, and arrived at an approach that was acceptable to the Nisga'a, to governments, and to third parties. She achieved the support of her Cabinet colleagues for the Nisga'a treaty and concluded the work on the legislation to eventually move the treaty to Parliament. Minister Nault rose to the challenge of being responsible for shepherding the legislation through Parliament in the face of the Reform Party's vigorous and vocal opposition. Both Minister Stewart and Minister Nault were continually monitoring the Nisga'a-Gitanyow overlap issues.

Senator Jack Austin rose to the same challenge when the legislation reached the Upper House.

The core provincial team included Jack Ebbels, a University of Saskatchewan law graduate who, since August 1991, was either the Chief Negotiator for the Province or the Deputy Minister of Aboriginal Affairs. He had been returned to the table by the Premier to "get the deed done," as he said, and because of his position could get the provincial government response in a timely fashion. Patrick O'Rourke, with years of previous experience, was extremely strong on provincial jurisdictions and authority at the table; he also hosted good Christmas parties. Trevor Proverbs succeeded Jack Ebbels as the Chief Negotiator when Jack became the Deputy Minister, and remained in that position when Jack returned to the table. The remainder of the core provincial team included Boris Tyzuk, a lawyer, and George Thom from the Treaty Advisory Committee. They, too, had a long cast of players, including Richard Inglis, John Cowell, and Marlyn Simpson.

I cannot overlook the important role of Nigel Wilford and his team. He and I have worked together since 1988, although not on the Nisga'a file; his efforts enabled me to remain in active negotiations with the Inuit of Northern Quebec on their offshore claims in northern Quebec and Labrador during this period.

Tara Hiebert, my secretary at MacPherson Leslie & Tyerman in Saskatoon, always managed to keep track of me and helped balance the work at two coasts with my law office in Saskatoon.

On the Nisga'a team, Nelson Leeson from Laxgalts'ap, where he had served as a councillor for twelve years, served as Executive Chairman. A former commercial fisherman like Joe Gosnell, he was a passionate voice for Nisga'a rights. Harry Nyce, Sr. was the Resources Negotiator. He is from Gitwinksihlkw, where he served seven years as Chief Councillor and five years as Band Manager. He, too, began as a commercial fisherman. Later he attended UBC and majored in political science. He was a strong proponent of Nisga'a culture and heritage. Edmond Wright, from the Gitlakdamix Band, was the Secretary Treasurer. His experience was primarily in the forestry sector, though he has been the Village of New Aiyansh Administrator since 1970. He put his financial and administrative experience to good use. The balance of the Nisga'a negotiating team was made up of members of the Band councils and other executive members ranging in total from fifteen to twenty people. The Nisga'a also engaged a number of legal counsel and consultants in the areas of fish, wildlife, forestry, fiscal issues, tax, mining, lands, land titles, highways, constitution, and dispute resolution. The advisors attended the negotiations on an as-needed basis.

The chief lawyer for the Nisga'a was Jim Aldridge, who had articled to Tom Berger. Jim brought to the final negotiations a life-long commitment to the Nisga'a treaty; if the Nisga'a had grown old at the negotiating table, so had Jim. He was hard nosed, tough, and extraordinarily knowledgeable about the most minute details of the Agreement in Principle and the provisions of the Final Agreement; he could recount the history of every word in every section. He could also get angry, but that would soon pass. For he has a highly refined sense of humour. He is a professional in every way, and always willing to look for a solution. There were not enough hours in a day, I'm sure, to satisfy him. Other key lawyers included Marcus Bartley, Bruce Campbell, and Ellen Gunn.

And of course, none of this would have begun had it not been for the courage, the vision, the compassion, and the sheer political will of Frank Calder and Joe Gosnell, to whom the people of Canada owe a debt that is now beginning to be realized.

The literary talent of Donald Ward breathed life into this story. The enthusiasm he brought to the task suggested to me that it was much more than just another assignment for him. An interesting and fun guy to work with.

Three people were instrumental in getting me started on this book and keeping me going: Ed Sebestyen, Bill Peterson, and Jayne Horachek.

Appendix II:
Nisga'a Final Agreement In Brief

....

PREAMBLE

The Final Agreement is intended to be the just and equitable settlement of the Nisga'a land question.

The Canadian courts have stated that reconciliation between Aboriginal and non-Aboriginal people is best achieved through negotiation and agreement, rather than through litigation and conflict. As such, the Parties intend the Final Agreement to establish a new relationship based on mutual sharing and recognition.

The Parties intend that the Final Agreement will provide certainty with respect to ownership and use of lands and resources, and the relationship of laws within the Nass area.

GENERAL PROVISIONS

The Nisga'a will continue to be an Aboriginal people under the *Constitution Act, 1982*.

The Nisga'a will continue to enjoy the same rights and benefits as other Canadian citizens.

Lands owned by the Nisga'a will no longer be reserve lands under the *Indian Act*.

The *Canadian Charter of Rights and Freedoms* will apply to the Nisga'a Government and its institutions.

Federal and provincial laws (such as the *Criminal Code of Canada*) will continue to apply to Nisga'a citizens and others on Nisga'a Lands.

The Treaty addresses the issue of certainty through a number of provisions. Key among these is a clause which provides that the Treaty is a full and final settlement of Nisga'a Aboriginal rights. Another provision clearly states that the Treaty exhaustively sets out the Nisga'a section 35 rights. There is also an agreement that the Nisga'a Aboriginal rights and title are modified and continue as set out in the Treaty. Finally, the Nisga'a agree to release any Aboriginal rights, including Aboriginal title, that are not set out in the Treaty or which are different in attributes or geographical extent from the Nisga'a section 35 rights set out in the Treaty.

The Final Agreement can only be amended with the consent of all three Parties. Canada would give consent to any proposed amendments by order of the Governor in Council, and British Columbia would do so by resolution of the Legislature.

The Aboriginal rights of other Aboriginal groups are protected by the Final Agreement. The Final Agreement directs the court to adjust any treaty rights under the Final Agreement, to the extent necessary, so that the Nisga'a treaty rights do not adversely affect any other First Nation's Aboriginal rights. The Treaty also provides for the negotiation of replacement rights in the event that Canada concludes another treaty which adversely affects Nisga'a treaty rights.

LANDS

The Nisga'a will own approximately 1,992 square kilometres of land in the lower Nass Valley. The land will be held in fee simple by the Nisga'a—the same kind of land ownership enjoyed by other landowners.

Nisga'a Lands will include approximately 1,930 square kilometres of transferred Crown land and 62 square kilometres of Indian reserves that will cease to be reserves on the effective date of the Treaty.

Nisga'a Lands will not include existing fee simple lands, or lands subject to agricultural leases and wood lot licences.

Mineral Resources
The Nisga'a will own all subsurface resources on the Nisga'a Lands.

Interests within Nisga'a Lands
Existing legal interests on Nisga'a Lands will continue or be re-issued on their current terms. The Nisga'a, as the owners of the Nisga'a Lands, will be able to set conditions on any new interests it grants in the future.

Fee Simple Lands Outside Nisga'a Lands
Land contained within 18 Indian reserves outside of the Nisga'a Lands, and a small amount of adjacent land, will become fee simple lands owned by the Nisga'a and subject to provincial laws. The Nisga'a will own the subsurface resources of these lands.

The Nisga'a will also own an additional 15 parcels of fee simple land, totaling approximately 2.5 square kilometres. Subsurface resources on these lands will continue to be owned by the province and will be under provincial jurisdiction.

Commercial Recreation Tenure
The Nisga'a will receive a commercial recreation tenure for guiding which will operate under provincial laws.

Heritage Sites and Key Geographic Features
Important cultural sites will be protected through heritage site designation.

Some key geographic features will be renamed with Nisga'a names.

Parks and Ecological Reserve
British Columbia's authority and responsibilities over the Nisga'a Memorial Lava Bed Park and Gingietl Creek Ecological Reserve will continue.

Nisga'a history and culture are, and will be promoted as, the primary cultural features of the Park.

Nisga'a citizens have the right to use the lands and resources within the Park and Ecological Reserve for traditional purposes.

Water Volumes
Existing water licences will remain in place.

British Columbia will establish a Nisga'a water reservation of 300,000 cubic decametres of water per year to meet domestic, industrial and agricultural purposes.

LAND TITLE

Nisga'a Lands will be owned by the Nisga'a. Any fee simple parcels within Nisga'a Lands that exist on the effective date will continue to be subject to the *Land Title Act* and the provincial land title system generally.

Individual parcels within Nisga'a Lands will initially be registered under a Nisga'a land title system and, following a transition period, may be registered under the provincial land title system.

FOREST RESOURCES

The Nisga'a will own all forest resources on Nisga'a Lands.

Existing licences will be in effect for a five year transition period to allow licensees to adjust their operations and will then be replaced by new licences. The licensees are required to meet certain obligations under the licences through the transition period and beyond, including silviculture obligations.

Following the transition period, the Nisga'a will manage forestry on Nisga'a Lands.

The Nisga'a Government will be able to implement forest management standards, provided that these meet or exceed provincial standards such as the Forest Practices Code.

Timber Processing
Provincial laws pertaining to the manufacture of timber products harvested on Crown lands will apply equally to timber harvested on Nisga'a Lands.

The Nisga'a will not establish a primary timber processing facility for 10 years after the effective date of the Treaty.

Forest Resources Outside Nisga'a Lands
The province agrees in principle to the Nisga'a purchase of forest tenure(s) with an aggregate allowable annual cut of up to 150,000 cubic metres. Any such acquisition would be subject to the Forest Act.

ACCESS

There will be reasonable public access to Nisga'a Public Lands for non-commercial purposes such as hunting, fishing and recreation.

Residents of Nisga'a Lands who are not Nisga'a will have access to their private land.

The Nisga'a Government may make laws regulating public access for the purposes of public safety, protection of environmental, cultural or historic features, and protection of habitat.

The federal and provincial governments will have access to Nisga'a Lands for purposes such as the delivery or management of government services and emergency response. Likewise, representatives of the Nisga'a Government may, in accordance with the laws of general application, have temporary access to lands other than Nisga'a Lands for similar purposes.

ROADS AND RIGHTS OF WAY

The province will continue to own the Nisga'a Highway (which is the main road through Nisga'a Lands) and will maintain the secondary provincial roads. The province may also acquire portions of Nisga'a Lands to create additional rights of way for road or public utility purposes.

The Nisga'a Government will regulate and maintain all Nisga'a roads.

FISHERIES

Nisga'a citizens will have the right to harvest fish and aquatic plants subject to conservation requirements and legislation enacted to protect public health and safety.

Salmon

The Nisga'a will receive an annual allocation of salmon under the Treaty and harvest agreement, which will, on average, comprise approximately 26 percent of the Canadian Nass River total allowable catch. In addition, the Nisga'a will be able to sell their salmon, subject to monitoring, enforcement and laws of general application. A Harvest Agreement, separate from the Final Agreement, allows for the harvesting of sockeye and pink salmon.

If, in any year, there are no directed Canadian commercial or recreational fisheries for a species of Nass salmon, a Nisga'a commercial fishery will not be permitted for that species.

Steelhead

The Nisga'a have the right to harvest steelhead for domestic purposes.

Enhancement

The Nisga'a Government may conduct enhancement activities for Nass salmon with the approval of the Minister of Fisheries and Oceans.

Non-Salmon Species and Aquatic Plants

The Nisga'a may harvest non-salmon species. The allocation will be for domestic purposes, meaning that the harvest cannot be sold. The Final Agreement provides for a shellfish allocation and the Nisga'a may negotiate an allocation for other species, such as halibut and crab.

Fisheries Management

The Minister of Fisheries and Oceans and the province will retain responsibility for conservation and management of the fisheries and fish habitat, according to their respective jurisdictions. In addition, the Nisga'a Government may make laws to manage the Nisga'a harvest, if those laws are consistent with the Nisga'a Annual Fishing Plan approved by the Minister.

The Parties will establish and be represented on a Joint Fisheries Management Committee (JFMC) to facilitate the cooperative planning and conduct of Nisga'a fisheries and enhancement activities. The committee will make recommendations to the federal and provincial governments on these matters.

The Nisga'a will prepare a Nisga'a Annual Fishing Plan for all species of salmon and other fish. The Nisga'a Annual Fishing Plan will be reviewed by the JFMC and, if satisfactory, approved by the Minister of Fisheries and Oceans.

The agreement also provides for Nisga'a participation in any future regional or watershed-based fisheries management, should the need arise.

Lisims Fisheries Conservation Trust
The Trust will be established to promote conservation and protection of Nass area fish species, facilitate sustainable management of the fisheries for the benefit of all Canadians, and promote and support Nisga'a participation in the stewardship of the Nass fisheries.

Canada will contribute $10 million to this initiative and the Nisga'a will contribute $3 million.

Nisga'a Participation in the General Commercial Fishery
The Nisga'a will receive $11.5 million from Canada and B.C. to participate in the general commercial fishing industry.

The Nisga'a will not establish large-scale fish-processing facilities within eight years of the effective date of the Treaty.

WILDLIFE AND MIGRATORY BIRDS

The Nisga'a will receive a wildlife hunting allocation for domestic purposes in the Nass Wildlife Area. There are specific allocations for moose, grizzly bear and mountain goat. In the future, mammals other than these may be designated and an allocation established.

Hunting will be subject to conservation requirements and legislation enacted for the purposes of public health and safety. The Nisga'a right to hunt cannot interfere with other authorized uses of Crown land and does not preclude the Crown from authorizing uses of or disposing of Crown land, subject to certain considerations.

The Nisga'a may also harvest migratory birds, subject to laws of general application and appropriate international conventions.

Wildlife Management
The Minister of Environment, Lands and Parks is responsible for all wildlife. A wildlife committee will be established to promote cooperative management of the resource in the Nass area and advise the Minister on management and Nisga'a hunting matters. The committee will have equal

representation from the Nisga'a and the province, with one representative from Canada.

The Nisga'a will develop an annual management plan for their hunt which will require provincial approval. The management plan will be reviewed by the wildlife committee and approved by the provincial Minister.

Nisga'a citizens who hunt outside the management area will be subject to provincial laws.

Trade, Barter and Sale
The Nisga'a will be able to trade or barter wildlife, wildlife parts and migratory birds among themselves, or with other Aboriginal people. The Nisga'a harvest of wildlife is for domestic purposes.

Trapping
Trapping will be regulated in accordance with provincial laws.

Guiding
Guiding activities will continue to be subject to laws of general application.

The Nisga'a may receive a guide outfitter's certificate in the Nisga'a Lands, if a current certificate ceases to apply.

The Nisga'a will receive an angling licence for certain watercourses outside of the Nisga'a Lands.

ENVIRONMENTAL ASSESSMENT AND PROTECTION

The Nisga'a Government will have the power to make laws relating to environmental assessment and protection. The environmental standards defined in these laws must meet or exceed federal and provincial standards.

The Nisga'a may undertake environmental assessments of proposed projects on their lands. Assessments will include public participation; and, the results will be available to the public, except where information must remain confidential by law. Federal and provincial environmental assessment processes continue to apply on Nisga'a Lands.

Canada and British Columbia will participate in environmental assessments in cases where a project will have effects outside the Nisga'a Lands. To avoid duplication, the agreement provides for the harmonization of Nisga'a environmental assessment processes with those of Canada and British Columbia.

NISGA'A GOVERNMENT

The Nisga'a will be governed by the Nisga'a Lisims Government (central government) and four Nisga'a Village Governments.

Nisga'a Constitution
The Nisga'a will adopt a Constitution which will set out the terms of governance and recognize the rights and freedoms of Nisga'a citizens. The Constitution must be passed by at least 70 percent of the voters who participate in the vote to ratify the Final Agreement.

Relations with Individuals who are not Nisga'a Citizens
The Nisga'a Government will be required to consult with other residents of Nisga'a Lands about decisions that significantly and directly affect them. Likewise, residents who are not Nisga'a will be able to participate in elected bodies that directly and significantly affect them. The means of participation can include opportunities to make representations, to vote for or seek election on Nisga'a Public Institutions, and to have the same means of appeal as Nisga'a citizens. Some local laws, such as traffic and transportation will apply to other residents of Nisga'a Lands, but in the majority of cases Nisga'a laws will only pertain to Nisga'a citizens.

Transitional Provisions
The first elections for Nisga'a Government will be held no later than six months after the effective date of the Treaty. Prior to the elections, the Nisga'a Tribal Council will continue to manage Nisga'a affairs, in accordance with the transition provisions.

Legislative Jurisdiction and Authority
The Nisga'a Government will have the power to make laws required to carry out its responsibilities and exercise its authority under this agreement. In addition, the Nisga'a Government may make laws governing such things as Nisga'a citizenship; Nisga'a language and culture; Nisga'a property in Nisga'a Lands; public order, peace and safety; employment; traffic and transportation; the solemnization of marriages; child and family social and health services; child custody, adoption, and education.

Federal and provincial laws continue to apply to Nisga'a citizens and Nisga'a Lands, and the relationship between these laws and Nisga'a laws has been clearly set out in the Final Agreement.

ADMINISTRATION OF JUSTICE

The Nisga'a Government may provide policing, correctional, and court services on Nisga'a Lands in accordance with the terms of the Treaty.

Police Services
If the Nisga'a Government decides to provide its own policing within Nisga'a Lands, it may do so with the approval of the Lieutenant Governor in Council. The Nisga'a Police Service will have the full range of police responsibilities and the authority to enforce Nisga'a, provincial and federal laws, including the *Criminal Code of Canada*, within the Nisga'a Lands. The police force will be required to meet provincial qualification, training and professional standards. It will also be independent and accountable.

Community Corrections Services
The Nisga'a may enter into agreements with Canada or British Columbia to provide community correctional services in accordance with generally accepted standards, and consistent with the needs and priorities of the Nisga'a Government.

Nisga'a Court
The Nisga'a may establish a Nisga'a Court for approval by the Lieutenant Governor in Council. The Nisga'a Court will adjudicate prosecutions and civil disputes arising under Nisga'a laws and review the administrative decisions of Nisga'a public institutions.

The judges will be appointed by the Nisga'a Government, according to a method of selection approved by the Lieutenant Governor in Council, and will comply with generally recognized principles of judicial fairness, independence and impartiality.

In proceedings where the accused could face imprisonment under Nisga'a law, he or she may elect to be tried in the Provincial Court of British Columbia.

Final decisions by the Nisga'a Court may be appealed to the Supreme Court of British Columbia on the same basis as decisions made at the Provincial Court of British Columbia.

INDIAN ACT TRANSITION

Provisions will be made to facilitate the transition from jurisdiction under the *Indian Act* to provincial or Nisga'a jurisdiction for such things as wills, administration of estates, and governance arrangements.

Capital Transfer and Loan Repayment

The cash settlement benefit of $190 million will be paid through capital transfers over a period of 15 years according to a schedule agreed to by the Parties.

The loans made by the Nisga'a to support their participation in Treaty negotiations over the years will be fully repaid over 15 years according to a schedule agreed to by the Parties.

Fiscal Relations

The Nisga'a Government will be responsible for ensuring the provision of programs and services at levels reasonably comparable to those generally available in northwest British Columbia.

Every five years, the Treaty requires the Parties to negotiate a fiscal financing agreement through which funding will be provided to the Nisga'a Government to enable the delivery of programs and services including health, education, social services, local services, capital asset maintenance and replacement, housing, and resource management.

The Fiscal Financing Agreement will take into account the Nisga'a Government's ability to raise its own revenues consistent with an own source revenue agreement. The first Own Source Revenue Agreement will provide for a phased-in contribution of Nisga'a revenues over a period of twelve years after the initial agreement. The Own Source Revenue Agreement will be renegotiable every two years, if requested by any of the Parties.

The Treaty confirms that the funding of Nisga'a Government is a shared responsibility of the Parties and that it is the Parties' objective that, where feasible, the reliance of the Nisga'a Government and the Nisga'a Villages on transfers will be reduced over time.

Taxation

The Nisga'a Government will have the power to tax Nisga'a citizens on Nisga'a Lands.

The Nisga'a Government, Canada and British Columbia may negotiate tax delegation agreements for other taxes and the Parties may make agreements to coordinate their respective tax systems on Nisga'a Lands.

The *Indian Act* tax exemption for Nisga'a citizens will be eliminated after a transitional period of eight years for transaction (e.g., sales) taxes and 12 years for other (e.g., income) taxes.

Pursuant to a taxation agreement, the Nisga'a Government and Nisga'a Village Governments will be treated in the same way as municipalities for tax purposes.

CULTURAL ARTIFACTS AND HERITAGE

The Royal British Columbia Museum and the Canadian Museum of Civilization will return a portion of their collections of Nisga'a artifacts to the Nisga'a. The museums will also retain some collections of Nisga'a artifacts for public exhibitions.

The Nisga'a Government and the province will coordinate their activities to manage heritage sites within Nisga'a Lands to preserve their heritage value from activities which may otherwise adversely affect them.

LOCAL AND REGIONAL GOVERNMENT RELATIONS

Nisga'a Lands will continue to be part of the Electoral Area "A" in the Regional District of Kitimat-Stikine.

The Nisga'a and the Regional District may enter into servicing agreements or otherwise coordinate their activities with respect to common areas of responsibility.

DISPUTE RESOLUTION

If disputes arise regarding the interpretation, application or implementation of the Treaty, the Parties will try to resolve them through cooperation and consultation. If the Parties are unable to resolve the dispute in this manner, they may resort to mediation or another form of dispute resolution that would facilitate the Parties' efforts to agree. If these efforts fail, the Parties will have recourse to arbitration, if they agree, or the British Columbia Supreme Court.

ELIGIBILITY AND ENROLMENT

To be eligible to receive benefits from the Nisga'a Treaty, a person must meet enrolment criteria that are largely based on Nisga'a ancestry.

The task of determining eligibility will be carried out by an eight-member Enrolment Committee, which will create a register of names during an initial enrolment period. Thereafter, the Nisga'a Government will maintain the register. The decisions of the Enrolment Committee and the Nisga'a Government with respect to eligibility and enrolment are final and binding, within the bounds of an appeals process.

RATIFICATION

The Final Agreement has no force or effect unless ratified by the Nisga'a, British Columbia, and Canada.

Those Nisga'a who are enrolled by the Enrolment Committee will vote on the agreement by secret ballot. A Ratification Committee, with Nisga'a, federal and provincial representatives, will oversee the conduct of the vote. To be approved, the agreement must be ratified by a majority (i.e., 50 percent plus one vote) of all eligible voters.

British Columbia and Canada will ratify the agreement in the British Columbia Legislature and Parliament, respectively, by the enactment of legislation giving effect to the Treaty.

IMPLEMENTATION

The Treaty will be implemented according to an Implementation Plan that is separate from the Final Agreement. The Implementation Plan sets out the steps to be taken to properly make the Treaty work on the ground. The plan will be for a term of ten years starting from the effective date of the Treaty.

* * *

Federal Treaty Negotiation Office
PO Box 11576
2700 – 650 W. Georgia St.
Vancouver, BC V6B 4N8

Notes

....

NOTES TO A NOTE ON TREATIES IN CANADA (PAGES 3–10)

1. *The Economist,* August 8, 1998, p. 34.
2. Cited in L. C. Green and Olive P. Dickason, *The Law of Nations and the New World* (Edmonton: University of Alberta Press, 1989), p. 18.
3. Cited in ibid, p. 40.
4. See Lewis Hanke, *The Spanish Struggle for Justice in the Conquest of America* (Boston: Little, Brown, and Co., 1965).
5. David E. Stannard, *American Holocaust: Columbus and the Conquest of the New World* (New York: Oxford University Press, 1992); see also Ward Churchill, *A Little Matter of Genocide: Holocaust Denial in the Americas, 1492 to Present* (Winnipeg: Arbeiter Ring Publishing, 1998); Robert Davis and Mark Zannis, *The Genocide Machine in Canada: The Pacification of the North* (Montreal: Black Rose Books, 1973).
6. George Manuel and Michael Posluns, *The Fourth World: An Indian Reality* (Don Mills, Ontario: Collier-Macmillan, 1974).
7. Richard White, *The Middle Ground: Indians, Empires, and Republics in the Great Lakes Region, 1650–1815 (Cambridge: Cambrige University Press, 1991).*
8. See Anthony Hall, "Indian Treaties," *The Canadian Encyclopedia,* CD-ROM Editions (Toronto: McClelland and Stewart, 2000).

NOTES TO CHAPTER TWO (PAGES 21–40)

1. British Columbia Legislature, *Sessional Papers,* 1887, p. 264.
2. William Trutch, "Report on the Lower Fraser Indian Reserves, 28 August 1867," British Columbia: *Papers Connected with Indian Land,* p. 42.
3. Joseph Gosnell, "Chief Gosnell's Historic Speech to the British Columbia Legislature," December 2, 1998 (http://www.ntc.bc.ca/speeches/gosnell4.html).
4. Paul Tennant, *Aboriginal Peoples and Politics: The Indian Land Question in British Columbia, 1849–1989* (Vancouver: University of British Columbia Press, 1990), p. 90.
5. Quoted in Donald Smith, "We should honour Sir John, eh?" *The Globe and Mail* (Toronto), January 11, 2000, p. A15.
6. *The Oxford English Reference Dictionary,* 2nd ed. (Oxford: Oxford University Press, 1996), p. 1151.
7. Paul Tennant, *Aboriginal Peoples and Politics,* p. 91.
8. Quoted in Joseph Gosnell, "Chief Gosnell's Historic Speech to the British Columbia Legislature."

9. Paul Tennant, *Aboriginal Peoples and Politics*, p. 92.
10. C. T. Fyfe, editor, *A Book of Good Poems* (Vancouver, Toronto, Montreal: The Copp Clark Publishing Co. Limited, 1959), p. 434.
11. E. Brian Titley, *A Narrow Vision: Duncan Campbell Scott and the Administration of Indian Affairs in Canada* (Vancouver: University of British Columbia Press, 1986), quoted on p. 50.
12. *Calder et al v. the Attorney-General of British Columbia*, 34 DLR (3d) 145.
13. Quoted in Thomas Berger, "The Importance of the Nisga'a Treaty to Canadians," Corry Lecture: Queen's University, Kingston, ON, February 10, 1999.
14. "The Nisga'a Tribal Council Framework Agreement Signed," News release issued jointly by the Government of Canada, The Province of British Columbia, and the Nisga'a Tribal Council, March 20, 1991.
15. The First Nations of British Columbia, the Government of British Columbia, and the Government of Canada, "The Report of the British Columbia Claims Task Force," June 28, 1991. As stated in the opening page of the report, "The Task Force was created on December 3, 1990 by an agreement between representatives of First Nations in British Columbia, the Government of British Columbia and the Government of Canada. The terms of reference asked the Task Force to recommend how the three parties could begin negotiations and what the negotiations should include."
16. *British Columbia Treaty Commission Agreement*, September 21, 1992, p. 7.
17. *In All Fairness: A Native Claims Policy*. Published under the authority of the Hon. John C. Munro, PC, MP, Minister of Indian Affairs and Northern Development (Ottawa, 1981), p. 13.
18. Ibid., Appendix.
19. "Nisga'a, British Columbia and Canada Release Historic Agreement-in-Principle," Press release issued jointly by the Government of Canada, the Province of British Columbia, and the Nisga'a Tribal Council, February 15, 1996.
20. Ibid.
21. Ministry of Aboriginal Affairs, Government of British Columbia, *Instructions on Open Negotiation*, September 19, 1994.
22. Indian and Northern Affairs Canada, "Federal Commitment to Openness of Treaty Negotiations." Speech by Mrs. Anna Terrana, MP, to the Treaty Negotiation Advisory Committee, Vancouver, September 30, 1994.
23. Indian and Northern Affairs Canada, "Government of Canada supports more openness," [communiqué], Vancouver, September 30, 1994.
24. Ministry of Aboriginal Affairs, Province of British Columbia, "Glossary of Treaty-related Terms As Used by the Province of British Columbia" (http://www.aaf.gov.bc.ca/aaf/pubs/glossary.htm).

NOTES TO CHAPTER THREE (PAGES 41–58)

1. Nisga'a Tribal Council, *Nisga'a: People of the Nass River* (Vancouver: Douglas & McIntyre, 1993), p. 1.
2. Department of Indian Affairs and Northern Development, "Federal Guidelines for the Settlement of Overlapping Comprehensive Claims or Treaties," Ottawa, June 15, 1994.
3. "Nisga'a negotiations openness protocol signed." Press release issued jointly by the Government of Canada, the Province of British Columbia, and the Nisga'a Tribal Council, December 15, 1996.

NOTES TO CHAPTER FOUR (PAGES 59–73)

1. Television interview. I am certain of the quote, less certain of the date and program.
2. Federal Treaty Negotiation Office, "Nisga'a Final Agreement: Issues and Responses" (http://www.inac.gc.ca).
3. Brian Laghi and Heather Scoffield, "Nisga'a treaty reveals conflicts in ideology," *The Globe and Mail* (Toronto), December 10, 1999, p. A7.
4. Shakespeare, *The Taming of the Shrew*, act 1, sc. 2, lines 281–82.
5. *Sim'oogit* means "chief."

NOTES TO CHAPTER FIVE (PAGES 75–85)

1. Ministry of Aboriginal Affairs, Province of British Columbia [news release], Victoria, July 29, 1997.
2. Select Standing Committee on Aboriginal Affairs, Mr. Ian Waddell, MLA, Chair, "Towards Reconciliation: Nisga'a Agreement-in-Principle and British Columbia Treaty Process," First Report, Second Session, Thirty-sixth Parliament, Legislative Assembly of British Columbia, July 1997.
3. Legislative Assembly, Province of British Columbia [news release], July 3, 1997.
4. Ian Bailey, "Irwin rules out quick wrapup of Nisga'a treaty to win votes," *Times Colonist* (Victoria), May 2, 1997, p. A5.
5. "Canyon City, B.C., Native re-elected third time," Calgary *Herald*, May 5, 1997.

NOTES TO CHAPTER SIX (PAGES 87–97)

1. "What is BC F.I.R.E.?" Photocopied handout published by the BC Foundation for Individual Rights and Equality, 113–437 Martin St., Suite 281, Penticton, BC, V2A 5L1.
2. Gordon Campbell, "Will of community must direct treaty talks, Liberal leader writes," Vancouver *Sun*, April 8, 1998, p. A17.

3. Heather Scoffield, "The one who brought the treaty home," *The Globe and Mail* (Toronto), December 14, 1999, p. A14.
4. "Nisga'a Education and Health" (http://www.schoolnet.ca/aboriginal/nisga1/ed-e.html).
5. Ibid.
6. *Delgamuukw v. Attorney-General of British Columbia*, 153 DLR (4th) 193.
7. Ibid.

NOTES TO CHAPTER SEVEN (PAGES 99–110)

1. Giovanni Boccaccio, *Decameron*, 3rd day, 2nd story. A more modern translation reads: "By holding his tongue his honour remained unimpaired, whereas if he were to talk he would make himself look ridiculous."
2. *Tædium vitæ*: literally, weariness of life.
3. Janet Steffenhagen, "Treaty talks discuss Delgamuukw effect impact: The federal Indian Affairs Minister is hoping to advance land claims talks," Vancouver *Sun*, May 8, 1998, p. A4.
4. Liberal Party of Canada, "The Aboriginal Peoples of Canada," Pamphlet, September 1993.
5. Liberal Party of Canada, *Creating Opportunity: The Liberal Plan for Canada*, Ottawa, 1993.
6. Liberal Party of Canada, *Our Future Together: Preparing Canada for the 21st Century*, Ottawa, 1997.
7. Royal Commission on Aboriginal Peoples, Interim Report, March 23, 1995.
8. Hon. A. C. Hamilton, Factfinder for Minister of Indian Affairs and Northern Development, *Canada and Aboriginal Peoples: A New Partnership*, Published under the authority of the Honourable Ronald A. Irwin. PC, MP, Minister of Indian Affairs and Northern Development, Ottawa, 1995.
9. Royal Commission on Aboriginal Peoples, Final Report, *People to People, Nation to Nation*, November 23, 1996.
10. *Delgamuukw v. Attorney-General of British Columbia*, 153 DLR (4th) 193.
11. Ibid.
12. Justine Hunter, "Clark cranks up effort to reach land-claim deal," Vancouver *Sun*, March 9, 1998, p. A1.
13. Ibid.
14. "Release the New Nisga'a Mandate, Campbell Urges Clark," Press release issued by the BC Liberal Official Opposition, March 11, 1998.
15. Gordon Campbell, Leader of the Opposition, "Will of community must direct treaty talks, Liberal leader writes," Vancouver *Sun*, April 8, 1998, p. A17; "Indians must 'surrender' rights in treaties, Liberal leader writes," Vancouver *Sun*, April 9, 1998, p. A23.

16. Suzanne Fournier, "We will never surrender land," Vancouver *Province*, April 12, 1998, p. A44.
17. Justine Hunter, "Clark to launch mail campaign on Nisga'a treaty," Vancouver *Sun*, April 18, 1998, p. A6.
18. Ibid.

NOTES TO CHAPTER EIGHT (PAGES 111–127)

1. *St. Catharine's Milling & Lumber Co. v. the Queen* (1888), 14 App. Cas. 46.
2. Carolyn Swayze, *Hard Choices: A Life of Thomas Berger* (Vancouver: Douglas and McIntyre, 1987), p. 81.
3. Wilson Duff, *The Indian History of British Columbia. Vol. 1: The Impact of the White Man* (Victoria: Royal British Columbia Museum, 1964), p. 8; quoted in *Calder v. Attorney-General of British Columbia*, 34 DLR (3d) 145, p. 179.
4. *Calder v. Attorney-General of British Columbia*, 34 DLR (3d) 145, pp. 181–82.
5. Ibid., p. 190.
6. Quoted in *Calder et al*, p. 176.
7. John Marshall (1755–1835), Chief Justice of the Supreme Court, 1801–1835.
8. *Worcester v. State of Georgia* (1822), 6 Peters 515, pp. 542–44.
9. Bill Henderson, "A Brief Introduction to Aboriginal Law in Canada," Virtual Law Office (www.bloorstreet.com).
10. *The Canadian World Encyclopedia* (http://tceplus.com/aborights.htm).
11. Henderson, "A Brief Introduction."
12. *Calder et al.*
13. "Statement on Claims of Indian and Inuit People," (Ottawa: Queen's Printer, 1973).
14. *Hamlet of Baker Lake v. Canada*, 5 WWR 193.
15. *Delgamuukw v. Attorney-General of British Columbia*, 153 DLR (4th) 193, p. 273.
16. "Joseph Gosnell's Speech at the Nisga'a Treaty Initialling Ceremony," August 4, 1998 (http://www.kermode.net/nisgaa/no_frames/initial.html).
17. *Ronald Edward Sparrow v. Her Majesty the Queen at al*, (1990) 1 SCR 1075.
18. Indian and Northern Affairs Canada, Price Waterhouse, "Economic Value of Uncertainty Associated with Native Land Claims in B.C.," March 1990.
19. KPMG, "Benefits and Costs of Treaty Settlements in British Columbia— A Financial and Economic Perspective," Project Report, Victoria, January 17, 1996.
20. E. Brian Titley, *A Narrow Vision: Duncan Campbell Scott and the Administration of Indian Affairs in Canada* (Vancouver: University of British Columbia Press, 1986), quoted on p. 50.

21. Government of Canada, "Government Launches Process for Negotiating Aboriginal Self-Government," [news release], Ottawa, August 10, 1995.
22. "Aboriginal Self-Government: The Government of Canada's Approach to Implementation of the Inherent Right and the Negotiation of Aboriginal Self Government," Federal Policy Guide, published under the authority of the Honourable Ronald A. Irwin. PC, MP, Minister of Indian Affairs and Northern Development, Ottawa, August 10, 1995.
23. Government of Canada, "Government Launches Process for Negotiating Aboriginal Self-Government."
24. "Aboriginal Self-Government: The Government of Canada's Approach to Implementation of the Inherent Right and the Negotiation of Aboriginal Self Government."

NOTES TO CHAPTER NINE (PAGES 129–140)

1. "Challenge to treaty gets date in court," *Terrace Standard,* May 20, 1998.
2. "Statement of the Gitanyow Hereditary Chiefs," [press release], Vancouver, July 29, 1998.
3. "Joseph Gosnell's Speech at the Nisga'a Treaty Initialling Ceremony," August 4, 1998 (http://www.kermode.net/nisgaa/no_frames/initial.html).
4. Lori Culbert and Lindsay Kines, "Plane crash seen as sign of need for road in Nass," Vancouver *Sun,* August 6, 1998, p. A3.

NOTES TO CHAPTER TEN (PAGES 141–150)

1. Nisga'a Tribal Council, *Nisga'a: People of the Nass River* (Vancouver: Douglas & McIntyre, 1993), p. 15.
2. From the "Convention Booklet of the 42nd Annual Convention, the Nisga'a Nation," April 1999.
3. Gordon Campbell, Leader of the Opposition, "Will of community must direct treaty talks, Liberal leader writes," Vancouver *Sun,* April 8, 1998, p. A17; "Indians must 'surrender' rights in treaties, Liberal leader writes," Vancouver *Sun,* April 9, 1998, p. A23.
4. Bill Vander Zalm, "Let's pay off the Nisga'a," *The Globe and Mail* (Toronto), November 12, 1999, p. A19.
5. Heather Scoffield, "Treaty will perpetuate poverty, Manning says," *The Globe and Mail* (Toronto), October 27, 1999, p. A4.
6. Brian Laghi and Heather Scoffield, "Nisga'a treaty reveals conflict in ideology," *The Globe and Mail* (Toronto), December 10, 1999, p. A14.
7. Quoted in the Right Honourable Adrienne Clarkson, Governor General of Canada, "Installation Speech," The Senate, October 7, 1999 (http://www.gg.ca/speeches/installation-speech_e.html)
8. Ibid.

9. John Ralston Saul, *Reflections of a Siamese Twin: Canada at the End of the Twentieth Century* (Toronto: Viking, 1997), p. 88.
10. Thomas R. Berger, *A Long and Terrible Shadow* (Vancouver: Douglas & McIntyre, 1991), p. 162.
11. "Chief Gosnell's Historic Speech to the British Columbia Legislature," December 2, 1998 (http://www.ntc.bc.ca/speeches/gosnell4.html).
12. "Joseph Gosnell's Speech at the Nisga'a Treaty Initialling Ceremony," August 4, 1998 (http://www.kermode.net/nisgaa/no frames/initial.html).
13. "Chief Gosnell's Historic Speech to the British Columbia Legislature."
14. "Triumph—Nisga'a Treaty Sends Signal of Hope & Reconciliation Around the World: Chief Joseph Gosnell," European and UK Tour, November 1998 (http://www.ntc.bc.ca/speeches/gosnell13.html).
15. Author's notes, August 21, 1999.
16. "Chief Gosnell's Historic Speech to the British Columbia Legislature."

NOTES TO CHAPTER ELEVEN (PAGES 151–165)

1. Department of Indian Affairs and Northern Development, "An Address by the Honourable Jean Chrétien, Minister of Indian Affairs and Northern Development, to the 12th Annual Convention of the Nishga [sic] Tribal Council, Kincolith, British Columbia, October 30, 1969, [press release].
2. Quoted in Thomas R. Berger, *A Long and Terrible Shadow* (Vancouver: Douglas & McIntyre, 1991), p. 151.
3. *Calder et al v. Attorney-General of British Columbia,* 34 DLR (3d) 145.
4. Nisga'a Ratification Committee, [press release], November 9, 1998.
5. Nisga'a Ratification Committee, Nisga'a Constitution Adoption Committee, "Executive Summary," Prepared for the President, Nisga'a Tribal Council, Eva Clayton, Chairperson.
6. Barbara McLintock and Ian Austin, "Come on in! Turned away in 1887, the Nisga'a got a red-carpet welcome yesterday," Vancouver *Province,* December 1, 1998, p. A1.
7. "Chief Gosnell's Historic Speech to the British Columbia Legislature," December 2, 1998 [http://www.ntc.bc.ca/speeches/gosnell4.html].
8. Jim Beatty, "Nisga'a treaty perpetuates past wrongs, Campbell says," Vancouver *Sun,* December 8, 1998, p. A3.
9. Canadian Press, "Nisga'a treaty sparks heated debate," *StarPhoenix* (Saskatoon), November 4, 1999, p. A11.
10. Ian Austin, "Papers told they oppose Nisga'a treaty," Vancouver *Province,* September 21, 1998, p. A3.
11. Quoted in ibid.
12. Nisga'a Tribal Council, "Nisga'a Object to Censorship," Media advisory, Vancouver, September 20, 1998.

13. Quoted in Jim McNulty's "National Affairs" column, Vancouver *Province*, September 25, 1998, p. A26.
14. "Straight Talk: Joe Gosnell Answers Treaty Critics," Vancouver *Sun* Forum, January 29, 1999 [http://www.ntc.bc.ca/speeches/gosnell5.html].
15. Office of the Premier, Province of British Columbia, "Historic Nisga'a Treaty passes milestone as second reading vote held," [news release], January 13, 1999.
16. Ibid.
17. BC Liberal Caucus, "Motion to end Nisga'a debate an unprecedented abuse of power," April 20, 1999, Article Archive [http://www.bcliberals.bc.ca/].
18. Louise Dickson, "Gosnell opposes vote: Nisga'a treaty debated on CBC phone-in show," *Times Colonist* (Victoria), December 7, 1998, p. C3.

NOTE TO CHAPTER TWELVE, (PAGES 167–182)

1. Louise Dickson, "Gosnell opposes vote: Nisga'a treaty debated on CBC phone-in show," *Times Colonist* (Victoria), December 7, 1998, p. C3.

NOTES TO CHAPTER THIRTEEN (PAGES 183–195)

1. Peter Macklem, "Letter to the Editor," *The Globe and Mail* (Toronto), July 29, 1998. Professor Macklem was responding to an editorial that appeared on July 24, 1998, p. A14.
2. Quoted in Vancouver *Sun*, July 30, 1998, p. A1.
3. Joel Bakan, "No referendum needed on Nisga'a deal, experts say," Letter to the Editor, Vancouver *Sun*, August 27, 1998, p. A19.
4. Peter Macklem, "Letter to the Editor."
5. Interview with Ann Petrie, *CBC Newsworld*, November 16, 1998.
6. Peter W. Hogg, "Referendum not desirable," Letter to the Editor, *The Globe and Mail* (Toronto), August 1, 1998, p. D7.
7. Quoted in John Robert Colombo, *Colombo's Canadian Quotations* (Edmonton: Hurtig Publishers, 1974). Look under "W."
8. R. M. Richardson and Associates, "A Comparative Cost Analysis of the Nisga'a Treaty," A study prepared for John Cummins, MP, 1999.
9. *Derrickson v. Derrickson*, (1986) 1 SCR 285.

NOTES TO CHAPTER FOURTEEN (PAGES 197–215)

1. *New York Times*, August 5, 1998, p. A1.
2. *The Economist*, August 8–14, 1998, p. 34.
3. Norman Spector, "Headaches over fish, Nisga'a in B.C.," *The Globe and Mail* (Toronto), October 20, 1998, p. A4; "Federal politicians are strangely silent on treaty," Unsigned Editorial, Vancouver *Sun*, November 12, 1998, p. A22.

4. Erin Anderssen and Edward Greenspon, "Historic Nisga'a treaty stalled: It's behind schedule already, and now Ottawa is considering a big delay," *The Globe and Mail* (Toronto), March 22, 1999, p. A1.
5. Quoted in the *Terrace Standard*, March 17, 1999, p. 4.
6. Norman Spector, "Headaches over Fish, Nisga'a in British Columbia," *The Globe and Mail* (Toronto), October 20, 1998, p. A4.
7. Doreen Mullins, Executive Director, Indian and Northern Affairs, "Molloy is accessible," Letter to the Editor, *The Globe and Mail* (Toronto), October 27, 1998, p. A3.
8. Bill Cleverley, "Nisga'a question on municipal ballots gets short shrift." *Times Colonist* (Victoria), September 24, 1999, p. C4.
9. Quoted in *The Globe and Mail* (Toronto), October 27, 1999.
10. Honourable R. D. Nault, PC, MP, Minister of Indian Affairs and Northern Development, "The Facts About the Nisga'a Treaty: Building Partnerships Through Negotiations," October 26, 1999, p. 1.
11. Daniel LeBlanc, "Odd couple keep House running smoothly," *The Globe and Mail* (Toronto), January 3, 2000. P. A4.
12. Office of the Leader of the Opposition, "People Deserve a Say on Nisga'a Bill: Manning and MPs call for province wide referendum on contentious bill," [press release], November 16, 1999.
13. Bill Vander Zalm, "Let's pay off the Nisga'a," *The Globe and Mail* (Toronto), November 12, 1999, p. A19.
14. Tom Molloy, "Why the Nisga'a treaty works: The chief federal negotiator defends the controversial agreement made with B.C. natives," *The Globe and Mail* (Toronto), November 22, 1999, p. A19.
15. Brian Laghi and Heather Scoffield, "Nisga'a treaty reveals conflict in ideology," *The Globe and Mail* (Toronto), December 10, 1999, p. A7.
16. Indian and Northern Affairs Canada, "Speaking notes for The Honourable Robert D. Nault, Minister of Indian Affairs and Northern Development to the Senate Committee on Aboriginal Peoples, March 23, 2000, Ottawa, Ontario."
17. Nisga'a Final Agreement Bill. Third Reading—Debate Suspended. Hon Jack Austin moved the third reading of Bill C-9, to give effect to the Nisga'a Final Agreement. Ottawa: *Hansard*, March 30, 2000.
18. Department of Indian Affairs and Northern Development, "Historic Nisga'a Treaty Ratified; Receives Royal Assent," [press release], April 13, 2000.

Index

....

Bisaillon, Claude, 216
Black, David, 159–60, 161
Blake, Edward, 23
Boudria, Don, 203, 206, 207, 209
Bourgue, Jocelyn, 168
Bownsey, Lorne, 13
Brinston, Lloyd, 159
British Columbia, land claims in, 21–23,
25–27, 96, 107–8; economic effects of,
118, 122–23, 127; history of, 18,
112–15; process of, 27–30, 38–39, 192;
public involvement in, 36–38, 80–81
British Columbia (government of): com-
mitment to NFA, 13, 18, 77, 79–81, 95,
107, 108, 159, 160; consultations with
government of Canada on NFA, 95,
110, 129, 130, 174, 193–95; cost of
NFA to, 174, 193–95; involvement in
NFA process, 47, 161, 162–63, 164,
202; NFA rights and responsibilities,
170–72, 174, 175–76, 177–78, 179. See
also Provincial negotiating team
British Columbia Federal Liberal Caucus,
48, 85
British Columbia Select Standing
Committee on Aboriginal Affairs,
79–81
British Columbia Treaty Commission
(BCTC) Agreement, 28–30, 36, 192
British North America, aboriginal and
treaty rights in, 5–9
British Privy Council, Nisga'a petition to,
23–24, 25
Brown, Martyn, 88
Buchanan, Judd, 158
Bulkley-Skeena Regional Advisory
Committee, 46, 72
Calder, Frank, 26, 53, 146, 149–50, 205. See
also Calder v. Attorney-General of
British Columbia
Calder v. Attorney-General of British
Columbia: as basis of Nisga'a land
claims, 26, 29–30, 36, 112, 126, 135,
151; effect on federal aboriginal policy,
118, 149; and legal theory of aborigi-
nal rights, 112, 114–15, 119; proceed-
ings of, 112–14

Calgary Herald, 82
Campagnolo, Iona, 158
Campbell, Bruce, 218
Campbell, Gordon: effect on BC ratification process, 108–9, 157, 159, 163;
opposition to treaty negotiations and
NFA, 88, 107, 133, 143, 145, 186
Canada (government of): aboriginal self-
government policy of, 123, 151,
181–82, 187, 188, 198; assimilation
policy of, 25–26; commitment to NFA,
77, 199–200, 201, 202, 203, 204–5;
consultations with BC government on
NFA, 95, 110, 129, 130; cost of NFA to,
174, 193–95; land claims policy of,
22–23, 26, 27–28, 29–31, 54, 162; NFA
rights and responsibilities of, 170,
173–74, 175–76, 177, 179, 184; passage
of NFA legislation through
Parliament, 47, 204–15; position on
interim protection measures, 38–39;
position on Openness Protocol,
36–38. See also Constitution Act, 1982;
Federal negotiating team
Canada and Aboriginal Peoples: A New
Partnership, 105
Canadian Museum of Civilization, 63, 127,
179, 182, 230
CANFREE (Canadians for Reconciliation,
Equality, and Equity), 211
Cantin, Lyse, 217
Canyon City. See Gitwinksihlkw
Capital and transfer payments, 66, 229. See
also Nisga'a Final Agreement, fiscal
and financial provisions
Carruthers, Major, 91
Cashore, John, 31, 56, 95, 96
Certainty: issue in NFA negotiation and
ratification process, 57, 70, 103–6,
107–8, 109–10, 122, 124–26, 152, 154;
Modified Aboriginal Rights Approach
to, 123–24; NFA provisions for, 62–63,
124–26, 164, 169, 173, 181. See also
Extinguishment
Certainty Working Group, 62
Certainty Working Group (TNAC), 71–72